UNBEARABLE LIFE

INSURRECTIONS: CRITICAL STUDIES IN
RELIGION, POLITICS, AND CULTURE

INSURRECTIONS: CRITICAL STUDIES IN RELIGION,
POLITICS, AND CULTURE

SLAVOJ ŽIŽEK, CLAYTON CROCKETT, CRESTON DAVIS,
JEFFREY W. ROBBINS, EDITORS

The intersection of religion, politics, and culture is one of the most discussed areas in theory today. It also has the deepest and most wide-ranging impact on the world. Insurrections: Critical Studies in Religion, Politics, and Culture will bring the tools of philosophy and critical theory to the political implications of the religious turn. The series will address a range of religious traditions and political viewpoints in the United States, Europe, and other parts of the world. Without advocating any specific religious or theological stance, the series aims nonetheless to be faithful to the radical emancipatory potential of religion.

For a full list of the books in this series, see pages 271–73.

UNBEARABLE LIFE

A GENEALOGY OF
POLITICAL ERASURE

ARTHUR BRADLEY

Columbia University Press   *New York*

Columbia University Press wishes to express its appreciation for assistance
given by Lancaster University's English Literature and Creative Writing
Department in the publication of this book.

Columbia University Press
Publishers Since 1893
New York   Chichester, West Sussex
cup.columbia.edu

Library of Congress Cataloging-in-Publication Data
Names: Bradley, Arthur, author.
Title: Unbearable life : a genealogy of political erasure / Arthur Bradley.
Description: New York : Columbia University Press, 2019. | Series:
Insurrections: critical studies in religion, politics, and culture |
Includes bibliographical references and index.
Identifiers: LCCN 2019005951 | ISBN 9780231193382 (cloth : alk. paper) |
ISBN 9780231193399 (pbk. : alk. paper) | ISBN 9780231550284 (ebook)
Subjects: LCSH: Citizenship. | Expatriation. | Biopolitics. | Sovereignty. |
Collective memory—Political aspects. | Political theology.
Classification: LCC JF801 .B69 2019 | DDC 320.01—dc23
LC record available at https://lccn.loc.gov/2019005951

Columbia University Press books are printed on permanent
and durable acid-free paper.
Printed in the United States of America

Cover design: Milenda Nan Ok Lee

Cover art: Roberta Maioli, *Damnatio memoriae*, 2016 (*detail*).
Photo by Luca Maggio.

For Aya

CONTENTS

ACKNOWLEDGMENTS

I would like to thank everyone—too many people to properly acknowledge here—who has helped me in all kinds of ways during the long process of writing this book.

Firstly, I particularly want to thank the small circle of personal and intellectual friends who have taken the time to read, talk to me about, and offer feedback on this work from its inception: Ward Blanton, Antonio Cerella, Michael Dillon, Charlie Gere, and Yvonne Sherwood. In particular, I'm very grateful to Mick—*il miglior fabbro*—for all his support.

I am also very grateful to a larger group of friends and colleagues who helped to shape my thinking in large or small ways during the writing process: Ian Almond, Robert Appelbaum, Simon Bainbridge, Agata Bielik-Robson, Howard Caygill, Rachid al-Daif, Bulent Diken, Kamilla Elliott, Ziad Elmarsafy, Michael Greaney, Laurence Hemming, Hilary Hinds, Gavin Hyman, William Large, Boštjan Nedoh, John Schad, Jackie Stacey, Simon Swift, and Andrew Tate.

I must also thank my extended family for all their love, encouragement, and support: my brother and sisters; my brothers-in-law and sisters-in-law; my parents-in-law, Hussein and Salwa Hamdar; my father, John Bradley, to whom I owe everything; and especially my mother, Anne Bradley, whom I miss more than I can say.

I'm very grateful to the editors of the Insurrections: Critical Studies in Religion, Politics, and Culture series—Clayton Crockett, Creston Davis, Jeffrey Robbins, and Slavoj Žižek—for their interest in and support of my work. I particularly want to thank Ward Blanton for his incredibly generous support and advocacy for this book. I am very grateful to the anonymous reviewers of the manuscript for their invaluable feedback, which has improved the book in many ways. I am also very grateful to Roberta Maioli for permission to use a detail from her artwork *Damnatio memoriae* on the cover of this book. Finally, I want to extend the warmest thanks to my editor Wendy Lochner, for her constant support of this project from the beginning; to Lowell Frye and Kathryn Jorge at Columbia University Press; and to copyeditor Adriana Cloud for all their editorial assistance in bringing the book into print.

I would also like to thank staff and students at the following institutions for invitations to deliver earlier versions of the material in this book and for very helpful feedback that improved it in many ways: University of Agder; American University of Beirut; University of Copenhagen; University of Cracow; University of Geneva; Georgetown University; Goldsmiths College, London; King's College, London; Kingston University; University of Innsbruck; University of Lausanne; London School of Economics; the Institute of Philosophy in the Research Centre in the Slovenian Academy of Arts and Sciences; University of Malta; University of Manchester; University of Nottingham; University of St Andrews; University of Sussex; University of Toronto; University of Uppsala; University of Warwick; and the University of York.

In addition, I am also reproducing some material that has been published before in new, expanded, and substantially reworked form: "Accelerator Despite Itself: Credo, Crisis, Katechon," in *Credo, Credit, Crisis: Reflections on Faith and Money*, ed. Aidan Tynan, Laurent Milesi, and Christopher John Müller (London: Rowman and Littlefield, 2017), 65–84; "Odnarejeno: Benjamin in prihodnost preteklosti," *Problemi* 55, nos. 3–4 (2017): 177–99; and "Let the Lord the Judge Be Judge: Hobbes and Locke on Jephthah, Liberalism, Martyrdom," in *Law, Culture and the Humanities* (published online on May 16, 2017).

Finally, and most importantly, I would like to thank Abir and Aya, who, in every sense of the word, make life bearable. This book is dedicated to Aya, who teaches me more about life and how to live it every day than I could ever hope to teach her.

UNBEARABLE LIFE

INTRODUCTION

I n ancient Rome, during the time of the imperial cult, a dead emperor famously underwent a process called "apotheosis": "becoming divine." It would be decreed by the senate that the dead man had become a god and should have a public cult dedicated to him for future worship. As many historians have documented, the imperial funeral rite signified this becoming-god by means of a curious deus ex machina. To take the Emperor Septimius Severus's funeral ceremony in AD 211, for instance, the sovereign's apotheosis was represented symbolically by a wax effigy that was treated as if the life of the dead man had been transferred into it. Yet, if the imperial funeral ceremony was explicitly designed to consecrate the afterlife of the emperor, it also possessed a curious afterlife of its own, which extended from ancient Rome into the modern political imaginary. If we turn to Ernst Kantorowicz's famous discussion of royal funeral ceremonies in renaissance France, for example, we find a similar ritual: a wax effigy is substituted for the physical body of the dead king to signify the mysterious perpetuity of the body politic. For modern scholars of sovereignty, from Elias Bickerman to Giorgio Agamben, Roman imperial apotheosis thus constitutes one possible (albeit heavily disputed) source for the most famous fiction of sovereign power from the Christian Middle Ages: "the King never dies" (*le Roi ne meurt jamais*).[1]

However, a dead sovereign could endure a very different and far more ignominious fate in imperial Rome, and, indeed, one such fate was inflicted upon Septimius Severus's son Geta, after his murder by his brother and co-emperor Caracalla in AD 211. For the senate, any emperor who had brought disgrace or discredit upon the state—or indeed any citizen found guilty of the crime of treason (*maiestas*)—could be subject to a judgment that was believed to be even more awful than death: *damnatio memoriae* (the damnation of memory). If this judgment was passed, every trace of the individual's physical existence would be removed from the public record in a ritual just as elaborate as apotheosis: his name would be scratched from inscriptions on tablets (*abolitio nominis*), his face chiseled from statues, his wax mask unparaded at funerals, his temples destroyed, his image on coins defaced, his will annulled, his property expropriated. In order to preserve the honor of Rome, the individual would be symbolically expunged from the city as if he had never existed in the first place.[2]

If the ritual of *damnatio memoriae* seemingly could not be further removed from apotheosis, though, it is paradoxically close to its exact and symmetrical mirror image—even down to the substitution of icons (effigies, statues, symbols, temples) of the sovereign in place of the sovereign's own organic body. On the one hand, we have a ritual of political recollection or commemoration that elevates the body of the dead man to a theological *dignitas*—symbolized in iconic form—above bare physical existence and that affirms the perpetual power of what never dies. On the other, we have a ritual of political forgetting or amnesia, which consigns the sovereign's dead body to an oblivion beneath even bare life—again symbolized by a process of iconoclasm—and which confirms the perpetual impotence of what seemingly

never lived in the first place. In the fate of Emperor Geta—
a becoming-nothing rather than a becoming-divine of the
sovereign—we encounter what might even be called a process
of reverse or backwards apotheosis: "the King has never lived"
(*le Roi n'a jamais vécu*).

This book seeks to explore something I want to call "unbearable life"—the sovereign power to render life unborn, unlived,
or nonexistent—from its origins in ancient Rome up to the
modern republic. It is obvious, after all, that the sovereign act of
damnatio memoriae possesses a political afterlife every bit as persistent and enduring—if not more so—than imperial apotheosis. As the political history of the last 200 years—from the French
Revolution to the War on Terror—has abundantly demonstrated,
this biopolitics of erasure has metastasized and radicalized in
modernity: what predominantly applied to the dead is now routinely performed on the living; what was once reserved for
images of the body is now exerted directly on the physical body
itself; what originally was focused upon individuals is now
extended to include social classes, racial and ethnic groups,
even entire states and peoples. To be sure, unbearable life passes
under many different names and assumes many different forms
in political modernity: "enemies of the people" (France, the
Soviet Union, the People's Republic of China) the "missing"
(Vietnam, Cambodia, Lebanon, Palestine, Northern Ireland,
and so on), the "disappeared" (Argentina, Chile, El Salvador,
Guatemala, Syria, and many other countries), all the way to so-
called ghost detainees policed by "black units" in "black sites"
now located all over the world. If the victims change and the
contexts differ radically across time and space, my wager is that
we can trace something like the same judgment of future ante-
rior sovereign annihilation in each case: *they will never have
existed*. For Banu Bargu, the politics of enforced or involuntary

"disappearance" today is defined precisely by the production of a life that never lived: what is at stake is "a kind of violence that seeks not only to eradicate the person who is the target of enforced disappearance but also to erase the fact that the person ever existed."[3] In what follows, I offer an (inevitably provisional, selective, and fragmentary) genealogy of sovereignty over unbearable life, from *damnatio memoraie* to contemporary biopolitics that seeks to pose the following ancient, yet also peculiarly modern, questions: What is the "life" of unbearable life? How does it change and endure across sovereign time and space, from empires to republics, from emperors to kings and presidents, from subjects to citizens? Why do we find a life that is seemingly unbearable at the very origin of sovereignty itself?

In order to begin to answer these unanswerably vast questions, I want to propose a working hypothesis that I will spend the rest of this book fleshing out in more detail. To axiomize: sovereignty is neither the power to make die and let live (as the famous ancient Roman formula puts it) nor the power to make live and let die (as Foucault's biopolitical reversal of the Roman dictum puts it) but rather the power *to make life neither live nor die.* It is not the power to decide upon life and death, in other words, but the more originary and fundamental power to decide upon the living and the nonliving, upon what *counts* as being alive and what does not, upon which lives are "bearable" (in every sense of that word, from the metaphysical through the juridico-political to the biological) and which are "unbearable." If the sovereign declares someone or something an unbearable life, in other words, they perform arguably the most radical biopolitical—or rather *nihilopolitical*—gesture imaginable: what is socially, politically, or philosophically intolerable in the eyes of the state, for whatever reason, is simply deemed to be ontologically or politically nonexistent in the first place. In ancient Rome, recall, *damnatio memoriae* was considered to be quite literally a fate worse than death.

To risk stating the obvious, "life" is arguably now the single most exhausted, overdetermined, and yet still curiously empty signifier within the modern political imaginary. It is hardly surprising that this should be the case, of course, because as Foucault was perhaps the first to show, modern politics is nothing less than "the politics of life itself"—where the "itself" refers to the pure positum or datum of biological species-being. As biopolitics increasingly hollows life of all meaning, however, biopolitical theory seems to expand to fill the vacuum: bare life (Giorgio Agamben), precarious life (Judith Butler), creaturely life (Eric Santner), and immunized life (Roberto Esposito) are just the most famous amongst its increasingly baroque declensions.[4] However, my master concept is subtly different from the proliferation of other contemporary attempts to articulate the biopolitical and thanatopolitical capture of life: unbearable life is not life that is not worthy of being lived, life that can be killed without committing murder or sacrilege and so on, but rather life that is never recognized as having lived or died. If Emmanuel Lévinas was surely right in *Totality and Infinity* (1961) to argue that even the act of killing the other bestows a minimal recognition upon her—because we can only kill what we first acknowledge to live or exist independently from us—we will see that the concept of unbearable life removes even this meager "dignity." In Hannah Arendt's famous account of Nazi thanatopolitics, for example, the Jews are clearly a "life" that lies beneath bare life, precarious or grievable life and all tropes that define life as the unconditional capacity to be injured or killed:

> The murderer leaves a corpse behind and does not declare that his victim has never existed; if he wipes out any traces, they are those of his own identity, and not the memory and grief of the persons who loved his victim; he destroys a life, but he does not destroy the fact of existence itself. The Nazis, with the precision peculiar to them, used to register their operations in the concentration camps under the heading "under cover of the night (*Nacht und Nebel*)."[5]

If unbearable life is qualitatively different from rival concepts within the field of biopolitical theory, as I will seek to argue, what follows will nonetheless seek to build on, gather together, and extend both forward and backward in time and space a set of diverse modern reflections about sovereign power by, in particular, Michel Foucault, Judith Butler, and Roberto Esposito. It takes as its main point of theoretical departure an intriguing but undeveloped observation of the later Foucault about the sovereign's power over the life and death of his subjects. As we will see in chapter 1, Foucault is the first to note that this—apparently commonplace—formula conceals a previously unnoticed aporia, or paradox. To put it in Foucault's own words, sovereignty of life and death places the subject in a position where, politically, they cannot even be considered to be *alive* until the sovereign decides: "the subject is, by rights, neither dead nor alive," he contends in *"Society Must Be Defended"* (2003), and it is "thanks to the sovereign that the subject has the right to be alive or, possibly, the right to be dead."[6] Yet, of course, Foucault was by no means the only theorist to hypothesize sovereign power as the power to decide upon the very appearance of life itself, and, in a certain sense, the work of many of his biopolitical successors can be read as an attempt to give concrete form to this subject caught somewhere between, or before, life and death. For Judith Butler, writing in the immediate aftermath of the 9/11 attacks, the sovereign decision upon life is famously accompanied by a biopolitical arithmetic that "counts" certain lives—and thus also certain deaths—more or less than others: "Violence against those who are already not quite living, that is, living in a state of suspension between life and death, leaves a mark that is no mark."[7] In Roberto Esposito's compelling recent discussion of National Socialist biopolitics—and in particular Nazi eugenics—he likewise argues that sovereignty consists in the power to create a state of exception outside life and death—a life that is not life—that precedes the power to kill: "sovereign law isn't so much the capacity to put to death as it is to nullify life in advance."[8]

What, if anything, does unbearable life add—or, better, take away—from bare life, precarious life, and the other shadowy dramatis personae on the crowded stage of contemporary biopolitics? To speak of a life rendered politically, theologically, or ontologically "unbearable" by sovereign power, I argue that we must subtract ourselves from a persistent biothanatopolitical gesture that extends from Foucault up to even Butler where sovereignty is conceived principally as the power to kill, and, correspondingly, life is construed in terms of its absolute exposure to violent death. It is revealing, for instance, that Foucault's remarkable observation about the sovereign's power over the life and death of his subjects in *"Society Must Be Defended"* is quickly foreclosed by the conclusion that such power really only expresses itself in, or as, the power to kill. As we will see in chapter 1, Agamben, too, consistently resorts to what we might call this thanatopolitical default position in his *Homo Sacer* project when he insists that *"life exposed to death (bare life or sacred life) is the originary political element."*[9] For Butler, the political decision upon whether life becomes, or fails to become, grievable likewise determines whether that life can be exposed to extreme physical violence or not: "certain lives are not considered lives at all, they cannot be humanized," she writes, and this "gives rise to a physical violence that in some sense delivers the message of dehumanization that is already at work in the culture."[10] Yet, as Butler certainly recognizes, what I am calling "nihilopolitics" contains a proliferation of virtual, conceptual, and biopolitical *dispositifs*, many of which cannot easily be gathered under the general sign of positive or physical "thanatopolitics." If nihilopower inevitably takes the form of war, murder, torture, and other kinds of extreme empirical violence, we will see in the following chapters that it really specializes in producing what Foucault intriguingly call acts of "indirect murder,"[11] which foreclose upon direct or positive killing—political, theological, and philosophical gestures of preemptive or retroactive erasure that render positive empirical violence redundant, tautological, or exorbitant. In our own dark biothanatopolitical imaginary, I suspect that (with apologies to Spinoza) no one has quite yet determined what we can do to a body.

In this book, I trace the history of unbearable life as it emerges across the western political theological imaginary, from Augustine of Hippo through William Shakespeare, Thomas Hobbes, Maximilien Robespierre, and Carl Schmitt up to Walter Benjamin. To quickly outline an argument that will be unpacked at length in the chapters that follow, I want to (1) focus on a series of crucial—yet still almost totally obscure, unread, and unexplained— moments in the canon of western political theology where a sovereign decision is taken that certain forms or modalities of life simply do not, could not, or will never exist. For the thinkers I will explore in what follows, this decision takes many forms (metaphysical, historical, political, literary), and the category of unbearable life is conjugated in many different ways (individuals, subject positions, symbolic figures, entire classes or peoples, even ethical or ontological categories), but, in each case, the conclusion remains the same: they (whoever "they" are) do not belong to the realm of life and death. Yet, as we begin to explore this sovereign decision in more detail, we will also see that it is never simply arbitrary, neutral, or superfluous, but (2) rather something that is integral to the operation of sovereignty itself and the domain of "life" that is its dominion. By rendering certain intolerable or undesirable forms of life inexistent—relegating them to an inaccessibly distant past, consigning them to parallel or virtual universes, or projecting them into an infinitely deferred future—the sovereign seeks to annihilate all resistance to his sovereignty over life via a series of nihilopolitical gestures without recourse to visible or positive murder or killing: exile, expulsion, proscription, nonrecognition, social death, preemptive or retroactive nullification. If someone does not exist, if they never possessed any natural or human rights, if there is no higher power (whether human or divine) bearing witness to the injustice of their suffering, then they become someone to whom literally anything can be done with total impunity and without possibility of redress. Finally (3), this book will propose that there is also one more bearer of unbearable life—one more life that was never born and can never die—in the history of sovereignty besides the victim, and this, of course, is the figure of the sovereign himself. In a paradoxical sense, recall, the emperors Septimius Severus and Geta are subject to the *same* fate, albeit from logically and diametrically opposite poles: both are placed in a political state of exception beyond—whether majestically above or miserably below—the living and the dead.

In one very obvious sense, of course, a "history" of unbearable life is something of a contradiction in terms because it can only be the history of an absence, of a constitutive exclusion, of that which is not permitted to enter history. It will quickly become apparent that what follows does not pretend to be remotely comprehensive and there is an extreme degree of contingency to the selection policy of authors and texts. As the reader will see, my choice of examples is just that—a choice—which probably says as much about my own idiosyncratic cluster of interests in religion, politics, philosophy, and literature as anything else. Yet, this is not to say that what follows is entirely arbitrary, either. To be absolutely clear about where I am coming from, this book is perhaps best read as a modest contribution to that ancient—and yet again now curiously timely—genre it seems we must still helplessly call "political theology."[12] If the essays that follow are all singular pieces—which can, if the reader wishes, be read independently of one another—they are also all new and interlocking reflections on a very familiar set of political theological themes and problems: sovereignty, rule, norm, exceptionalism, messianism, apocalypticism, divine violence, the so-called empty space or groundlessness of the political.[13] Finally, though, I should add that—like every genealogy—this book is not actually a history of the past at all but of the present and it seeks to contribute to, and intervene in, a set of absolutely contemporary political questions. In the conclusion of each chapter, I thus seek to fashion or construct what Walter Benjamin famously calls a historical constellation between past and present, then and now, the premodern and the late modern: what still remains of the theological in the political as we move through time and space is, as we will see, a very particular sovereign cut or de-cision between the existent and the nonexistent, bearable and unbearable lives. What forms, then, does this sovereign decision take? How does it change as we move from Augustine through Shakespeare, Hobbes, Robespierre, and Schmitt to Benjamin? To what extent is unbearable life necessarily synonymous with abjection, lack, vacancy—or might it be resisted or lived otherwise?

To begin to map what is largely unchartered territory, chapter 1 gives a provisional genealogy of nihilopolitics in contemporary biopolitical theory. It is the later Michel Foucault who first begins to pose the question of unbearable life in a fascinating thought experiment in his Collège de France lectures. As I have already suggested, the French thinker argues that the classic sovereign power over life and death contains a hidden paradox. For Foucault, sovereignty over life and death logically requires that the sovereign place the political subject in a position *outside* the order of the living: the subject is paradoxically neither dead nor alive until the sovereign takes the decision one way or another. However, as we have begun to see, Foucault goes on to insist that such unbearable life exists only in theory; in practice, classical sovereignty always takes the form of the power to kill a life whose existence precedes its jurisdiction. If Foucault himself thus returns the question of unbearable life to critical obscurity, this chapter goes on to argue that it emerges from the shadows once again in the work of his biopolitical successors— such as Roberto Esposito, who argues that a subject who precedes the order of life and death is more than a mere "theoretical" hypothesis. In Esposito's work on Nazi eugenics, we get a kind of answer to Foucault's question of what sovereign power over the very *possibility* of life itself might look like. Finally, though, chapter 1 will also raise a question that will, in one way or another, persist throughout the chapters that follow. What, if anything, can be done to resist the rule of unbearable life?

It is my aim in the remainder of the book to offer a series of close textual case studies of unbearable life loosely—sometimes very loosely—drawn from the corpus of western "political theology." Accordingly, chapter 2 returns to one of the foundational texts of Christian political theology and, indeed, of western political theory itself: Augustine of Hippo's *City of God against the Pagans (De Civitate Dei contra Paganos).* To be precise, I focus on a curious moment in the celebrated Book 19 of Augustine's text—which sets out his own theological and political vision of the City—where he recalls that Virgil's *Aeneid* speaks of a terrifying savage called Cacus, who lived all alone, preying upon his fellow man, until he was finally slain by Hercules. Yet, in a mysterious gesture that has attracted almost no attention whatsoever in the vast canon of Augustine criticism, the theologian asserts that Cacus could never really have existed. For Augustine, Cacus must be excluded from the City of God because he constitutes an ontological threat to the theologian's Neoplatonic metaphysics, and chapter 2 goes on to explore the political theological implications of this exclusion. If Cacus becomes the name for the absolute "outside" of Augustine's universe, this chapter shows that (like all the other species of unbearable life we will encounter in this book) he remains paradoxically *inside* that universe—indeed, even in the person of the sovereign himself. In Augustinian political theory—and in subsequent retellings of the myth of Hercules and Cacus by such diverse figures as Maximilien Robespierre and Carl Schmitt—the sovereign himself becomes a kind of Cacus.

After Augustine's *City of God*, chapter 3 turns to a very different dramatization of the political theology of sovereign violence: William Shakespeare's *Macbeth*. To be sure, Shakespeare is—as figures as diverse as Benjamin, Schmitt, Kantorowicz, and, more recently, Eric Santner have all powerfully testified—a dramaturge of what we might call (in the full Lacanian sense of the term) our political theological "imaginary": *Richard II*, *Hamlet*, and *King Lear* do not so much stage fictions of sovereignty as something closer to the sovereignty *of* fiction.[14] However, chapter 3 will argue that *Macbeth* is also the site of a very particular—and, as we will see, uncannily prescient—political theological fantasy of sovereignty. If Macbeth is to secure his place on the Scottish throne, it is not only necessary to dispense with his present rivals but also to stop his future rivals from ever being born in the first place: Macbeth kills Banquo, not because the latter personally has a claim to the throne, but because the Weird Sisters prophesize that he will be the father to a line of kings. For Macbeth, sovereignty over unbearable life thus takes the form of an increasingly frenzied war upon the child and ultimately the *unborn* child: Duncan's son Malcolm, Banquo's son Fleance, and Macduff's son are all material signifiers of a virtual future that must be prevented from ever becoming actualized. In the final section of chapter 3, I pursue Macbeth's war against unbearable life through a series of scenes of early modern and modern political terror: the Gunpowder Plot, the English Civil War, the camp.

For Thomas Hobbes, whose political theory is the subject of chapter 4, unbearable life assumes a very specific form: the religious martyr. It is in Hobbes's famous attempt to found his Commonwealth upon man's natural and rational desire for self-preservation that we find the promise and the threat of a life that is radically *uncommon*. As we will see, he takes seriously only one possible exception to his political anthropology, and this is the category of the religious believer who is, apparently, willing to deny her own nature and reason and lay down her life for her God. Yet, Hobbes concludes his discussion of religious martyrdom in *Leviathan* with an abrupt gesture: the modern religious martyr is not merely vainglorious or irrational but historically and theologically *impossible*. To Hobbes's sovereign gaze, the very existence of a human being who could freely choose death over life constitutes such a threat to his precious Commonwealth that she must be rendered unbearable life: *Leviathan* restricts the category of "martyrdom" only to those who personally bore witness to the Resurrection of Jesus, so that no modern citizen can possibly be a martyr no matter how much blood she sheds. If the religious martyr appears to be the absolute exception to political subjectivity in the Commonwealth, we will see that it returns to become "the rule" in the form of Hobbes's strong apology for absolute sovereign power over the life and death of his subjects: the social contract becomes a kind of sacrificial cult and the political subject a species of civic martyr. In the conclusion of chapter 4, we will re-constellate the Hobbesian struggle between love of life and love of death in a contemporary figure: the suicide bomber.

If the previous chapter takes place against the explosive backdrop of the English Civil War, chapter 5 jumps forward to one of the bloody primal scenes of modern popular sovereignty: the French Revolution. To ground my own reading, I focus here upon the (still largely unread and unexamined) political writings and speeches of one of the Reign of Terror's main philosophical architects: the Jacobin leader Maximilien Robespierre. It was arguably Hegel—in the "Absolute Freedom and Terror" chapter of the *Phenomenology of Spirit*—who first recognized that the Terror was a kind of war on unbearable life: the guillotine produced "the coldest and meanest of all deaths," he famously claimed, "with no more significance than cutting off a head of cabbage or swallowing a mouthful of water."[15] However, what is particularly remarkable in the case of the Terror is that unbearable life is not merely the subject position of the victim, who has already been condemned to the philosophical guillotine by abstract reason. For Robespierre, as critics as diverse as Maurice Blanchot and Slavoj Žižek have had cause to observe, the ideal revolutionary subject *himself* occupies a state of living death long before the vulgar event of his empirical death: he famously describes himself in his final speech to the National Convention as a living martyr to the French Republic who has *already* given his life to the Revolution. In Robespierre's political imaginary, this uncanny state outside of life and death—the living martyr, the already dead—becomes the site of a new revolutionary sovereignty, and chapter 5 concludes by tracking this spectral figure from the French Revolution to a series of modern revolutionary movements like the Mexican Zapatista National Liberation Army.

In chapter 6, I turn to the controversial figure with whom political theology is, for better or worse, synonymous in the modern epoch: the German legal and political theorist Carl Schmitt. It focuses, in particular, on Schmitt's reflections on a mysterious figure in the Apostle Paul's Second Letter to the Thessalonians: the *katechon*. As is now well-known, Paul speaks of a "restrainer" who will hold back the appearance of the "lawless one"—a figure who the early Church associated with the Antichrist of John's Gospel—until the end of the world (2 Thessalonians 2:6–7). To begin with, Schmitt's *katechon* seems expressly designed to reconcile the competing demands of politics and theology, history and eschatology, worldly power (*potestas*) and sacred power (*auctoritas*) by giving historical forms of power such as the Roman Empire a certain legitimacy as "restrainers" of the Antichrist. If the Pauline figure of the restrainer thus seeks to (at least temporarily) render the Antichrist unbearable life, chapter 6 will go on to argue that, once again, this life will not remain where he puts it: the lawless one returns to the heart of sovereignty itself in the form of a kind of state anomia or anarchy. For Schmitt, to recall the title of the obscure 1942 article where the Pauline figure makes its very first appearance in his work, the *katechon* turns out to be not simply a restrainer but an "accelerator despite itself" (*beschleuniger wider willen*): it paradoxically maintains order *through* chaos, paralyzes by catalyzing, preserves the status quo by accelerating the forces of change. In the final section of chapter 6, I trace this aporetic logic of sovereign acceleration—in which *nomos* and anomia, law and lawlessness increasingly coincide—into contemporary biopolitics of security.

What, finally, might be the *future* of unbearable life? It is this question that prompts chapter 7, which takes as its focus the modern German Jewish philosopher Walter Benjamin's philosophy of history and, in particular, his celebrated but mysterious claim that the present generation is bestowed with a "*weak* Messianic power" to redeem the past. As Benjamin knew, a certain obscure tradition of Christian theology that extends from Pietro Damiani through Duns Scotus to William of Ockham argued that God's absolute power means that He can at any point undo something that has already happened: a "fallen" woman (in Damiani's famous example) can regain her virginity as if she never lost it in the first place. To be sure, Benjamin's theory of the redemption of history has many plausible origins, but my hypothesis here is that it can also be read as a radically profane or immanent rewriting of the concept of divine omnipotence over the past, or what we might almost term (recalling Jacob Taubes's

famous verdict on Carl Schmitt) a "divine power from below."
If the past appears to be a realm of pure necessity—where nothing whatsoever can change because it has already happened—
Benjamin goes on to argue (via an idiosyncratic synthesis of
Judeo-Christian messianism and materialist cosmology) that, on
the contrary, the past always contains a kind of virtual or potential remainder where things could have happened otherwise. For
Benjamin, this unlived remainder within the past is not simply
the hypothetical question of "what might have been," but a real
and open possibility: what Benjamin famously calls "*weak* Messianic power" is, I will argue, precisely the unlived or unrealized
past's claim to retroactive actualization and fulfilment. In this
sense, unbearable life—or what Benjamin famously calls the
happiness that "exists only in the air we have breathed, among
people we could have talked to, women who could have given
themselves to us"[16]—continues to live on as the unfinished or
incomplete work of the past.

In closing this introduction, though, I want to try and state as
clearly as possible what I see as the larger political, philosophical, and theological issues that are at stake in this book. To
rewrite the title of a celebrated collection of essays edited some
twenty-five years ago by Eduardo Cadava, Peter Connor, and
Jean-Luc Nancy, I really want to ask a new kind of political question: who or what comes—not after—but *before* the subject?[17]
If this book has a central hypothesis, it is that there is a virtual
and obscure field of sovereign power that precedes, forecloses, and
arguably even seeks to render redundant the classical sovereign
decision upon the life and death of the subject that historically

opens up the entire field of subject formation. For Foucault, as we have already begun to see, what we all too prematurely call "the subject" first exists in a state of exception where it is neither living nor dead—neither alive enough to be killable nor dead enough to be forced to live—until the sovereign decision is taken and what follows seeks to map this (metaphysical, political, and juridical) subject position of a priori neutrality or indifference. What if we are *not yet* subjects?

To extend this hypothesis a little further, I also seek to re-pose an ancient question in a new way: what kind of sovereign body can possess power over both life and death? It is a remarkable constant of political theory from the imperial cult, through renaissance theological absolutism to modern liberal constitutionalism, that sovereign power must, in one way or another, be radically subtracted from the order of life and death: Roman apotheosis, Ernst Kantorowicz's legal fiction of the king's two bodies, Jean Bodin's sovereign perpetuity, Thomas Hobbes's vast "artificiall man," Rousseau's general will, Schmitt's political theology, even the simple constitutional distinction between the person and the office, all seek to install a certain unliving remainder—whether divine, artificial, or representational—within the body of the ruler that survives his finitude.[18] At the same time, modern biopolitical theory has constantly observed an uncanny symmetry between this privileged sovereign body at the heart of the political order and that of his most destitute or marginalized subject: the tortured body of the condemned man (Foucault), the abject body of *homo sacer* (Agamben), even the apparently world-impoverished body of the animal or creature (Derrida).[19] Yet what follows seeks to bring together these two insights in a different way. For my purposes, to recall the curious symmetry between Septimius Severus and Geta with which we began one last time, the sovereign who is above all life finds his dark mirror image, not in bare life, animal, or creaturely life, but in the unbearable life that is beneath life, a life that does not live or die, a life that is *not*. If the sovereign is able to decide not merely upon life and death but on what counts as life in the first place, in other words, it may not be because he is the highest form of life but, to borrow an intriguing hypothesis of Jean-Luc Nancy, because sovereignty itself logically occupies a kind of infinite or supreme *void* that is entirely excepted from, and incommensurate with, the life/death nexus over which it presides: "sovereignty is not located in any person; it has no figure, no contour; it cannot be erected into any monument. It is, simply, the supreme. With nothing above it. Neither God nor master."[20] In his radical nihilism, the sovereign is thus arguably the first unbearable life.

In conclusion, though, this book will also continually raise the classic Leninist question: what—if anything—is to be *done* under the sovereignty of unbearable life? Is it a matter of asserting all the more strongly our right to life, to a voice, to human dignity, to political subjectivity? Or might unbearable life itself become a new kind of political subject position from which to speak and act? It is worth observing here the silent irony that inevitably attends any discussion of *damnatio memoraie*. After all, we would not even know of the existence of such memory sanctions (let alone that of their intended targets like Geta) if they worked as they were supposed to—and this inevitably raises the question of *why* they do not work, or, better, why they set in motion a certain *worklessness*. To be sure, biopolitical theory has offered many possible solutions to the political capture of life, but arguably the most popular response is that there is something within "life" itself that stubbornly and inherently resists sovereignty: Hannah Arendt's natality, Jacques Derrida's sur-vival, Gilles Deleuze's virtuality, Giorgio Agamben's potentiality, and so on, all, in their radically different ways, posit a (metaphysical, ontological, biological or political) residuum within the order of the living that somehow precedes or exceeds political seizure. However, as we will see in chapter 1, it is possible to detect a suspiciously virtuous circularity in the attempt to argue that life itself, in all its infinite plenitude, always already supplies us with the resources to combat the political control over life. If life is pure potentiality, if life's potentiality just *is* stronger than all the biopolitical powers that seek to control life, if biopolitics can only but fail to capture the singularity, potentiality, and plurality of the living, then the uncomfortable question arises of why such powers do not merely continue to exist but to expand, multiply, and proliferate on a planetary scale. Perhaps (or so I want to propose in what follows) a new political answer to the sovereign capture of life may be found not in some neo-vitalist or "positive" biopolitics but in the nihilopolitical state that is being unbearable itself. By embracing, and capitalizing upon, their fate as beings radically outwith the order of life and death, political actors have been able to transform that fate into a ground of immanent resistance or even insurrection: a life that neither lives nor dies cannot, after all, easily be killed or forced to live in servitude. For the parliamentarians of the English Civil War, the Jacobins of the French Revolution, and all the way up to contemporary resistance movements like Mexico's Zapatista National Liberation Army and the Invisible Committee, we will see this state of exception outside life and death becomes the laboratory in which a new set of—paradoxically affirmative—conjugations of political subjectivity are produced: monstrous or unnatural births, the never born, the already dead, the living dead, the people to come. In the political death that is unbearable life, a new politics is struggling to be born.

1

UNBEARABLE

Foucault and the Birth of Nihilopolitics

What does having the right of life and death actually mean? In one sense, to say that the sovereign has a right of life and death means that he can, basically, either have people put to death or let them live, or in any case that life and death are not natural or immediate phenomena which are primal or radical, and which fall outside the field of power. If we take the argument a little further, or to the point where it becomes paradoxical, it means that in terms of his relationship with the sovereign, the subject is, by rights, neither dead nor alive. From the point of view of life and death, the subject is neutral [neutre], and it is thanks to the sovereign that the subject has the right to be alive or, possibly, the right to be dead. In any case, the lives and deaths of subjects become rights only as a result of the will of the sovereign.

—Michel Foucault, *"Society Must Be Defended":*
Lectures at the Collège de France, 1975–76

I n a lecture first delivered on March 17, 1976, at the Collège de France, and published posthumously in *"Society Must Be Defended"* (2003), Michel Foucault briefly proposes an intriguing thought experiment about sovereignty. It is, rightly

or wrongly, a commonplace of political theory that the fundamental right of the classical sovereign is the power of life and
death (*vitae necisque potestas*) over his subjects.[1] As Foucault
observes, the sovereign power to put people to death or let them
live has its origins in the Roman right of the father (*patria potestas*) to dispose of his children's lives. Yet, he contends, this classic formula also contains a previously unnoticed aporia, or paradox, that extends sovereignty into a new virtual territory. To put
it in Foucault's own terms, sovereign power over both life and
death—if it really does what it claims to do—logically positions
the political subject in an a priori state of political exception outside the life/death matrix unless and until the sovereign decision is taken: "the subject is neutral and it is thanks to the sovereign that the subject has the right to be alive or possibly, the
right to be dead." If he does not go on to unpack the full implications of this thought experiment anywhere in his later work,
I want to propose that Foucault nonetheless offers the first, most
succinct, and penetrating formulation of what this book will call
"unbearable life": a life rendered unlived, nonexistent, unbearable by sovereign power. For classical sovereignty, sovereign
power is not merely the power to decide upon whether a living
subject should continue to live or die but, fundamentally, to
decide on whether that subject (now radically divested of any
intrinsic natural rights or properties) ever possessed the right to
be considered "alive" in the first place: sovereign is he who
decides, not on life and death, but on unbearable life.[2] This opening chapter proposes that Foucault's famous history of the
"birth" of biopolitics—of the politics of making life live and letting die—from early modern social contract theory to the Nazi
camps is also the story of the *naissance* of nihilopolitics, of the
politics of making life neither live nor die. In what follows, I offer
a counter-genealogy of Foucault's thought experiment that tracks

the historical production of a very singular set of sovereign bodies, that could all be said to exist outside the life/death matrix: the never born, the living dead, the already dead. What, then, is the "life" of unbearable life? How does it emerge across the field of modern political theory from Hobbes through Rousseau to contemporary biopolitical theorists like Esposito? To what extent might it be possible for the subject to resist this sovereign power over life and death?

In the Collège de France lectures and contemporaneous texts, Foucault famously narrates a larger historical story about the passage from absolute to popular sovereignty, sovereignty to governmentality, and, more broadly, sovereign power to biopower. To quickly reconstruct this genealogy, I begin by returning to the French philosopher's famous claim in the opening sentence of the chapter "Right of Death and Power over Life" from *The Will to Knowledge*: "one of the characteristic privileges of sovereign power was the right to decide life and death."[3] For Foucault, recall, classical sovereignty is essentially a right of seizure: "of things, time, bodies, and ultimately life itself; it culminated in the privilege to seize hold of life in order to suppress it."[4] Yet, in the nineteenth century classical sovereignty metastasizes into a proliferation of new disciplinary regimes, apparatuses, and technologies, he argues, which supplement, and reverse, its classical privilege. If the basic signature of sovereign power over the individual subject was "to make die and let live" (*faire mourir ou laisser vivre*), biopower exerts itself not over citizens but over populations, races, and species-existence itself with the exact opposite imperative: to "make live and let die" (*faire vivre et*

laisser mourir).[5] This new power is dedicated to "generating forces, making them grow, and ordering them" rather than "impeding them, making them submit, or destroying them."[6] In inaugurating a new epoch in the history of power, biopolitics also brings about a radical transformation in the subject of power from Aristotle's political animal (*zoon politikon*) to a new man who has been animalized *by* politics: "For millennia, man remained what he was for Aristotle: a living animal with the additional capacity for a political existence; modern man is an animal whose politics places his existence as a living being in question."[7] What is the place of Foucault's thought experiment on the classic sovereign power of life and death within this larger genealogy?

To start with, Foucault's hypothesis seems to problematize this story of the irreversible historical mutation of sovereign power into biopower: what the French philosopher calls the sovereign "right of life and death" is neither the power to make live nor make die, strictly speaking, but the power to make life neither live nor die, to render life neutral. It is not surprising, then, to see *"Society Must Be Defended"* immediately go on to reinforce the very opposition it has just inadvertently called into question. According to Foucault, the "theoretical paradox" he locates in the classical theory of sovereignty contains "a practical disequilibrium," which (conveniently) permits him to disregard it altogether. If a sovereign "obviously" (*bien entendu*)[8] cannot grant life in the same way that he inflicts death—and we will return in a moment to this unargued assumption that "life" must precede sovereignty—then his supposed power over life and death is always exercised in an unbalanced way that tips the scales in favor of death. For Foucault, sovereign power over "life" is in reality nothing but the tautological repetition of the "right of the sword": "it is at the moment when the sovereign can kill that he exercises his right over life."[9] This is why *The Will to Knowledge* famously redescribes the sovereign "power of life and death" as the power to take life or let live, to kill or refrain from killing.[10] In Foucault's genealogy, it will only be with the birth of the epoch of biopolitics proper that biological life ceases to be merely the pre-political substrate or condition of politics and becomes something close to its end or goal—and so he returns unbearable life to the critical obscurity where he first found it.

In what follows, though, I want to argue that Foucault's remarkable thought experiment on classic sovereignty exceeds the various conceptual antinomies (theory versus practice; sovereign power versus biopower; killing and making live) in which he seeks to capture it: unbearable life will never quite stay where he seeks to put it. It is worth noting at the outset here that this attempt to reduce the sovereign right of life to nothing more than the tautological repetition of the right to kill comes at the risk of what we will see to be a curiously retroactive depoliticization and re-naturalization—even a revitalization—of "life" under sovereignty that reverberates through the history of biopolitics. After all, any attempt to limit sovereign power to nothing but the power to kill can only mean that the subject would no longer really be "neutral" vis-à-vis life and death, but must already somehow be given as a living being (*zoon*), as if life really were a "natural or immediate" phenomenon. To take Foucault's hypothesis about sovereignty over life and death seriously, we must thus begin to imagine a counter-genealogy—a kind of unbearable life—of his familiar genealogy of "life" as the historical passage from sovereign power to biopower, sovereignty to governmentality, making die to making live, and so on—in short, of the entire history of what has come to be known as "biopolitics." If sovereignty is not simply reducible to the power to kill, if a sovereign really does have the power to "grant life in the same way that he can inflict death,"[11] if life was never a natural or immediate phenomenon that was simply outside the domain of the political but something that has always been permeated by political power, then arguably an obscure form of power starts to emerge in the theoretical, historical, and philosophical interstices between sovereignty and biopolitics, life and death, killing and living. In rereading Foucault's history of the birth of biopolitics against itself, we can begin to glimpse the *naissance* of nihilopolitics.

In the March 17 lecture, Foucault intriguingly goes on to assert that the birth of biopolitics—which he normally dates to the beginning of the nineteenth century—is already under way more than 150 years earlier in social contract theory: "The jurists of the seventeenth and especially the eighteenth century were, you see, already asking this question about the right of life and death."[12] It is with the canonical signatures Hobbes, Locke, and Rousseau (who, though never explicitly named, are some of the likely targets here) and the classic debates around the social contract (natural versus civil rights, individual liberties versus political obligations) stretching from the English Civil War to the French Revolution that we can begin to glimpse the emergence of something like biological life as the referent object of political power. To say the very least, Foucault's attempt to reclaim a figure like Thomas Hobbes as a theorist of biopower *avant la lettre* here is somewhat surprising, because, of course, the twentieth-century French philosopher axiomatically sets his own theory of politics against that of the seventeenth-century English political theorist: Foucault famously insists here and elsewhere that we must "eschew the model of Leviathan in the study of power" in order to understand the new architecture of the political.[13] In Foucault's lecture, though, he also seems to identify something close to Hobbesian social contract theory less as the dying breath of sovereign absolutism, say, and more as the birth pangs of what will become known as biopower. What if, contrary to everything Foucault previously led us to believe, Hobbes had already cut off the king's head?[14]

To quickly unpack Foucault's hypothesis here, Hobbes's apology for the classic sovereign power to make die and let live ironically ends up anticipating the equal and opposite biopolitical power to make live and let die.[15] It is our natural right to preserve our own physical existence; recall, that is the foundation of what Hobbes famously calls "the mutual Relation between Protection and Obedience."[16] According to Foucault, though, social contract theory's recognition that the subject's natural right to life—a right that Hobbes famously argues cannot be alienated by society—necessarily precedes and delimits the sovereign power to kill is the thin end of a wedge that will ultimately lead to the demise of sovereignty itself. For Foucault, Hobbes's theory of sovereign power is thus ironically delegitimized by the very authority—the natural right to life—that brought it into existence in the first place:

The jurists ask: When we enter into a contract, what are individuals doing at the level of the social contract, when they come together to constitute a sovereign, to delegate absolute power over them to a sovereign? They do so because they are forced to by some threat or by need. They therefore do so in order to protect their lives. It is in order to live [*pouvoir vivre*] that they constitute a sovereign. To the extent that this is the case, can life actually become one of the rights of the sovereign? Isn't life the foundation [*fondatrice*] of the sovereign's right, and can the sovereign actually demand that his subjects grant him the right to exercise the power of life and death over them, or in other words, simply the power to kill them? Mustn't life remain outside the contract [*hors contrat*] to the extent that it was the first, initial, and foundational reason [*motif*] for the contract itself?[17]

Yet, it is again possible to suspect what I have called a certain vitalism in Foucault's implication that "life" thus constitutes a point of external, or pre-political, resistance to Hobbesian sovereign power. If Foucault's reading of the state of nature is curiously literal here—as though Hobbes were claiming it was a real, chronological epoch prior to the establishment of society rather than a retroactive projection or naturalization by the social order itself—what his naturalist critique of social contract theory's account of the sovereign right to kill ironically also misses is the fact that the English philosopher expressly claims that the "foundation" of the right of life and death does not lie in society at all, but in that (allegedly "natural" but actually naturalized) state: Hobbes famously argues that the sovereign alone *retains* his own natural right to do anything to anyone to survive in the state of nature, in the form of the right to punish and kill in society.[18] This is why Hobbes is able to argue that the sovereign's naturally founded right to kill any one of his subjects with impunity is not (as we will see in chapter 4) contradicted in any way by the subjects' equal and opposite natural right to physically resist their sovereign in cases (such as war, self-sacrifice, capital punishment) where he puts their life in danger. In contradistinction to Foucault's claim that the subject's natural right to life constitutes a point of pure, pre-political resistance to sovereign power, we might thus begin to suspect that the Hobbesian sovereign's right to kill was always virtually or embryonically "inside," so to speak, what we all too prematurely persist in calling natural or pre-political life.

In the sense that sovereignty is virtually present at the very origin of "life" itself or, better, that "life" itself is already a ret-roactive sovereign production, Hobbes's political philosophy arguably does not bear witness to the birth of modern biopower, of making live and letting die, but of that more obscure sovereign power we have called nihilopower: making life neither live nor die. It is ironically possible to find something close to Foucault's own thought experiment of sovereign power over life and death in Hobbes's discussion of those explosive "controversies"— monstrous births, miracles, martyrdom, and other biopolitical states of exception—that threaten the stability of the Common-wealth and can, in his view, only authentically be settled one way or another by a sovereign decision. To take Hobbes's own hyper-bolic example of the deformed newborn baby from *De Cive* (1642), for example, he is clear that the civil sovereign—not right reason, morality, or Aristotelian philosophy—is who ultimately decides what *counts* as human life and what does not:

> For example, if a woman bring forth a child of an unwonted shape, and the law forbid to kill a man; the question is, whether the child be a man. It is demanded therefore, what a man is. No man doubts but the city shall judge it, and that without taking an account of Aristotle's definition, that man is a rational creature.[19]

For Hobbes, the sovereign right to decide whether a human being *ever* lived in the first place thus takes precedence over the right to kill a human being whose natural existence is simply assumed to preexist the political decision. If human biological life is defined by this sovereign decision, rather than being a prior natural right or capacity to which politics is merely super-added, then Hobbesian sovereign power thus anticipates the very theory of sovereignty over life and death that Foucault himself deems to be impossible: Hobbes places the subject in a neutral position—neither quite alive enough to make die nor dead enough to let live—until the sovereign decision is taken one way or the other. In this sense, Hobbes's "unwonted" (unusual, uncommon, exceptional) child—who is placed in a kind of suspended animation until a sovereign decision on whether it is a human being or not is taken—could perhaps be the obscure historical, political, and philosophical ancestor of Foucault's Francisco Franco, who is equally suspended between life and death at the other end of existence:

> To symbolize all this, let's take, if you will, the death of Franco, which is after all a very, very interesting event. It is very interesting because of the symbolic values it brings into play, because the man who died had, as you know, exercised the sovereign right of life and death with great savagery, was the bloodiest of all the dictators, wielded an absolute right of life and death for forty years, and at the moment when he himself was dying, he entered this sort of new field of power over life which consists not only in managing life, not only in making live, but finally in keeping individuals alive after they are dead. And by a power that is not simply scientific prowess, but the actual exercise of the political biopower established in the eighteenth century, we have become so good at keeping people alive that we've succeeded in keeping them alive when, in biological terms, they should have been dead long ago. And so the man who had exercised the absolute power of life and death over hundreds of thousands of people fell under the influence of a power [*coup d'un pouvoir*] that managed life so

well, that took so little heed of death, and he didn't even realize that he was already dead and was being kept alive after his death.[20]

In his March 17 lecture, Foucault also seems to implicitly identify another social contract theorist under whose signature we may observe the first appearance of "life" as a political object: Jean-Jacques Rousseau. To remember his larger place in the general narrative of Foucault's 1975–1976 lecture series, Rousseau's social contract theory—and more particularly his theory of the natural right of man—is expressly invoked by the revolutionary bourgeoisie in the eighteenth century as a universalist, anti-historicist reaction against the new historiography of the sixteenth and seventeenth centuries, privileging the historical struggle between tribes, peoples and races, which was the political province of the aristocracy: "The Rousseauism of the bourgeoisie at the end of the eighteenth century, before and during the Revolution, was a direct response to the historicism of the other political subjects who were fighting in the field of theory and historical analysis."[21] If Foucault recognizes that Rousseau remains at all times a theorist of sovereignty,[22] it is nonetheless possible to see this revolutionary appeal to the natural right not merely to life but to freedom and equality over and against the historicism of the aristocracy as another decisive moment in the emergence of biopower. In Foucault's genealogy of eighteenth-century political theory, Rousseau's "*beau sauvage*"—who precedes society as its natural constituent power—is pitted against Henri Boulanvillier's "barbarian," who is constituted retroactively by the social order itself as its defining negative.[23] What, though, if (again contrary to Foucault's own explicit genealogy) Rousseau's noble savage is already a "barbarian"?

To begin by stating the obvious, Rousseau's own remarkable description of the birth of society in book 2 of the *Social Contract* is (just as we have seen in the case of Hobbes) clearly something vastly more complex than any mythical "return to nature": "Anyone who dares to institute a people must feel capable of, so to speak, changing human nature," he famously writes, "of transforming each individual who by himself is a perfect and solitary whole into part of a larger whole from which that individual would *as it were receive his life and his being* [*en quelque sorte sa vie et son être*]."[24] It is not merely that man's passage from nature and society is irreversible, in other words, but something more radical: "human nature" itself—and hence natural right or law—is once again a retroactive construction bestowed by society. As readers of Rousseau as radically different as Leo Strauss, Jacques Derrida, and Bernard Stiegler have observed, "man" in the state of nature was not a human being at all but a species of subhuman or "animal"[25] who is essentially defined by a lack or absence of human nature: "There is no natural constitution of man to speak of," Strauss contends, "everything specifically human is acquired or ultimately depends on artifice or convention."[26] For Stiegler—revolutionizing Derrida's theory of the supplement in the *Grammatology* (1967)—Rousseau's allegedly natural man in the *Discourse on Inequality* is again constituted by what he calls a necessary default of origin (*le défaut qu'il faut d'origine*), which finds itself always already supplemented by technical prostheses: man is a "being without qualities" in the state of nature.[27] If Rousseau's natural man receives his life and being from society— rather than from any intrinsic natural law or right—then we might again detect a certain political vitalism in Foucault's claim that "life" simply predates the social contract as its necessary foundation: what allegedly exceeds sovereignty as its condition of possibility—animal or biological existence—is once again folded back into a sovereignty that turns out to be the quasi-transcendental political condition of its own "natural" condition. In Rousseau's own apology for the sovereign right of life and death—which is revealingly even more uncompromising than Hobbes's—the citizen's "natural" right to life is thus no defense whatsoever against capital punishment or warfare: "Whoever wills the end, also wills the means and these means are inseparable from certain risks and even certain losses."[28]

In many ways, then, Rousseau's account of the sovereign power to decide on life or death ends up (like Hobbes's before him) raising the question of whether the subject *ever* possessed a right to life independently of sovereign decision. It is in his discussion of the right of life and death (*vitae necisque potestas*) that Foucault's genealogy of biopower once again seems to open up the possibility of a genealogy of nihilopower: the right to make the citizen neither live nor die. As is well documented, Hobbes asserts the subject's inalienable right of physical resistance against sovereign acts (war, capital punishment) that put their lives in danger. Yet, Rousseau's own defense of capital punishment from chapter 5, book 2 of *The Social Contract*, "Of the Right of Life and Death," refuses this natural right to life by insisting, again *contra* Foucault, that life is less the foundation of the social contract than its product. To put it in Rousseau's words, the citizen has already "promised" her life to the sovereign as the very condition of entering society in the first place:

> Whoever wants to preserve his life at the expense of others ought also to give it up for them when necessary. Now, the Citizen is no longer judge of the danger the law wills him to risk, and when the Prince has said to him, it is expedient to the State that you

die, he ought to die; since it is only on this condition that he has
lived in security until then, and his life is no longer only a bounty
of nature, but a conditional gift of the State [*un don conditionnel
de l'État*].[29]

For Rousseau, as we have already seen in the case of Hobbes,
the sovereign right to kill is underwritten by a more obscure sovereign power to decide whether a human being ever genuinely
"lived" in the first place. If the subject's life does not precede the
sovereign as a free gift of nature, but is a kind of vital "loan"
extended by the sovereign that can be recalled at any moment,
then the sovereign right to kill does not negate a living being so
much as it once again confirms the subject's originary default or
lack of human life: what we call the "death penalty" might be
more properly described as the state's retroactive annulment of
its own conditional gift of life or even a kind of "life penalty." In
this sense, Rousseau universalizes the Hobbesian sovereign's
decision on the humanity (or lack thereof) of the exceptional
or "unwonted" child: every citizen is put in the position of the
"unwonted" child, whose very existence is a question of sovereign decision.

In the remainder of his lecture of March 17, Foucault goes on
to pose a famous question that has continued to reverberate
across generations of biopolitical theorists: why does a technology of power that "takes life as both its object and its objective" and even aims "to improve life" go on to "demand deaths"
not only amongst its "enemies" but also "its own citizens"? To
answer the question of why biopolitics seems so inevitably to

bleed into thanatopolitics, Foucault turns from the race wars of the early modern period to the emergence of what he calls "modern racism": racism in modernity has become "primarily a way of introducing a break into the domain of life that is under power's control," he contends, "the break between what must live and what must die." If National Socialist biopolitics waged a military war against its foreign enemies, to take only the most blatant example, it also presided over an act of internal biological "cleansing" of its own population (Jews, homosexuals, the mentally ill, and so on), which was predicated on the assumption that the strength and purity of the "good race" would increase in proportion to the decline of the "inferior race." For Foucault, biopolitics justifies political killing or letting die (*laisser mourir*) "only if it results not in a victory over political adversaries, but in the elimination of the biological threat to and the improvement of the species or race." In the March 17 lecture, revealingly, killing should be understood not simply as the positive or physical act of murder but "also every form of indirect murder: the fact of exposing someone to death, increasing the risk of death for some people, or, quite simply, political death, expulsion, rejection, and so on."[30] What, though, if modern racism is less an entirely new biopolitical power—one that breaks decisively with classical sovereignty—than the empirical outworking of the aporia we have been tracing in the theory of sovereign power over life and death from Hobbes to Rousseau?

To be sure, we can glimpse the entire future history of biopolitical theory in Foucault's March 17 lecture: what will become Agamben's bare life, Butler's precarious life, and Esposito's immunized life are, with the luxury of hindsight, all virtually present in the French philosopher's account of the biopolitics of racism. It is nonetheless possible to wonder whether—for all their claims to more or less "complete" or even perfect Foucault's unfinished project—Foucault's biopolitical successors genuinely pursue his thought experiment about the sovereign right of life and death to its logical conclusion. As I have already hinted in the Introduction, they remain largely within the (residually vitalist) conceptual perimeters of his genealogy of biopolitics, where sovereign power is nothing more than the right to kill a life that is always already naturally given. For Agamben, whose multivolume theory of sovereignty in *Homo Sacer* (1995–2005) explicitly begins where Foucault's genealogy of biopolitics ends, this sovereign right of life and death is famously reconceptualized as the political power to produce the subject called "bare life" (*nuda vita*): "*It can even be said that the production of a biopolitical body is the original activity of sovereign power.*"[31] If Foucault's thought experiment of a subject who is "by rights, neither dead nor alive" until the sovereign decides seems in certain respects to be the theoretical prototype for Agamben's *Homo Sacer* project—as well as the whole dramatis personae of that project, from the Roman *Devotus* through the *Muselmänn* to the "braindead" coma patient Karen Quinlan—it is striking that (like Foucault) Agamben continues to define this body suspended between life and death purely in terms of its unconditional capacity to be killed: "*Not simply natural life, but life exposed to death (bare life or sacred life) is the originary political element.*"[32] In his definition of sovereignty as the capacity to produce bare life, Agamben not only reinforces Foucault's original decision to reduce sovereign power over life and death to nothing more than the power to kill, but also recapitulates what we have seen to be Foucault's own retroactive "naturalization" of life: the political subject must already somehow be given as a living being before she is produced as killable life.

In many ways, Roberto Esposito's compelling genealogy of biopolitics—which is unpacked in his trilogy *Communitas* (1998),

Immunitas (2002), and *Bios* (2004)—comes closest to giving concrete political form to Foucault's thought experiment: sovereignty consists in the power to place the subject in a kind of originary state of political ontological suspension outside life and death before the decision to make them live or die is taken.[33] It is in Esposito's compelling reimagining of National Socialist biopolitics in *Bios* that we can find an implicit answer to Foucault's question of what a sovereign power over life and death might actually look like. As Esposito reminds us, Nazism was not originally a politics of death at all but of birth: natural birth, albeit always seen through the optic of racial heredity, became the basic determinant of German citizenship (or the lack thereof). Yet, of course, it was not so much birth that determined political status as the other way around, because political status—or rather the particular bio-racial arithmetic that calculated one's position within the political order—predetermined the value of birth, which births counted, and which did not. To put it in Esposito's words, this fatal logic is the beginning of an obscure Nazi biopolitical *dispositif* he calls "the anticipatory suppression of birth":[34] what was taking place in such phenomena as the mass compulsory sterilization of men and women suffering from hereditary diseases or genetic disorders was not so much the killing of bare or subhuman life than (think of Hobbes's unwonted child again) the preemptive foreclosure of potential lives from every being born in the first place.[35] If a decision could be taken that certain potential lives were not worthy of being born, it was but an extension of that logic to declare present lives (the real people who would have gone on to father and mother those future children) to also be legally and politically inexistent—the infamous biolegal category of "life unworthy of being lived" (*Lebensunwertes Leben*). For Esposito, this is why Hannah Arendt's remark about the abject position of the concentration camp inhabitants in her

Origins of Totalitarianism (1951) also carries an exact and chilling biopolitical purchase: "the status of the inmates in the world of the living, where nobody is supposed to know if they are alive or dead, is such that it is as though they had never been born."[36] In this sense, Nazi biopolitics represents the political culmination of the nihilopolitical gesture we have been tracing from Hobbes to Rousseau: "sovereign law isn't so much the capacity to put to death as it is to nullify life in advance."[37]

In preparing the ground for the remainder of this book, though, I want to consider one last question that is inevitably raised by Foucault's thought experiment and will continue to concern us throughout what follows: resistance. To return to the famous closing chapter of *The Will to Knowledge*, "Right of Death and Power over Life," Foucault claims that political resistance to the biopolitical capture of life consists not in the return to ancient discourses and rights of law, but in a new contestation and mobilization of the very domain of "life" itself. "It is not that life has been totally integrated into techniques that govern and administer it," he remarks, but quite the opposite: "it constantly escapes them."[38] If biopolitics is the politics of life itself—the politics that takes biological life as its referent object—Foucault's famous hypothesis is that life somehow also exceeds biopolitical capture as an irreducible excrescence produced within the system itself that, nonetheless, cannot be metabolized by it: "life as a political object" could even be "turned back against the system that was bent on controlling it."[39] In this claim, Foucault's residual vitalism—which consistently and retroactively posits "life" as radically exterior to sovereignty—breaks out into the open as a site of political resistance: *life itself seems to contain the capacity to resist sovereign power over life*. What, then, is to be done under the sovereignty of unbearable life?

To risk belaboring the obvious once more, Foucault's assertion that life exceeds sovereign capture has become something of an article of faith of any affirmative biopolitics over the last thirty years, but its exact philosophical ground remains notoriously opaque. It goes without saying that his "theory of resistance"—if there is one—is one of the most controversial areas of his thought precisely because it seems to imply the very a priori ontological or normative foundation *for* resistance that, axiomatically, any genealogy refuses.[40] As Gilles Deleuze was arguably the first to note of the *History of Sexuality* project, Foucault "must have come up against the question of whether there was anything 'beyond' power—whether he was getting trapped in a sort of impasse within power relations."[41] Yet, of course, the famous discussion of "method" is equally insistent that there is no pure transcendental "outside" of sovereign power—call it life, the body, the subject, or whatever you like—from which its "inside" may be criticized, because this apparent outside is itself produced by that very inside.[42] For the later Foucault, the power of resistance seems to be the property neither of a pure transcendental will or subject but an immanent effect of the system itself: resistance is something analogous to the "noise" generated by the homeostatic or cybernetic feedback loop of power/knowledge. If this purely immanent theory of resistance might seem at first blush to solve the problem of the transcendental "outside" identified by Deleuze, it arguably does nothing more than internalize Deleuze's aporia within the entropic machine of power/knowledge itself: Foucault still does not answer the central question of *why* power/knowledge must inevitably produce internal resistance—an outside within the inside—let alone why this resistance should be consistently named "life."[43] In Esposito's reading, the later Foucault's famous claim about life's capacity to resist the forces seeking to control it begs a fatal question about the status of the biothanatopolitical project itself, which haunts the latter's genealogy: "If life is stronger than the power that besieges it, if its resistance doesn't allow it to bow to the pressure of power, then how do we account for the outcome obtained in modernity of the mass production of death?"[44]

In seeking to articulate his own affirmative theory of biopolitics, Esposito revealingly appeals to one more *tableau vivant* of a sovereign body suspended neutrally between life and death: Roger "Rogue" Riderhood, a minor character in Charles Dickens's novel *Our Mutual Friend* (1865), who is also, of course, the subject of a famous late reading by Gilles Deleuze.[45] It was Deleuze's original claim that this Dickensian villain, who is rescued unconscious from the River Thames after almost drowning, arouses the interest of the company assembled at his bedside, not out of any sympathy for Riderhood as an individual, but because they detect a "spark of life"[46] within him that is independent of any subjectivity and which they all, as living beings, share.[47] According to Esposito's rereading of Dickens's novel, Riderhood's comatose body becomes the site of a positive biopolitics that contests the Nazi thanatopolitical reduction of life to bare or killable life. To recall Esposito's fascinating argument here, Riderhood's "spark of life"—which everyone around him equally possesses—signifies the production of a virtual impersonal "life," which precedes and exceeds the actualized life and death of the individual subject: "What Dickens calls 'outer husk' or a 'flabby lump of mortality' has not a little to do with the 'empty shells' and 'life unworthy of life' of Binding and Hoche—with Treblinka's flesh of the ovens—yet with a fundamental difference that has to do with a change in orientation;

no longer from life seemingly to death, but from death seemingly to a life in which Riderhood awakes."[48] If Esposito's own affirmative theory of biopolitics has an ontological foundation, it thus appears to lie in a Simondonian and Deleuzean politics of virtuality, which, again, insists upon life's intrinsic resistance to biopolitical capture, its perpetual becoming in new forms, and its extension across the entire field of the living to the point where no element of it can be isolated and destroyed in favor of another.[49] In valorizing a "spark of life" that resists every attempt to capture it politically, though, Esposito's biopolitics arguably describe a similar politically vitalist circle as Foucault: life is taken to ontologically exceed power, and so, in turn, power is deemed to be politically incapable of mastering life.[50]

In Michel Foucault's remarkable thought experiment upon sovereign power over life and death, then, we arguably begin to glimpse an alternative past, present, and future for biopolitical theory. To reiterate my central hypothesis: sovereignty consists not merely in the power to decide upon life and death—in the Roman right of life and death, in *vitae necisque potestas*—but in the power to make life neither live nor die, to position the political subject in an "unbearable" state of exception outside the spectrum of life and death. If this opening chapter has begun to trace the *naissance* of nihilopolitics via a singular set of unbearable bodies suspended between life and death—Hobbes's unwonted child, Rousseau's condemned man, Foucault's Franco, Agamben's comatose victim, Deleuze and Esposito's Roger "Rogue" Riderhood—what follows will continue to map this genealogy of nihilopolitics backward and forward in time from

Augustine to Benjamin by tracing the theological, literary, and philosophical dramatis personae of unbearable life. In drawing this opening chapter to a close, though, I want to re-pose the question that haunts Foucault's own unfinished genealogy of biopolitics and will continue, in one way or another, to concern us here. What positive or affirmative form of life might an "unbearable" political subjectivity take between the false antinomies of vitalism and nihilism?

To offer a preliminary sketch of an answer, I want to return to our final spectacle of a figure suspended in a state of neutrality between life and death: Roger "Rogue" Riderhood from Charles Dickens's *Our Mutual Friend*. It is striking that not one of the many discussions of this minor villain by Deleuze, Agamben, Esposito, or their exegetes remarks upon the character's eventual fate. As we will see, this omission may be no coincidence, because Riderhood's eventual demise casts doubt upon the very political vitalism—the spark of life—they all proffer as an antidote to sovereign biopolitics.[51] For Dickens, Riderhood awakens from his coma only to revert to his former criminal life before finally drowning in a struggle with his accomplice, and the novel's principal antagonist, Bradley Headstone:

> Bradley was drawing to the lock edge. Riderhood was drawing away from it. It was a strong grapple, and a fierce struggle, arm and leg. Bradley got him round, with his back to the lock, and still worked him backward.
>
> "Let go!" said Riderhood. "Stop! What are you trying at? You can't drown *me*. Ain't I told you that the man as has come through drowning can never be drowned? I can't be drowned."
>
> "I can be!" returned Bradley in a desperate, clenched voice. "I am resolved to be. I'll hold you living, and I'll hold you dead. Come down!"[52]

If this deadly struggle is literally a kind of Hegelian master-slave dialectic (and Riderhood addresses the schoolteacher Headstone as "master" or "governor" throughout the book), it is also possible to read it as a dramatization of the very sovereign power over life and death that we have begun to track in this chapter. On the one side, Headstone is apparently the classical sovereign asserting his right of life and death over his subject: "I'll hold you living, and I'll hold you dead." On the other, Riderhood is seemingly the classical subject whose life and death subsist entirely at the behest of sovereign will and decision: "Bradley got him round, with his back to the Lock, and still worked him backward." In his deadly determination that Riderhood will have no life or death independent of his own, Headstone's nihilistic act of suicide-murder dramatically exemplifies Foucault's hypothesis that, to the sovereign gaze, "the subject is, by rights, neither dead nor alive."

In conclusion, though, I would like to speculate that Riderhood and Headstone's master-slave dialectic can be read (just like Hegel's original rendition) less as a confirmation of the sovereign status quo than as a dramatization of resistance, of the emergence of a new form of political subjectivity, of the slave becoming (in Jean Hyppolite's phrase) the "master of the master."[53] To pursue this hypothesis, I want to focus on the fact that Riderhood and Headstone's deadly conflict at the end of *Our Mutual Friend* nonetheless conceals an unspoken *agreement* between the two characters about the former's uncanny position: Roger "Rogue" Riderhood cannot die because he is, in some paradoxical sense, *already* beyond life and death. It is Riderhood's defiant claim, remember, that "You can't drown me," because, according to a river worker's superstition he recounts earlier in the book, a man who has already "come through" drowning once can "never be drowned." As Headstone's own counterclaim—"I can be!"—seems implicitly to concede, Riderhood is quite correct: the master cannot directly kill his (seemingly unkillable) "slave" but only enclose or capture him within his own act of self-killing or destruction. Yet, Riderhood's act of resistance against the sovereign power over life and death is clearly not the product of some positive Simondonian or Deleuzean *élan vital*, which simply exceeds political capture. By asserting "I can't be drowned" because he has *already* "come through" drowning, Riderhood is not affirming the existence of some inextinguishable spark of life within him that resists sovereignty, so much as seeking to transform his passive status as a being in a state of exception outside the order of life and death—neither alive nor dead, always already dead—into a (potential) new form of power.[54] If I have read this scene in any way legitimately, Dickens's novel thus seems to obliquely point a way toward an immanent critique of the sovereignty of unbearable life without falling into the negative biopolitical trap of simply accepting it as an inescapable condition or the positive biopolitical trap of prematurely valorizing some external position that allegedly exceeds its grip: someone who exists outside life and death can, after all, be neither killed by a master nor forced to live as a slave. For Roger Riderhood—"Rogue" that he is[55]—unbearable life becomes not simply an abject fate to be passively endured, but the site upon which a powerful new sovereign body can be produced. In affirming his status as a being radically outwith the order of life and death, this political subject can resist the sovereign power to make die or make live—and turn unbearable life itself into a new form of "life."

2

UNGOOD

Augustine's City of Cacus

*Perhaps, after all, he never existed or, more probably, he was
not like the description given by poetic fantasy.*

—Augustine of Hippo, *City of God*, book 19

In book 19 of *City of God Against the Pagans* (*De Civitate Dei
contra Paganos*), Augustine of Hippo excludes only one figure from his famous city. It is in chapter 12 of that book,
"Peace Is the Instinctive Aim of All Creatures, and Is Even the
Ultimate Purpose of War," that this curious gesture appears. As
the theologian relates, all human beings, no matter how vicious,
self-centered, or evil they may appear, ultimately desire a state
of peace: a warrior wages war in order to impose his own idea of
peace; a robber takes care to maintain peace with his fellow
thieves, and even a solitary killer lives in peace with his wife and
family. Yet, it is at this point that he invokes one last example
of human vice, which seems to exceed all the others. To put it
in Augustine's own words: "Let us, however, suppose such a
man as is described in the verse of epic legends, a creature so
unsociable and savage that they perhaps preferred to call him a
semi-human rather than a human being."[1] For the Christian

theologian, we can find exactly such an "unsociable and savage" creature in a book that (as he recalls in the *Confessions*) he first read as a child: Virgil's *Aeneid* tells the story of Cacus (Κακός), the son of Vulcan, a monstrous savage who vomited black smoke and fire, whose kingdom was a solitary cave reeking of blood and festooned with the body parts of his victims, and who waged nothing less than a one-man war against society before he was finally destroyed by Hercules as punishment for stealing a herd of the god's cattle.[2] In what follows, I explore a series of political theological iterations of the unbearable figure of Cacus, from Augustine through Robespierre and up to Barack Obama. This chapter argues that Cacus is both the constitutive "outside" of Augustine's universe (his name, as the theologian helpfully reminds us, is the Greek word for "bad") but paradoxically he also haunts the inside of that universe, even or especially in the figure of the sovereign himself. Why does Augustine come to the conclusion that Cacus, like so many "similar poetic fictions," is a mere "fantasy"?[3]

In one obvious sense, Cacus—Κακός, bad, evil—represents a kind of hyperbolic thought experiment by Augustine to vindicate his own Neoplatonic theology of the good. It is only necessary to quickly recall here Augustine's famous argument about the privative nature of evil to understand the savage's (otherwise mysterious) appearance in book 19. According to the theologian, all being is good inasmuch as it emanates from the same one substance, namely, God: "There is no such entity in nature as 'evil.'"[4] To posit evil as a thing in itself, we would effectively oppose a rival substance to the one God as well as everything that emanates from him and thus fall into Manicheanism. If Augustine thus denies the existence of an absolute or ontological evil, of course, this is not to say that he does not accept that evil really exists in the world but, rather, that evil is merely "a name for the privation of good [*privatio boni*]"—an absence in or lack of the good—brought about by sin, as opposed to an ontological thing in itself.[5] For Augustine, all being, no matter how sinful or corrupt it may appear, thus necessarily contains a relation to the good, which means that all being is potentially redeemable. In the theologian's account, this conclusion even extends to the embodiment of evil himself: Satan cannot be wholly evil precisely because he really exists.[6]

It might appear, then, that this is the reason why Cacus must be regarded as a mere fancy of the classical poets: the savage (unlike Satan) *is* wholly evil and so he, alone, must be deprived of existence. As a result, his brief appearance in book 19 is a strange anomaly in Augustine's corpus—like a Hobbesian *homo lupus* turning up some one thousand years before the fact. However, there is a revealing moment of equivocation before the theologian finally takes the radical decision to consign the savage to the realm of nonexistence, almost as if he were aware of the philosophical inelegance of such a drastic solution. To try to explain away the existence of this mythical monster, Augustine toys with the possibility that Cacus (like the soldiers, robbers, and murderers described earlier) may simply have acted out of will or necessity when performing his vicious deeds: "it may be that it was not lust for inflicting injury but the necessity of preserving his life that made him so savage." In Augustine's words, Cacus (like all other existent beings) may well have desired a state of peace—albeit in this case only with *himself*:

> Now although his kingdom was the solitude of a dreadful cavern, and although he was so unequalled in wickedness that a name was found for him derived from that quality (he was called Cacus,

and κακός is the Greek word for "wicked"); although he had no
wife with whom to exchange endearments, no children to play with
when little or to give orders to when they were a little bigger, no
friends with whom to enjoy a chat, not even his father, Vulcan (he
was happier than his father only in this important respect—that
he did not beget another such monster as himself); although he
never gave anything to anyone, but took what he wanted from anyone he could and removed, when he could, anyone he wished to
remove; despite all this, in the very solitude of his cave, the floor of
which, in the poet's description "reeked ever with the blood of
recent slaughter" his only desire was for a peace in which no one
should disturb him, and no man's violence, or the dread of it, should
trouble his repose. Above all, he desired to be at peace with his own
body; and in so far as he achieved this, all was well with him.[7]

If he briefly entertains the possibility that Cacus may not have
been absolutely evil, though, Augustine just as quickly goes on
to dismiss it out of hand. It is quite clear that within the terms
and conditions of the theologian's theory of natural law there can
be no such thing as the savage's purely private—which is to say
entirely antisocial—peace. To recall Augustine's precise argument in this context, Cacus's decision to keep the peace solely
with himself, rather than with any of his fellow men or creatures,
means that this "semi-beast" breaks with the inherent sociabil-
ity dictated by natural law, and so, strictly speaking, he is not
only not human, but not even an animal. In this pre-Hobbesian
universe, where apparently even wolves desire to live in peace
with their fellow wolves rather than wage a war of all against
all, Cacus thus turns out be something lower than the *lupus*:

> We observe, then, that even the most savage beasts, from whom
> Cacus derived the wild-beast side of his nature (he was in fact

also called a semi-beast), safeguard their own species by a kind of peace, by coition, by begetting and bearing young, by cherishing them and rearing them; even though most of them are not gregarious but solitary—not, that is, like sheep, deer, doves, starlings, and bees, but like lions, wolves, foxes, eagles and owls. What tigress does not gently purr over her cubs, and subdue her fierceness to caress them? What kite, however solitary as he hovers over his prey, does not find a mate, build a nest, help to hatch the eggs, rear the young birds, and, as we may say, preserve with the mother of his family a domestic society as peaceful as he can make it? How much more strongly is a human being drawn by the laws of his nature, so to speak, to enter upon a fellowship with all his fellow-men and to keep peace with them, as far as lies in him. For even the wicked when they go to war do so to defend the peace of their own people, and desire to make all men their own people, if they can, so that all men and all things might together be subservient to one master.[8]

Why, then, does Augustine take the decision to expel Cacus into the realm of unbearable life? To put it in a word, Cacus—or radical evil—is an ontological impossibility within his theologico-political universe. It is not possible to explain this creature's existence within a monist theory of virtue because he far exceeds any mere privation of the good in a sinful, postlapsarian world. Accordingly, we might go so far as to argue that Cacus is not technically "evil" at all: "even what is perverted must of necessity be in, or derived from, or associated with—that is, in a sense, at peace with—some part of the order of things among which it has its being or of which it consists," the theologian argues in chapter 12 of book 19, "otherwise it would not exist at all."[9] Yet, Cacus constitutes just such an absolute, and so ontologically impossible, vice. For Augustine, this rarest of beasts thus does

not fit any of the categories around which his (remarkably variegated) ontology is organized: Cacus is neither natural nor monstrous, neither human nor animal, neither good nor evil, neither
virtuous nor sinful, born too late for a world of Christian Neoplatonism and too early for the Hobbesian state of nature.[10] Perhaps most importantly, Cacus can also have no place in either
the City of Man or the City of God: he is both ungovernable by
temporal authority (because he exists purely for himself) and
unredeemable by spiritual authority (because he is the embodiment of absolute evil). If Augustine were to grant Cacus entry
into the city, the price would be nothing less than the destruction of his theologico-political monad: either God himself would
have created something radically evil (which would contradict
the theologian's Neoplatonism) or something evil could come
into existence entirely independently of God's creation (which
would contradict his anti-Manicheanism). Finally, this may also
be why the Christian theologian cannot accept Virgil's own solution to the problem of Cacus, which is less a matter of redemption by a loving creator so much as annihilation by a superior
force: Cacus, recall, is killed by Hercules in revenge for stealing
a herd of cattle from the god. In order to kill Cacus, though,
Augustine would have to permit the evil one to be born in the
first place, so it is little wonder that the theologian deems it saf-
est to believe that he simply never existed at all: "Perhaps, after
all, he never existed or, more probably, he was not like the
description given by poetic fantasy."

In this way, we might say that Cacus becomes a figure for the
absolute exteriority of Augustine's theologico-political order,

but—despite or because of his radical excrescence—I want to argue that the savage continues to trouble that order in its interiority as well. It is already possible to detect warning signs in earlier renditions of the story, for example, that Hercules might be something less than a hero and Cacus may be something more than a savage. To begin with the earliest iteration of the Hercules-Cacus myth, Pindar's famous fragment 169, "*Nomos Basileus*," appeals to the labors of Heracles to explain its enigmatic claim that *Nomos* "justifies what is most violent": Heracles himself, Pindar recalls, had violently seized the giant Geryon's cattle *before* the same cattle were stolen from him by Cacus.[11] For Carl Schmitt, who famously rereads Pindar's fragment in *The* Nomos *of the Earth* (1950),[12] Heracles's act of appropriation can thus be seen as a mythical dramatization of the originary violence of the sovereign gesture itself: "Heracles is the mythical foundation of order. Given that he 'appropriated' the cattle of the three-headed giant [Geryon], he created law; the *Nahme*—the *nomos*—transformed power into law. That is the significance of the often cited Pindar fragment *nomos basileus*."[13] If Heracles establishes sovereign order, Mika Ojakangas argues, it is not simply because he is exercising the natural right of the stronger over the weaker, but also because he is performing what Schmitt sees as the foundational act of *nomos*: land appropriation (*Landnahme*).[14] This natural act of appropriation—the settlement or capture of territory over which to exercise dominion—"constitutes the original spatial order, the source of all further concrete order and all further law."[15] In reading Heracles's original act of theft as the myth of the passage from nature to society—from anomia to *nomos*—Schmitt's own (violently appropriative)[16] account is clear that something of Cacus's monstrosity still endures in the Herculean figure of the monster-killing sovereign: "The point of departure of thinking: from chaos to cosmos; from the state of nature to the state; in the displacement, however, there exists a brute that is the cause of the displacement. Hercules who kills monsters and survives as the last monster."[17]

To return to Virgil's own iteration of the Hercules-Cacus myth, we can arguably find something of the same "monstrosity" at work in his representation of Hercules as well. It is a long-held view in Virgil scholarship that the Cacus myth in particular, and the *Aeneid* more generally, can be read as a panegyric on behalf of the new Roman regime of Augustus. According to this reading, Hercules and Cacus's struggle is not only a struggle between good and evil—Cacus is Κακός (bad, wicked) after all—but (recalling Schmitt's reading of Pindar) also between the state of nature and society, anomia and *nomos*, civilization and savagery. For K. W. Gransden, the heroic Hercules's triumph over Cacus thus becomes an allegory both of Aeneas's triumph over Turnus and ultimately of Augustus's triumph over Mark Anthony.[18] If this reading of the text as an exercise in political propaganda was for a long time the orthodoxy, however, it has recently been challenged by a new wave of Virgil scholarship that has (once again) emphasized the uncanny similarities between the forces of good and evil. In his reading of the *Aeneid*, for example, R. O. A. M. Lyne has painstakingly demonstrated how Virgil uses identical tropes to describe the power of Cacus, Hercules, Aeneas, and Augustus.[19]

For Lyne, to take just one simple but telling example, Cacus is by no means the only figure in book 8 of the *Aeneid* who is said to "vomit" (*uomunt*) smoke and fire: the heroic Aeneas's new helmet also vomits fire (*flammasque uomentem*) (*Aeneid*, 8.620), as does the boss of his shield (10.271). By using the same (undoubtedly pejorative) image to describe the *uis*—the power or force—of Aeneas and Cacus, Virgil complicates any simple attempt to morally oppose the two: "force on the 'right' side may not only be as passionate as the enemy's but monstrous like an enemy's."[20] If Aeneas seems closer to Cacus than first appears, this is arguably even more true of the heroic Hercules: Hercules himself (as we will see later on) is said to be "exulting in the slaughter of the triple-bodied Geryon and the spoils he had taken" when he arrives on the scene, and "the black bile of his fury [*furiis*]" upon the theft of his cattle is every bit as wild as Cacus's own (8.219). In the same way, Llewelyn Morgan observes that Virgil's vivid description of Cacus's cave as "warm with freshly shed blood" (*semperque recenti / caede tepebat humus*) (8.195–96) anticipates the later representation of Augustus's own victory at the Battle of Actium, where "the fresh blood began to redden the furrows of Neptune's fields" (*arua noua Neptunia caede rubescunt*) (8.695).[21]

Why, if the *Aeneid* is supposed to be a simple panegyric to Augustus, does the battlefield of the new Roman sovereign triumphing over his enemies recall nothing so much as the slaughter chamber of a savage? To anticipate the argument of the rest of this chapter—Virgil's retelling of the story of Hercules and Cacus may not be a means to praise or blame one particular sovereign (Augustus) so much as a prolonged meditation upon the inherent monstrosity of the sovereign lawmaking decision itself. It is significant here that Cacus's cave is located at the exact same spot where Rome itself will later be built and, even more revealingly, at the inaugural station of Remus.[22] Accordingly, Hercules's killing of his own dark "twin" Cacus prefigures Romulus's killing of his twin brother Remus. For Virgil, at least according to recent readings of the *Aeneid*, they are both acts of what we might call sovereign murder: Hercules's killing of Cacus preserves the proto-Rome of Evander, and Romulus's killing of Remus founds modern Rome. If the state of Rome is indistinguishable from Cacus's own blood-streaked cave, then it is little wonder, again, that Augustine (his own criticisms of empire not-withstanding) prefers to believe that Cacus can only be a fiction. In a kind of preemptive pagan strike against Augustine's Christian Platonism, Virgil does not see Cacus as the unbearable exception to theologico-political rule but something uncomfortably close to the—savage—rule itself.

In the same way, Livy's reiteration of the Hercules-Cacus myth further problematizes the opposition between what the later Derrida would famously call the beast and the sovereign.[23] It is arguably in Livy's account that some of the ambiguities latent in Virgil's original rendition break out into the open. As the former's *History of Rome* recounts, Cacus is a humble shepherd rather than Virgil's fire-breathing monster, but the rest of the story is broadly the same: he steals a herd of cattle from Hercules and takes them to his solitary cave (which is again the historic site of Rome) before being tracked down and murdered by the god for his crime. To an arguably greater degree than Pindar or Virgil, though, Livy stresses the ethico-political violence of Hercules's own sovereignty. If Hercules is supposedly the representative of civilization, imposing order upon chaos, we are again reminded that he arrives on the scene replete with the spoils of his labor against the giant Geryon: he has himself forcibly removed from Geryon the herd of cattle that Cacus will then proceed to take from him. Perhaps more intriguingly, Livy's account also suggests (at least fleetingly) that Hercules's killing of Cacus is not divine vengeance at all but an act of simple murder. In the aftermath of his death, Cacus's outraged fellow shepherds accuse Hercules of "flagrant murder" (*manifesta caedes*), and it is only

Evander's revelation that Hercules is in fact a god that saves him from bloody vengeance at their hands.[24]

To turn now to what is (so far as I am aware) the only modern retelling of the Hercules-Cacus myth, Michel Serres's fascinating discussion of Livy's *History of Rome* in his *Rome: The Book of Foundations* (1991) points to what we might even call a certain radical evil—a Κακός—at work in the figure of Hercules himself.[25] It is only via the recursive mimetic logic that Serres famously calls "parasitism" that this uncanny parallel between Hercules and Cacus can be understood. According to the French philosopher, the truncated version of Livy's narrative—whereby Cacus simply takes away a herd of cattle belonging to Hercules— must be seen within an infinite regress of taking without giving that is the aporetic "origin" of Rome itself. Firstly, Serres reiterates that the original thief is none other than Hercules himself: the god (1) steals the herd of cattle from Geryon as part of his tenth labor. (2) By stealing the cattle from Hercules, Cacus is thus merely repeating Hercules's original act of robbery: it is the theft of a theft. Finally, (3) Hercules's own reclamation of the cattle from Cacus is not so much an act of natural or divine restitution of the goods to their original owner as a repetition of Cacus's own repetition: Hercules is stealing back from Cacus what he himself had stolen in the first place. If each act of parasitism mimetically reenacts its precursor, it increasingly becomes impossible to tell one parasite from another: Hercules and Cacus are equally thief, victim, and murderer at different points along the mimetic chain.[26] In a total reversal of Augustine, Serres's version of the myth of Cacus is less a Platonic exercise in proving the essential goodness of all being than a demonic study in the universality of human evil: "History hides the fact that man is the universal parasite, that everything and everyone around him is a hospitable space. Plants and animals are always his hosts; man is always necessarily their guest. Always taking, never giving."[27]

In what Serres revealingly calls his own "book of evil,"[28] we thus discover a provocatively different account of why Hercules must rule the polis and Cacus must be expelled from it. It poses the same question as Pindar, Virgil, and Livy—how order emerges out of anarchy, law from violence, *nomos* from anomia— but its answer to that question is arguably even more disturbing than its predecessors'. According to Serres's political ontology, the key question is how man—the parasite par excellence—can overcome the Hobbesian war of all against all that is universal parasitism and learn to live in peace with his fellow man. To break out of this literally vicious circle—and here the influence of René Girard's mimetic theory upon his philosophy is unmistakable[29]—Serres appeals not to the agreement of a collective social contract but rather to the collective nomination and exclusion of a scapegoat. By excluding and sacrificing one individual as a parasite, we not only cover over, but bind together in guilt, the parasitism of the collective. If there is a principal candidate for the role of scapegoat in Livy's text, it is, of course, Cacus, whose killing for the crime of "stealing" Hercules's cattle comes to expiate the crimes of the community as a whole. For Serres, Evander's revelation to the collected shepherds that Hercules is the son of Zeus—rather than merely the latest parasite in a long line—is the moment when the community is finally able to break with the mimetic sequence of parasitism by nominating Cacus as its scapegoat: Hercules's killing of Cacus is not just one more act of taking without giving but an act of divine sovereign violence that enables the collective to forget its own complicity and form itself anew. In this sense, Serres's retelling of the story proposes another provocative, albeit post facto, pagan challenge to Augustine: Cacus is excluded not because he is the exception but because he is the rule, not because he has no place in the world but because he belongs too completely to it, not because there is nothing essentially evil in the universe but because there is nothing essentially good.

To what extent, then, might Augustine (like Pindar, Virgil, and Livy before him and Serres afterward) invite a strange kind of parallel between Cacus and the sovereign, between the state of nature and society, between anarchy and law? It is this possibility—a possibility that is arguably only latent in Augustine's own text but is nonetheless there—that I wish to pursue in the remainder of this chapter. As we have already begun to see, the theologian himself briefly speculates that Cacus's own private war against society may have been nothing more than an attempt to impose peace upon the rebellious demands and desires of his own body. For Augustine, Cacus—the absolute outlaw—may well be a kind of sovereign after all, albeit only over himself and his own household:

> He gave the orders and his limbs obeyed. But his mortal nature rebelled against him because of its insatiable desires, and stirred up the civil strife of hunger, intending to dissociate the soul from the body and to exclude it; and then he sought with all possible haste to pacify that mortal nature, and to that end he ravished, murdered, and devoured. And thus, for all his monstrous savagery, his aim was still to ensure peace, for the preservation of his life, by these monstrous and savage methods. Accordingly, if he had been willing to maintain, in relation to others also, the peace he was so busily concerned to preserve in his own case and in himself, he would not have been called wicked, or a monster, or semi-human.[30]

If Cacus is "sovereign" over his own private polis, though, the analogy cuts both ways: we will also see that the Christian ruler who presides over the city is—juridically, politically, and even theologically—at times perilously close to a kind of "Cacus." Perhaps we should again recall the violence that underwrites Serres's story of the birth of the state here: Hercules the sovereign god is himself a parasite, and the community that will become Rome is founded on a murder long before Romulus's slaying of Remus. In book 19 of *City of God*, I want to argue that we can see a similar ambiguity at work: the ideal Christian ruler of Augustine's city is not simply outwith the law (in the exceptional sense made famous by Carl Schmitt) but also operating at the very limits—if not beyond—the Augustinian sphere of virtue.

In order to explore this disturbingly intimate relation between Cacus and the Christian ruler, I now turn in more detail to Augustine's theory of political rule. It is important to preface any discussion of Augustinian political theory with a large *caveat lector*: Augustine had no "politics" as such that can be divorced from his theology. As Robert A. Markus shows in his study *Saeculum* (1970)—which arguably remains the most influential modern study of Augustine's politics—all we can do is extrapolate an Augustinian "political theory" from the theologian's particular remarks on the position of the Roman Empire within a Christian history of salvation.[31] To reconstruct Markus's classic reading here, the late Augustine of book 19 of *City of God* seeks to pursue a "middle way" between the Graeco-Roman theory of the polis as the defining site where man achieves virtue and the

Judeo-Christian theory of the kingdom as irreducible to any temporal state. On the one side, he famously rejects Eusebius's virtual sacralization of the Roman Empire under the reign of Constantine: we cannot adequately embody or represent the kingdom of God in any worldly political authority or organization because the latter is inherently fallen. On the other side, he also repudiates the Donatist demonization of Rome as wholly profane or even diabolical: we still have an inescapable social and religious duty to participate in worldly forms of power notwithstanding their very real flaws.[32] What, then, is the middle way between Jerusalem and Rome?

For Augustine, at least according to Markus's proto-secularist reading, what emerges is a kind of polis degree zero organized around nothing but the basic principle of securing order in a fallen universe on the brink of total disintegration: its "object was no longer to embody an over-arching rational order in society, but to secure its fabric against the forces of disintegration, helping to check conflict, to minimize its disruptive power."[33] To resolve the competing demands of kingdom and empire, Augustine thus constructs a Rome that is necessary but insufficient, absolute in its power but limited in its jurisdiction, essential to maintain order in a world threatened with chaos and yet inimical to the realization of the final, extra-worldly, good of human existence.[34] If the Greek polis was the place where the citizen could attain virtue, the Roman *imperium*'s purpose is merely to secure a space free from sin where the citizens may pursue virtue by themselves.[35] In our context, we might go as far as to say that the Augustinian state, "poised over an abyss of chaos,"[36] also stands against that unbearable parallel universe that would be the reign of Cacus: a universe in which created order is no longer redeemable, natural and social law have disintegrated into atomistic parasitism, and the last vestiges of good have been extinguished by absolute evil.

What exactly must the Christian sovereign do, then, in order to defend the City of God against the permanent threat of disintegration into chaos that is (at least theoretically) embodied by the rival City of Cacus? It is in chapters 5–9 of book 19 of *City of God*—in which he maps out his concept of the political realm in detail—that Augustine gives his most systematic answer to this question. As has been well documented by contemporary scholars, the Christian theologian progressively reviews the four defining spheres of politics: the household, the city, the world and, finally, the universe.[37] Yet, in each case, it would appear, his conclusion is the same. For Augustine, political authority is necessary to human beings as a finite redoubt against worldly evil but, once again, it remains wholly insufficient as a means of achieving our ultimate extra-worldly good: "All the institutions of political and judicial authority, with their coercive machinery, serve this purpose: 'while they are feared, the wicked are held in check, and the good are enabled to live less disturbed among the wicked.'"[38] In chapter 6 of book 19, which is revealingly entitled "The Mistakes of Human Judgment, When the Truth Is Hidden," though, we arguably find the theologian's most disturbing apology for the—necessary but imperfect—rule of the Christian sovereign over the city: torture.

In this famous or notorious discussion of the fragility of worldly sovereignty, Augustine effectively offers a (qualified) defense of a judge's power under Roman law to torture a person accused of a crime in order to extract a confession.[39] To make his case, he begins by anticipating and readily conceding every modern argument against the practice of torture. It is not only horrifically cruel in itself but utterly ineffective as a means of determining guilt or innocence, because the guilty may well never confess whereas the innocent will say anything at all to make their suffering stop. As always, Augustine remains insistent upon the inherent fallibility of postlapsarian rule: a judge cannot see into the consciences of men and so can never eliminate the possibility that they are putting an innocent man to torture and even death in order to prove his innocence. Yet, even so, he remains equally emphatic that, for all this epistemological uncertainty, the ruler must rule. If a judge unwittingly puts an innocent man to death to prove his innocence, he still remains more virtuous than a judge who fails to judge at all and thus surrenders to a state of chaos. For the theologian, the fragile wisdom of the Christian judge—"who has no intention to harm but who does so because his ignorance compels him"—is seemingly the only barrier against the war of all against all that would be the rule of Cacus:

> In view of this darkness that attends the life of human society, will our wise man take his seat on the judge's bench, or will he not have the heart to do so? Obviously, he will sit; for the claims of human society constrain him and draw him to this duty; and it is unthinkable to him that he should shirk it.
>
> In fact, it is not to him an unthinkable horror that innocent witnesses should be tortured in cases which are no concern of theirs; or that the accused are frequently overcome by the anguish of their pain and so make false confessions and are punished despite their innocence; or that, even if not suffering capital punishment, they very often die under torture or as a result of torture; or that the prosecutors, whose motive may be a desire to benefit human society by ensuring that crimes do not go unpunished, are at times themselves condemned. The witnesses may give false evidence, the defendant may hold out under torture with savage resistance and refuse to confess, and the accusers may be

incapable of proving the truth of their charges, however true those charges may be; and the judge, in his ignorance, may condemn them. All these serious evils our philosopher does not reckon as sins; for the wise judge does not act in this way through a will to do harm, but because ignorance is unavoidable—and yet the exigences of human society make judgement also unavoidable.[40]

In book 19, then, the Christian ruler is intended to secure order against the reign of terror theoretically symbolized by Cacus, but the question inevitably arises here of whether he can only do so by inflicting something perilously close to that state of terror itself upon his own citizens. It is Augustine himself who unflinchingly leads us to this dramatic conclusion by insisting upon the absolute undecidability of guilt or innocence within the postlapsarian city. Accordingly, the task of the sovereign can no longer be to describe or "read off" a preexisting natural order, but to impose, violently if need be, such order in the absence of any temporal guarantee as to its virtue. To the extent that there is no longer any recognizable underlying order to adjudicate upon, the Augustinian sovereign judges not necessarily because he can, but because he *must*: political judgment, however fallible, is essential to the preservation of the state against chaos. If he unwittingly ends up torturing the innocent, the sovereign remains guiltless because such an evil is still preferable to the greater evil of abandoning human solidarity altogether. In Augustine's apology for sovereign torture, though, the two extremes of civilization and the state of nature arguably begin to meet in the middle. What exactly is the difference between a political order that exposes every citizen (innocent or guilty) to arbitrary violence and the chaos of total anarchy?

To pursue this logic to its (literally fatal) conclusion, I suspect that the Christian ruler's decision to torture, in spite of the absolute undecidability of guilt or innocence, sets in motion a judicial machine that will lead, irrespective of his own good intentions, to a situation where the innocent not only can, but will, and (without the intervention of the grace of God) even must be tortured and put to death.[41] It would be a case of special pleading to describe such innocent victims as merely accidental casualties or "collateral damage" of the justice system because their potential death is already built into the torture machine as the necessary blood price to be paid for order. If the ruler must rule to protect the virtuous, then he must equally face the fact that the principle of the unknowability of virtue applies to *everyone*, whether it be the accused, members of one's own household, one's fellow citizens, or rival states in the world.[42] In seeking to decide upon the guilt or innocence of citizens from such a position of radical undecidability, the Christian ruler thus inevitably exposes every human being to the threat of being put to death to prove their innocence: life in the city becomes something close to a suspended death sentence.

If Augustine's Christian ruler would obviously object here that his goal is only to torture and kill enough people to secure the safety of the city from chaos, we might reply that Michael Dillon's haunting question to modern liberal sovereigns who profess to wage only "humanitarian" warfare arguably also begins to have purchase in this much older, premodern context: "how much killing is enough?"[43] To answer this bloody question, Augustine can only helplessly say "more": what makes torture and killing necessary in the first place—the sheer unknowability of the virtue of our fellow men in a postlapsarian universe—also ensures that it can never come to an end. For Oliver O'Donovan and Joan Lockwood O'Donovan, who offer arguably the best defense of Augustine's own defense of torture, we must not "refuse to lend our best efforts to the judicial process, though we do so with a grim sense of our limitations and a prayer for deliverance on our lips"[44]—but this only begs the question of what happens if our prayers are not answered and deliverance never comes. In a world where there can never be enough killing, the peace of the virtuous becomes indistinguishable from the peace of the grave.

In the Augustinian city of the Christian ruler, we can thus begin to glimpse the return of the unbearable figure of Cacus. To be sure, the ideal Christian ruler and the mythical figure of Cacus seem (quite literally) to occupy different philosophical universes: one seeking to uphold the good, the other embracing evil; one participating fully in human society, the other retreating to the solitude of a cave; one punishing his fellow man only out of duty and ignorance, the other robbing and killing out of pure, blind self-interest. Yet, of course, none of this would make any difference to the innocent man tortured to death to prove his innocence: either way he ends up dead. For Augustine—and, again, it is entirely to his credit that he does not flinch from exposing the bloody reality of worldly rule—the Christian ruler's lonely responsibility thus all too quickly begins to resemble the solitude of the savage; the judicial punishment of the accused cannot help but turn into a total war against the city, and the Roman Empire starts to resemble Cacus's own private kingdom: a torture chamber reeking of the slaughter of its countless victims. If Cacus thus seems to return from the dead to haunt Augustine's Rome, it may be because, in another sense, he never really left in the first place: the barbarian was always already inside the gates. This may finally be why Augustine takes the decision to render Cacus unbearable life: he becomes what we might call the ontological scapegoat whose sacrifice expiates the crimes of the sovereign. In bloodlessly annihilating Cacus with his own act of divine violence, Augustine himself thus ironically assumes the role of Hercules in his own work: a killer of monsters who survives to become the last monster.

In Augustine's retelling of the myth of Hercules's killing of Cacus, I thus think we encounter something more complex than the classic foundational mythologeme (which begins with Pindar, continues through Virgil, and endures to at least Schmitt) of how sovereignty triumphs over, and exits from, the state of nature: what passes under the proper name "Cacus" is not simply a historical moment or external space to be confronted, overcome, and ultimately forgotten but rather a structural anomia that is integral to the sovereign machine itself. It should not be forgotten here that Augustine is one of the philosophical architects not only of the modern state but of that state's overwhelming raison d'être: security. As Jean Bethke Elshtain observes, Augustine's modern reputation is, for better or worse, still as the theological godfather not only of Christian realism but also of that tradition of political realism that extends from Machiavelli, through Hobbes, up to Schmitt, Strauss, and even contemporary neoconservatism.[45] For Janet Coleman as well, Augustine's combination of a firm belief in the necessity of absolute authority to maintain order in a realm threatened with chaos, on the one hand, and deep skepticism about the capacity of political authority to do anything more than maintain order, on

the other, becomes nothing less than the metaphysical foundation of the modern secular state.[46] If all this is more or less common knowledge, though, what I want to hypothesize here is
that Augustine's political theology—and in particular his expo-
sition of the problem of Cacus—can also be read as the metaphysical origin of that intractable set of political, juridical, and
philosophical aporias that modern international relations theorists call "the security dilemma."[47] Who is the enemy? How, in
a permanently uncertain and changing world, can we ever know
if we are secure? Why does the effort to secure the state against
terror inevitably risk turning into a form of state terror?

To introduce the first of this book's historical constellations
between past and present, I would now like to turn away from
the premodern universe of the late Roman Empire to consider
some more political reimaginings of the killing of Cacus at critical moments in the foundation of the modern republic. It is
already well documented, for instance, that the figure of Hercules plays a revealing symbolic role in the political birth of both
the United States of America and, particularly, revolutionary
France. As John Adams describes in a 1776 letter to his wife, his
own (rejected) proposal for the image of the seal of the United
States was the judgment of Hercules: "the Hero resting on his
Clubb" would be accompanied by the figures of Virtue and
Sloth.[48] Yet, as Lynn Hunt recounts, it is postrevolutionary
France, rather than the new United States, that is most associated with the Greek hero.[49] The original image upon the revolutionary seal of state after the Declaration of the Republic in 1792
was the famous Marianne, but the National Convention voted
little more than a year later to replace this feminine figure with
a new, masculine and distinctly more belligerent, signifier of the
people. In the words of the new seal's designer, the artist and
deputy Jacques-Louis David, "This image of the people *standing*

should carry in his other hand the terrible club with which the Ancients armed their Hercules!"[50]

For David, the classical figure of Hercules—ironically enough a traditional symbol of French kingship dating back to the Renaissance[51]—was thus recruited by an increasingly embattled young Republic to perform various symbolic "labors" against its seemingly ever-proliferating internal and external enemies. To take just one example amongst many here, the revolutionary Hercules's debut appearance at a public festival organized by David in 1793 depicted him in colossal statuesque form vanquishing the many-headed "Hydra" of federalism. If the figure of Hercules was intended to embody the strength and unity of the French People under its new Jacobin government, the mythical Hydra (who apparently grew two heads for every one cut off) in turn symbolized the disunity and factionalism of supposedly counterrevolutionary groups such as the recently purged Girondins. Perhaps most importantly, however, Hercules—his club raised above his head to deliver the death blow to his prostrate enemy—also served to signify and legitimize the Jacobin decision to monopolize sovereign violence in order to prevent the disintegration of the revolution into total anarchy. In this way, Hercules became the symbolic face of the prompt, severe, and inflexible justice Maximilien Robespierre called "Terror."

In many ways, though, the Herculean republic's most dangerous and insidious enemy was arguably yet to appear: itself. It was Robespierre himself in his "Report on the Political Situation of the Republic" on 27 Brumaire, Revolutionary Year 2 (December 17, 1793), who ironically came closest to articulating the vicious circularity that drove the Terror to inevitably turn in upon itself. At this moment of supreme danger for the republic, the Jacobin leader surveys the political scene and finds massed enemies both outside and inside its borders—whether it be the

European monarchies of Austria or England or the insidious counterrevolutionary forces in France itself. To defeat the internal enemies of the Revolution who are conspiring to destroy it from within, Robespierre—a former prize-winning classical scholar—thus summons up the French Hercules for one more heroic labor:

> Carry the light into the dens of these modern Cacuses, where they share the spoils of the people while conspiring against its liberty. Suffocate them in their lairs, and punish at last the most odious of all crimes, that of dressing up counter-revolution in the sacred emblems of patriotism, to assassinate liberty with its own weapons.[52]

For Robespierre, however, as we will see in more detail in chapter 5, the French Hercules can, once again, never kill enough Cacuses to secure the republic against an—essentially unknowable—set of enemies: what is remarkable about his injunction to "punish *at last* [*enfin*] the most odious of all crimes [emphasis mine]" is the clear implication that, in spite of the execution of the king, the purging of the Girondins, and so on, the real and just act of punishment has apparently *yet* to take place. If conspiracy almost by definition disguises itself in the sacred emblems of patriotism—just as Cacus himself concealed the tracks of the cattle he stole from Hercules in Virgil's original account—then patriotism itself becomes inherently suspect: conspiracy is everywhere, even or especially amongst the most openly or apparently patriotic, and thus no amount of suspicion and no degree of punishment can ever be enough. In this self-fulfillingly paranoiac logic, the revolutionary Hercules depicted on the seal of state could *himself* be exposed as a Cacus at any moment—and indeed this was precisely what happened when

former heroes of the Revolution (Georges Danton, Camille Desmoulins, or even Robespierre himself after the coup of 9 Thermidor) were inevitably revealed to have been enemies of the state all
along and put to death. What if the only monster Hercules can
never kill is the Cacus that permanently resides inside himself?

In bringing this chapter to a close, I want to consider the
(reported) melancholy of another sovereign monster Hercules,
in another fragile empire, in another time of terror. To preserve
peace, this sovereign, like so many of his predecessors, is compelled to institute another judicial death machine: a targeted
killing strategy against individuals designated "terrorists" operating in foreign territory. It is the final step of a bureaucratic
process every bit as banally macabre as Robespierre's Committee
of Public Safety: every week or so the sovereign is presented by
his officials with a "kill list" of carefully selected targets, deemed
to pose an imminent threat, to approve for judicial execution. As
an aide admits, though, bureaucracy alone will not get the job
done: the ruler realizes that "this isn't science," that judgments
are the result of "human intelligence," and so he insists on taking the final life-or-death sovereign decision himself. Yet, we can
rest assured that he is well versed in the "just war" theories of
Christian philosophers like Augustine, and the lesson he takes
from them is that he should personally take "moral responsibility for such actions." For Augustine, recall, the Christian ruler
must rule even or especially when confronted with the sheer
impossibility of seeing into the hearts of men, of telling the
innocent from the guilty, of knowing precisely how much killing
is enough. By embracing a "disputed method for counting civilian

casualties," our modern sovereign tries to ease his own troubled conscience: he effectively counts "all military-age males in a strike zone as combatants," unless there is "explicit intelligence posthumously proving them innocent." If the Augustinian ruler must inevitably sanction the torture and death of the innocent to prove their innocence, his modern equivalent thus extends and perfects this logic: everyone is already guilty unless they can be (posthumously) proved innocent. This overwhelming presumption of guilt would explain why, according to official records, the targeted killing program has resulted in an extraordinarily low number of collateral deaths, with civilian casualties in the "single digits." Perhaps the only Augustinian aporia that our new Christian ruler cannot kill his way out of, however, is the aporia of killing itself that is captured so disturbingly in the unbearable myth of Cacus: President Obama "understood that they could not keep adding new names to a kill list," his former chief of staff admits, but "what remains unanswered is how much killing will be enough."[53] In his solitary kingdom, surrounded by the ever-increasing corpses of his victims, Cacus still reigns.

3

UNTIMELY RIPPED

Macbeth's Children

Despair thy charm,
And let the angel, whom thou still hast served
Tell thee, Macduff was from his mother's womb
Untimely ripped.

—William Shakespeare, *Macbeth*

In 1932, a young literary critic called L. C. Knights delivered a paper to the Shakespeare Association entitled "How Many Children Had Lady Macbeth?"[1] It was a question that had been exercising Shakespeareans—and particularly members of the school of "character criticism" established by the distinguished Victorian critic A. C. Bradley—for some time. As Carol Chillington Rutter reminds us, Shakespeare's play is at best ambiguous, and at worst even contradictory, on the subject: Lady Macbeth asserts that "I have given suck, and know / How tender 'tis to love the babe that milks me" (1.7.54–55), but Macbeth himself later bemoans that he is the wearer of a "fruitless crown" (3.1.60), and Macduff blankly asserts that the tyrant and usurper "has no children" (4.3.219).[2] Yet, Knights's intention was not to resolve this question once and for all—and, as Rutter notes, his paper magisterially never deigns to address it at any point—so much as to satirize what he saw as the kind of "pseudo-critical investigations which are only slightly parodied by the title of this essay."[3] To be more precise, Knights—an advocate of the New Criticism associated with such figures as T. S. Eliot and G. Wilson Knight—saw "How Many Children Had Lady Macbeth?" as a kind of literary equivalent to what philosophers call a category error: *Macbeth* was less an exercise in psychological or historical realism, which obeyed the rules of "real life," than a complex dramatic poem or "well-wrought urn" that should be read according to the internal rules of its own imaginative logic. If Knights sought to consign Macbeth's (living, dead, or nonexistent) children to history as a particularly anachronistic example of the realist fallacy, though, it seems Macbeth's progeny would not be so easily dispatched from the critical stage—and, indeed, casual readers today often mistakenly but revealingly assume "How Many Children Had Lady Macbeth?" to be precisely the sort of pseudo-critical investigation it set out to parody. Perhaps one sign of the peculiar timeliness of Macbeth's children was that, less than twenty years after Knights's attempt to kill them off once and for all, they returned in Cleanth Brooks's classic essay "The Naked Babe and the Cloak of Manliness" (1949), which reads the figure of the "new born babe" not as some kind of literal Bradleyan character but as a powerful poetic symbol of "the future" that Macbeth "would control and cannot control."[4] For Brooks, Macbeth's "war with the future"—his increasingly desperate attempts to preserve his own sovereign power in perpetuity—necessarily takes the form of a Herod-like "war on children,"[5] which seeks to eliminate all actual or potential rivals to the Scottish throne. In this chapter, I track Macbeth's war on children across time and space, from crises of sovereignty in the Jacobean court of the 1600s up to the biopolitics of the camp in the 1930s and 1940s. This chapter argues that Macbeth's war on the child—his attempt to secure mastery over the future by preventing alternative or parallel futures from ever being realized—becomes another signifier of the attempt to gain sovereignty over not just bearable but also unbearable life.[6] Who exactly are Macbeth's political "children"?

In a very literal sense, *Macbeth* is about time. Its first word is "when"—"When shall we three meet again?" (1.1.1)[7]—and the play contains more references to time than any other work by Shakespeare.[8] At the same time, *Macbeth* is also a series of philosophical reflections *upon* time: Macbeth and his wife's soliloquies famously explore the relation between cause and effect, deed and consequence, anticipation and retrospection, as well as the (variously chronological, kairological, or eschatological) constellation between past, present, and future times. However, it is what Kathleen Davis calls the *politics* of time—the classic question of how to gain sovereignty over time by predicting it, transcending, ordering it, or otherwise mastering it—that is the play's persistent theme.[9] To recall Banquo's penetrating question to the Weird Sisters at the very beginning of act 1, Macbeth is a play about the politics of sovereign perpetuity: sovereign is he (or rather she) who has the power to "look into the seeds of time, / And say which grain will grow, and which will not" (1.3.58–59). If "the king" is the play's official answer to the question of who will and should own the future—Duncan is the beginning of an illustrious line of Kings that will stretch from his own son Malcolm, through Banquo's descendants, all the way up to the present king of England and Scotland—*Macbeth* is the story of a power struggle not merely over the ancient throne of Scotland but over possession of a sovereign future that clearly extends up to, and includes, the Stuart monarchy of Shakespeare's own time. This is, of course, a play about Shakespeare's own present (*Macbeth* is now generally agreed to be some kind of political allegory of James VI of Scotland's accession to the English throne in 1603 and, more particularly, his attempted assassination in the Gunpowder Plot of 1605) that seeks to give the new English king both a historical past and, arguably, a political future.[10] In killing James's predecessor Duncan, Macbeth does not merely seek to change Scotland's past but England's present and future: he wants "solely sovereign sway and masterdom" over "all our nights and days to come" (1.5.69–70). What, then, is Macbeth's own sovereign time?

To become truly sovereign, Macbeth recognizes from the very beginning that it is not enough to merely commit regicide, he must also perform a kind of *temporicide*: an act of time killing. It will not suffice to merely kill Duncan and his heirs and replace their dynastic future with his own because he must also annihilate the political theological timespace—the "blessed time" (2.3.93)—over which the king presides. As Macbeth himself recognizes in a famous soliloquy at the end of act 1, a successful regicide requires an act of force so powerful that it is capable of short-circuiting the relation between cause and effect, act and consequence, past and future:

> If it were done, when 'tis done, then 'twere well
> It were done quickly. If th' assassination
> Could trammel up the consequence, and catch
> With his surcease, success: that but this blow
> Might be the be-all and the end-all, here,

But here, upon this bank and shoal of time,
We'd jump the life to come

(1.7.1–7)

For Macbeth, Duncan's murder is here imagined as a kind of metaphysical fishing expedition where the catch is the future. If he could kill Duncan so quickly that he could preempt ("trammel up") any consequences or retribution for his actions either in this world or the next, Macbeth imagines that this blow might become the "be-all and the end-all" that would not only stop ("surcease") the chronological progression of time itself but forestall any divine act of judgment. By this untimely gesture, the regicide not only aspires to reduce all future time to an infinite now but to collapse the transcendent cosmology of Christian political theology—"the life to come"—onto the pure immanence of "here, upon this bank and shoal of time."[11] In this fantastic *passage a l'acte*, Macbeth seeks to inaugurate a new sovereign time of what we might call immanent transcendence: sovereign is he who is master over *this*, bare time.

It is possible to detect the emergence of this sovereign order—"New hatched to th' woeful time" (2.3.59)—in the apocalyptic aftermath of Duncan's assassination at the beginning of act 2. As a play apparently written to ingratiate its author with the Jacobean court, *Macbeth* is frequently taken to reflect James I's own somewhat recherché political theology of kingship: absolutism, divine right, the king's two bodies.[12] For the loyal Macduff—who is first on the scene to discover Duncan's body—the killing of the king is thus not merely a criminal act but a heinous sin: "Most sacrilegious murder hath broke ope / The Lord's anointed temple, and stole thence / The life o' th' building!" (2.3.67–69).

Yet, a new immanent sovereign timespace competes with, and undercuts, the old transcendental order articulated by Macduff, because Macbeth's faux-naïf reply—"What is 't you say? the life?" (2.3.69)—telescopes the macro-universe of political theology down into the micro-universe of biopolitics. If Macbeth seems to be merely repeating Macduff's own word—did you say "life"?—"life" undergoes a subtle transformation in meaning here as it passes from one mouth to another: what was first the signifier of an entire theological cosmology—"the life o' th' building"—is now simply, only, "life." This "life" is no longer the *corpus mysticum* of the king's two bodies—a life that cannot be destroyed by mere homicide but which, like the royal touch of Edward the Confessor, is always left "to the succeeding royalty" (4.3.155)—but a bare life that can be killed without leaving any transcendental remainder. By depriving life of its baroque political theological architecture—the Lord's anointed temple— Macbeth also divests his killing of its transcendental implications. In the new king's own ambiguous words, "There's nothing serious in mortality; / All is but toys" (2.3.94–95).

What is at stake—historically, politically, and philosophically—in this untimely act of sovereign violence? It could be contended (with Kristen Poole) that Shakespeare's play foreshadows the larger crises of timespace at work in the early modern period between the competing cosmologies of, for instance, Thomas Hooker and John Calvin.[13] After a theological cosmology in which everything possesses an intrinsic spatial and temporal order and hierarchy—"I have begun to plant thee," the unwitting Duncan tells his protégé Macbeth, "and will labour / To make thee full of growing" (1.4.28–29)—we move into a new concept of timespace as a radically arbitrary and contingent field of force: "If chance will have me King, why chance may / crown me" (1.3.146–47). However, whereas Calvin argues that a recognition of the essential instability of the laws of time and space gives us a greater sense of God's omnipotence, Shakespeare's play anticipates the kind of extreme political nominalism of Machiavelli or even Hobbes in which time and space become a force field that can be entered, grasped, and reorganized by a political actor.[14] To put it in the words of Lady Macbeth, who grasps this new time much more quickly than her indecisive husband, sovereignty now becomes the godlike capacity to make and remake a time that no longer possesses any internal transcendental order or fixity: "Nor time nor place / Did then adhere, and yet you would make both" (1.7.51–52). By killing his political father Duncan, Macbeth demonically overthrows the medieval universe of Christian natural law theory—day becomes night, the hunter becomes the prey, and Duncan's horses, the "minions of their race," turn "wild in nature" as if they "would / Make war with mankind" (2.4.10–17)—but, read outside the play's tragic genre, the king-killer also reveals a strangely modern universe that no longer has *any* order outside his own sovereign act of making. This reading arguably only ever remains virtual within Shakespeare's play, however, because its official royalism obviously cannot permit its protagonist's act of regicide to go unpunished: Macbeth can never quite bring himself to believe in the new universe he has created and remains tortured by Christian guilt over the violence he has wrought upon the old order. Perhaps most crucially, of course, *Macbeth* also imposes an absolute biological finitude upon its protagonist's sovereignty that leaves him stranded, historically speaking, somewhere between the old time and the new, the premodern and the modern, the king's two bodies and Leviathan. If Duncan's version of sovereign perpetuity is made possible by the principle of dynastic succession—and the convenient biological fact that the king always seems to have a son and heir, whether it be Malcolm or the successor to the childless Elizabeth, the "cradle king" James I himself—Macbeth is tortured by the awareness that his own biopolitical project is famously stillborn: "He has no children" (4.3.219). In order to "jump the life to come," here and now, Macbeth must impossibly seek to become his *own* future, his own successor, even his own child.

In the sense that they are the most visible sign of the "life to come," *Macbeth* is also a play about children. It is famously haunted by the promise and threat of new life: Macbeth imagines "pity, like a naked new-born babe" (1.7.21), Lady Macbeth would have "dashed the brains out" of the "babe that milks me" (1.7.55–58); Hecate conjures up "*a bloody child*" (4.1) and "*a child crowned, with a tree in his hand*" (4.1), and Macduff is a child "from his mother's womb / Untimely ripped" (5.8.15–16). As an heirless king, Macbeth is tortured by the Sisters' prophecy that he will found no future dynasty: he is the wearer of a "fruitless crown," bearer of a "barren sceptre" who is to be "wrenched with an unlineal hand, / No son of mine succeeding" (3.1.60–63). To keep this empty future at bay, Macbeth must thus, Carol Chillington Rutter argues, crush the "seeds of time" (1.3.58) that are its present material form: "the children."[15] If previous answers to the question "How many children had Lady Macbeth?" take either a psychological (Bradley) or a poetic (Brooks) form, then, I want to propose that the Shakespearean child is also the site of a curious—and, as we will see, obscenely timely— biopolitical war over possession of the future. In order to jump the life to come, Macbeth must kill the sons and heirs who would enable the restoration of Duncan's original bloodline or the establishment of a new line of descent: Malcolm, Fleance, Macduff's son.

To Macbeth's new sovereign gaze, the son and heir is not simply a living being but a glimpse of the "future in the instant" (1.5.58)—a possible future amongst many others that must be consigned to the hypothetical past. It is only this proleptic logic that justifies not just the pursuit of Malcolm and Fleance but the—otherwise gratuitous—murder of Macduff's children. For Macbeth, his rival's son must die, not for what he is, but for what he and his own sons will become: "The castle of Macduff I will surprise, / Seize upon Fife, give to th' edge o' th' sword / His wife, his babes, and all unfortunate souls / That trace him in his line" (4.1.149–52). If Lady Macduff tells her child he is now "fatherless" (4.2.27)—because Macduff has fled to England—the boy seems to intuitively grasp the inexorable biopolitical logic that insists that, no matter what happens, he will always be his father's son and heir: "My father is not dead, for all your saying" (4.2.39). In this dynastic context of bloodlines stretching backward and forward across time, Macduff's son's claim is true regardless of whether Macduff is physically alive or not, because his father lives on in him—and this, of course, is why he must die: "What, you egg! / Young fry of treachery!" (4 2.85–86).

For Macbeth, however, the war on the child is not just an exercise in killing new life but also a preemptive war waged against the very *possibility* of new life—what we might almost call an ever-expanding exercise in state-sponsored "birth control." It is not enough to merely slaughter the children, because the (as yet unconceived) children of those children also pose an existential threat to his sovereignty. After Duncan's murder, the newly crowned king reflects that the Weird Sisters had prophesied that Banquo, not himself, would beget a line of future Kings: "They hailed him father to a line of kings" (3.1.59). To the childless Macbeth's evident horror, his killing of Duncan has turned him into nothing more than a political midwife to the line of Banquo:

> If 't be so,
> For Banquo's issue have I filed my mind;
> For them, the gracious Duncan have I murdered;
> Put rancours in the vessel of my peace
> Only for them; and mine eternal jewel
> Given to the common enemy of man,
> To make them kings, the seeds of Banquo kings

(3.1.63–69)

If Macbeth is in any doubt about who will own the future, the Weird Sisters confirm his worst fears by summoning up a spectral procession of Scottish Kings that begins with Banquo's descendants and stretches through James I and onward to "th' crack of doom" (4.1.116). This is the very political theology of time—of fathers succeeded by sons in the undying perpetuity of what Kantorowicz calls royal *dignitas*[16]—that Macbeth sought to destroy in killing Duncan. By making the decision to murder Banquo, Macbeth is thus not dispensing with a living rival for the throne (because he well knows that Banquo himself will never become king) so much as preventing the future line of kings that will issue from him from ever being born in the first place. In depicting the attempted annihilation of James I's own historic ancestors, Shakespeare's play thus implicitly asks its audience to contemplate a counterfactual reality in which the reigning English king never had the chance to exist.

In this larger sense, Macbeth's war against the child is a war on unbearable life: a preemptive act of *virtual* infanticide that

seeks to prevent future children from ever becoming real or actualized in the first place. It is this virtual gesture—of preventing,
reversing, or jumping over the progression of time from past to
future, from seed to plant, and, most importantly, from father
to son—that characterizes Macbeth's own untimely sovereignty
throughout the play. As we have already suggested, this political temporicide begins with the regicide of Macbeth's symbolic
father Duncan—"But here, upon this bank and shoal of time, /
We'd jump the life to come" (1.7.6–7)—and persists in the
genocide of Duncan's numerous political "children": Malcolm,
Banquo, Fleance, Macduff's son. Yet, arguably, it also endures
all the way up to Macbeth's own eventual death (or assisted suicide?) at the hands of Macduff in act 5. To reread it in this particular context, Macbeth's final confession before going into
battle that "I 'gin to be aweary of the sun / And wish th' estate
o' th' world were now undone" (5.5.48–49) should arguably be
read less as a somber recognition that his power is inevitably ebb-
ing away from him than as one last imaginary attempt to achieve
mastery over time and space through the act of (self-) killing. If
the killing of Duncan, Banquo, and Macduff's son were all
attempts to undo a certain predetermined future incarnated in
privileged material bodies—a glorious patrilineal succession that
inevitably consigns the childless Macbeth to a miserable prehis-
tory or past—this last imagined act of what we might even call
auto-infanticide is nothing less than an attempt to kill the progress of *all* time: *après moi, le néant*. For Emmanuel Lévinas, who
offers a famous reading of this speech in his *Totality and Infinity*
(1961), Macbeth's fantasy of total sovereignty in death takes
the form of an act of imaginative cosmological decreation: "Macbeth wishes for the destruction of the world in his defeat and
his death . . . or more profoundly still, he wishes that the noth-
ingness of death be a void as total as that which would have

reigned had the world never been created."[17] In killing himself, Shakespeare's tragic hero seeks to render the entire universe unbearable.

Why, in this philosophical context, do Macbeth's sovereign attempts to "undo" the estate of the world necessarily fail? It is Lévinas's claim that Shakespeare's play dramatizes the horror of that impersonal, bare existence that precedes all subjectivity he famously calls the "There is" (*Il y a*): "The '*there is*' inasmuch as it resists a personal form, is 'being in general.'"[18] According to the critique of Heideggerian fundamental ontology mounted in *Existence and Existents* (1947), what Macbeth's killing spree dramatizes is less being-toward-death (*Sein-zum-Tode*)—in which *Dasein* resolutely assumes death as his ownmost individuating possibility—than something close to the exact opposite: "the impossibility of death, the universality of existence even in its annihilation."[19] To the early Lévinas, whose immanent critique of ontology paves the way for the arrival of ethics as first philosophy, Macbeth's relentless attempts to kill his way out of being paradoxically only serve to confirm being's still more relentless indestructibility: "To kill, like to die, is to seek an escape from being, to go where freedom and negation operate. Horror is the event of being which returns in the heart of this negation, as though nothing had happened. 'And that,' says Macbeth, 'is more strange than the crime itself.'"[20] By killing Duncan, Banquo, and so on, Macbeth seeks to escape from being but he finds himself continually confronted by its return as though he had done nothing at all: Duncan's murder does not turn out to be the be-all and end-all, Banquo's ghost returns to preside at the triumphal feast, and, despite everything, Duncan's son Malcolm succeeds to the Scottish throne. For the later Lévinas of *Totality and Infinity*, Macbeth's final desire that his own death bring about the destruction of the world falls victim to this same self-defeating return of the repressed: "Suicide is tragic, for death does not bring a resolution to all the problems to which birth gave rise, and is powerless to humiliate the values of the earth—whence Macbeth's final cry in confronting death, defeated because the universe is not destroyed at the same time as his life."[21] If Macbeth seeks to create a "void as total as that which would have reigned had the world never been created," this vacuum is quickly filled—in fact was always already filled—by the oxygen of the "*Il y a*": "The void that hollows out is immediately filled with the mute and anonymous rustling of the *there is*," Lévinas writes in *Otherwise than Being* (1974), "as the place left vacant by one who died is filled with the murmur of the attendants."[22] This may be why the final scene of the play depicts not only the glorious coronation of Duncan's son Malcolm but also the apparent restoration of the very estate of the world Macbeth sought to overthrow at the beginning: King Malcolm revives the language of orderly temporal succession associated with his father when he promises his gathered subjects that his sovereign acts will be "planted newly with the time" (5.9.31) and performed "in measure, time and place" (5.9.39). In the end, it would seem that Macbeth's attempts to undo being are themselves undone—as though nothing had ever happened—by being itself.

In all these senses, Shakespeare's answer to the question "How many children had Lady Macbeth?" would seem to be very clear: Macbeth has no heirs, founds no dynasty, the estate of the world endures, and the political theological timespace he sought to destroy unfolds serenely into the future as if he had never existed. It is equally possible to argue, of course, that the play contains a much more unsettling answer to this question because, as many critics have observed, one of its most remarkable features is the way in which it continually blurs the line between legitimate and illegitimate violence, between sovereigns and usurpers, kings and king-killers.[23] According to John Drakakis—who is the author of one of the surprisingly few biopolitical readings of the play—*Macbeth* artificially imposes a reassuringly linear sovereign order, where rebellions are seen as merely temporary deviations from an enduring state of peace, on a history that could just as easily be depicted as a permanent cycle of violence and counterviolence. To give just one example, Shakespeare's play revealingly opens *after* MacDonwald's murder of Duncan's predecessor King Duff—which is extensively recounted in Holinshed—and the inclusion of which would have placed Macbeth's own, apparently singular, act of regicide in a longer context of mimetic king-killing.[24] Perhaps Malcolm's accession to the Scottish throne at the end is not necessarily the restoration of immemorial law and order it first appears either: this scene has regularly been staged in productions of the play as merely the prelude to a new wave of sovereign violence.[25] If Macbeth appears to be the demonic or unnatural exception to sovereign rule, in other words, it is possible to contend that he actually exposes the Benjaminian "becoming-rule" of the exception: the violence of the sovereign lawmaking and preserving gesture itself. In usurping the throne, Macbeth lays bare the *arcanum imperii* that sovereignty is itself an act of originary usurpation: sovereign is he who kills the sovereign. What if all the play's past and future sovereigns—Duncan, Malcolm, James—are Macbeth's political "children"?

It is striking that Banquo's very first question to the Weird Sisters in a play so heavily invested in James I's neopolitical theology is the kind that could normally only be addressed to a divinely ordained king: "Live you, or are you aught / That man may question?" (1.3.42). After all, the king and the Sisters occupy a supernaturally liminal position within and without the sphere of the living: both "look not like th' inhabitants o' th' earth, / And yet are on 't" (1.3.41–42). Yet, what Chris Laoutaris calls this "unsettling symmetry"[26] between the demonic power of witchcraft and the divine power of kingship persists throughout the play. For Macbeth and Banquo, the Sisters possess the very sovereign mastery over time—a kind of demonic equivalent to royal *dignitas*—that should be the sole preserve of the monarch: they have the power to "look into the seeds of time, / And say which grain will grow, and which will not" (1.3.58–59), in the same way that Duncan promises Macbeth that he will "labour / To make thee full of growing" (1.4.28–29). The Sisters' magic enables them to see into the future, and Edward the Confessor—the English king who shelters Malcolm and lends material support to his restoration—possesses an equivalent supernatural power of prescience: the "healing benediction" called the royal touch, which he leaves to "the succeeding royalty" and which is "a heavenly gift of prophecy" (4.3.155–57). In the first of a series of uncanny symmetries the play draws between sovereignty and exceptionality, the king must overthrow satanic magic by resorting to what Laoutaris nicely calls a "divinely sanctioned form of counter-magic."[27]

To pursue this thread a little further, Malcolm is also a curious kind of child on which to wager the political future in a play that allegedly valorizes a sentimental biopolitics of natality. It should be recalled that he is Duncan's appointed, rather than hereditary, successor in a Scotland where the law of primogeniture is only beginning to be established: "We will establish our estate upon / our eldest, Malcolm" (1.4.37–38). After Macbeth usurps the throne—a throne that could potentially have devolved to him before Duncan's decision—the play quietly turns Malcolm back into a born rather than a made king: "The Son of

Duncan, / From whom this tyrant holds the due of birth, / Lives in the English court" (3.6.24–26). Yet, this is a retroactive naturalization of an elective monarchy, which reflects the play's larger aim of retrofitting James I's theory of kingship via primogeniture into history. While (politically at least) he is fatherless— insofar as his succession does not proceed naturally from paternity—Malcolm is also literally without a mother. For Laoutaris, the young king's identity is marked throughout by his alienation from the maternal, feminine sphere: Macduff recalls that the young king's mother "Died every day she lived" (4.3.111) in the long discussion between the two, and the virginal Malcolm himself later confesses that he is "yet / Unknown to woman" (4.3.125–26).[28] In an uncanny sense that recalls nothing so much as Macbeth's murder of his own political "father" Duncan, Malcolm's succession thus seems to involve an act of symbolic matricide: the child king must "kill" a parent in order to reign.

Perhaps most famously, Macduff's restoration of the son of Duncan to the Scottish throne is enabled by a series of spatial and temporal reversals every bit as untimely as those that accompanied Macbeth's own seizure of power. It is the usurper Macbeth who becomes the upholder of spatiotemporal order, bizarrely, and the usurped Malcolm, Macduff, and Fleance who now seek to remake that order, arbitrarily, violently, and contingently, in their own image. After he becomes king, Macbeth seems to assume that the old timespace he destroyed will reassert itself as if nothing had happened: Banquo will stay dead, Great Birnam Wood will not come to Dunsinane Castle, all men will be born from women, and, thus, "our high-placed Macbeth / Shall live the lease of nature, pay his breath / To time, and mortal custom" (4.1.97–99). To the contrary, however, Macduff is very much a creature of the new time, who well recognizes that political agents do not have to obey natural law but can seize it in their own interest—just as the trees of Birnam can be hewn down and transported to Dunsinane. If Malcolm is one uncanny child king, Macduff—a man who abandons his family to their death at the hands of Macbeth—is another curiously exceptional figure on whom to stake the reestablishment of the natal order: "Why in that rawness left you wife and child— / Those precious motives, those strong knots of love— / Without leave-taking?" (4.3.26–28). This is a Scotland in which "Each new morn / New widows howl, new orphans cry" (4.3.4–5), but Macduff's own disregard of those "strong knots of love" has left him childless and wifeless. In another mimetic repetition of Macbeth's acts of parricide and infanticide, Macduff can only secure Malcolm's succession to his father's throne by equally real or symbolic acts of natal violence: fathers killing sons, sons killing mothers.

What, finally, of Macduff's famous revelation at the end of the play that he was "from his mother's womb / Untimely ripped" (5.8.15–16)? It is hardly surprising that contemporary Shakespeare criticism throws up numerous—often directly competing— interpretations of this moment: Macduff's birth has recently been taken as everything from an escape out of the maternal space into patriarchal parthenogenesis[29] to a harbinger of a new epoch of elective monarchy.[30] According to Cleanth Brooks, of course, Macduff's cesarean section is final proof of the futility of Macbeth's war upon the future: the child inevitably evades sovereign capture and still finds a way of being born. Yet, the play enables a less sentimental reading of the child that exposes Brooks's interpretation as another retroactive naturalization of a political decision, because this "naked babe" is not born at all but unbearable, *made*, in another act of sovereign temporicide. To read it this way, Macduff's birth is still a harbinger of the political future, but it is a future that symbolically belongs to Macbeth himself rather than the old order: what sets the kingdom right is somehow "wrong," what heals the sickly weal is itself unnatural, what counters the war on unbearable life is itself unborn. If Macbeth could only imagine that he could jump the life to come—short-circuit the order of temporal succession itself from past to future—Macduff's birth physically enacts this moment of immanent transcendence: a child untimely ripped from a dead mother by a doctor's knife is, of course, nothing less than the future in the instant, here and now, upon this bank and shoal of time. This material embodiment of the untimely political timespace Macbeth midwifed into being ironically secures for the usurper the very sovereign perpetuity—the royal *dignitas*—he has been seeking all along at the very moment of his own downfall and death. In this sense, Macduff is less Macbeth's tragic nemesis than something closer to his (il-)legitimate successor, his sole political son and heir: the "child" of unbearable life.

In closing, I want to return to the untimely question with which we began. It is now increasingly commonplace, of course, to read and stage Shakespeare's play as itself a kind of meditation upon, or prophecy of, future political terror from the English Civil War in the 1640s to African genocide in the 1990s. After all, *Macbeth* is generally assumed to be the product of, and a reaction to, a failed act of what Robert Appelbaum calls "terrorism before the letter," namely, the attempted regicide of James I in the Gunpowder Plot of 1605.[31] To be sure, Shakespeare's dramatization of the Gunpowder Plot in *Macbeth* has again provoked a spectrum of critical responses—which read it as everything from a simple exercise in pro-Jacobean propaganda to even a coded act of solidarity with the Catholic plotters[32]—but what I want to underscore here again is the remarkable extent to which the play captures and performs the radical "untimeliness" of this moment of political theological terror. For Guy Fawkes and his group of Catholic dissenters, the Gunpowder Plot was not merely an attempt to kill one single king but, once again, to jump the life to come. They hoped to kill "the King, Queen, Princes, Clergy, Nobility and Judges," as the Venetian ambassador Nicolo Molin reported back to his superiors, "and thus to purge the kingdom of perfidious heresies," leaving the throne empty for a king who would return England to Catholicism.[33] In Attorney General Sir Edward Coke's famous description of the events at the plotters' trial, their goal was nothing less than to render Protestant England itself unbearable: "but this treason doth want an apt name, as tending not only to the hurt, but to the death of the king; and not the death of the king only, but of his whole kingdom, *Non regis sed regni*, that is, to the destruction and dissolution of the frame and fabric of this ancient, famous and ever-flourishing monarchy, *even the deletion of our whole name and nation*."[34] Who, then, are Macbeth's political "children"?

It might be possible to find another, very different, answer to this question in the memorable final scene of the play when the severed head of the traitor king is brandished aloft for the assembled company by Macduff: "Behold where stands / Th' usurper's cursed head" (5.9.20–21). As we know, the Weird Sisters' prophecy of a line of kings extending from Banquo to "th' crack of doom" (4.1.116) would be exploded within fifty years of the play's first production by the trial and execution of James I's son and heir, Charles I, in 1649. To read the proceedings of Charles's trial in the context of the Scottish play today, we cannot but be struck by an untimely sense of dramatic déjà vu as Shakespeare's power struggles between competing versions of kingship—Duncan versus Macbeth, hereditary versus elective monarchy, a neopolitical theology of divine right absolutism versus a proto-Hobbesian political physics—are played out on this new, yet strangely familiar, stage. In Charles's own martyrological imaginary, as Ernst Kantorowicz has shown, it was the Christlike figure of the deposed Richard II who offered the proper dramatic precedent for his own fate—but his revolutionary opponents might have found the Scottish play to be a more fitting rehearsal of the regicide to come.[35]

As the exchanges between Charles I and John Bradshawe, lord-president of the High Court of Justice, reveal, the revolutionaries sought not merely to kill the king but to decapitate the entire political theology of kings upon which his life depended. To Charles's persistent demand to know "by what lawful authority I am seated here," Bradshawe replied by returning the king to the timespace of the elective monarchy in place at the beginning of *Macbeth*: "in behalf of the People of England, by which people you are elected King."[36] By claiming the hereditary monarchy of the present had its origins in the (albeit very limited) elective monarchies of the ancient kings, the Commons thus attempted to retroactively turn Charles back into the fatal Duncan: an elected king, who forgot where his power came from, and established his estate upon his eldest son. For an indignant Charles, of course, Bradshawe's claim was a flagrant rewriting of history: "Nay, I deny that," he replied. "England was never an elective kingdom; it was an hereditary kingdom for near this thousand years."[37] If he had ever seen *Macbeth*, though, he would have known that this line of defense was on distinctly shaky ground, at least where the Scotland of his ancestors was concerned. This revolutionary restaging of the Scottish play, which exposes the naked political contingency—the untimeliness— that lies beneath the political theology of kingship, unmistakably bears the political signature of Macbeth himself. In revealing that kings are always made, and can equally be unmade, the

English revolutionaries proved themselves to be the first (but by no means the last) of the Scottish regicide's political heirs.

To further trace Macbeth's (poisonous) political gift to modernity, I want to jump from this defining premodern act of regicide to what is arguably its most notorious modern equivalent: the Red Army's decision to kill not only Czar Nicholas II but the entire Romanov family in May 1919. It was apparently deemed necessary to kill Nicholas's children along with their father to ensure that none of them could be proclaimed czar in his place by the advancing White Army—and thus become a living rallying point for the forces of counterrevolution. According to Michael Walzer, the Russian royal family thus became the first casualties of a new epoch of revolutionary justice—not even the French Jacobins, after all, had ever contemplated killing Louis XVI's brothers or his son the dauphin for the virtual "crime" of being potential kings.[38] While Walzer sees the Russian regicide as an entirely unprecedented event, Leon Trotsky, recalling the events from exile some fifteen years later, preferred to argue that the Romanovs were in fact the victims of a much older political, indeed almost Shakespearean, logic. For Trotsky, the czar's family died as they lived: they "fell victim to that principle which constitutes the axis of monarchy: dynastic succession."[39] In killing Nicholas's entire family—"all unfortunate souls / That trace him in his line" (4.1.151–52)—the Bolsheviks arguably also proved themselves to be something close to Macbeth's modern political successors: they knew that it was not enough to merely eliminate the present czar in order to preserve their own power, but the very possibility of future czars.

If the Bolsheviks thought they had killed the principle of "dynastic succession" once and for all with the last of the Romanovs, it arguably returned (like Banquo's ghost) only fifteen years later under a new name: racial heredity. It is possible to see the Nazi race laws—already in place at the time Trotsky was writing in 1935—as an extension (even a perverse kind of democratization) of the dynastic principle to entire peoples and races: everyone, not just the aristocracy, now possessed a "bloodline." To return once more to Roberto Esposito's critique of Nazi biopolitics, I find it significant here that he sees post-Darwinist biological hereditary theory as the "secularization" of two distinct political theological trajectories—dynastic succession and Calvinist predestination—which will already be very familiar to readers of the Scottish play: "What needs to be highlighted is that post-Darwinian hereditary theory is situated exactly at the point of antinomic confluence between these two trajectories; on one side, it completely secularizes the dynastic tradition of the aristocratic sort; on the other, it reproduces the dogma of predestination in biopolitical terms."[40] For Esposito, political dynasticism and theological predestination coalesce in the kind of biopolitical determinism that gave rise to Nazi biopolitics: they all agree that the "destiny of the living being is completely preformed—naturally, with the variant that the soul is not immortal, but rather blood, which is transmitted immutably through the bodies of successive generations."[41] In National Socialist race laws, we might go as far as to argue that the bloody normativity that was always at work in Jacobean and Calvinist political theologies was secularized in the form of racial genocide. What were Nazi biopolitics, at least in this context, if not a kind of obscene political theological machine for deciding between the racially worthy and unworthy, the biologically elect and the damned?

For Esposito, as we have already seen in chapter 1, the Nazi politicization of blood also gave rise to a very particular immunitary *dispositif*, which will again provoke a sense of déjà vu to readers of *Macbeth*: "*the anticipatory suppression of birth.*"[42] It is now well documented that the Nazis' first legislative act after coming to power in 1933 was a law making possible the compulsory sterilization of any citizen suffering from a list of hereditary diseases and genetic disorders. Yet, if we read what took place in the camps against this longer biopolitical context, the Jews' eventual fate might be described as a belated extension of this eugenic policy of preemptively foreclosing upon birth, or even as a kind of untimely a posteriori "abortion": "the human masses sealed off in [the camps] are treated as if they no longer existed," Hannah Arendt powerfully observes, "as if what happened to them were no longer of any interest to anybody, as if they were already dead and some evil spirit gone mad were amusing himself by stopping them for a while between life and death."[43] If the Nazi anticipatory suppression of birth has many sources, of course, it is at least possible to argue that it is itself anticipated by the kind of preemptive strikes against the prenatal order we have traced in Shakespeare's play—the real or attempted killings of Malcolm, Banquo, Fleance, Macduff's son. In Macbeth's acts of virtual infanticide—which seek to prevent an ever-increasing number of potential children from ever being born—we can perhaps begin to see the long political archive of regicide begin to mutate into an early form of political eugenics: the Baroque prince becomes a perverse kind of doctor and the court a hospital, a laboratory, a camp.

In Nazi biopolitics and thanatopolitics, then, King Macbeth's endless war upon unbearable life continues to be waged on a racial and genetic scale: "sovereign law isn't so much the capacity to put to death," as Esposito presciently observes of the Nazis, "as it is to nullify life in advance."[44] To bear witness to this unbearable logic at work one last time in Shakespeare's play, I want to conclude this chapter by recalling the grisly ingredients that the Weird Sisters throw into their womb-like cauldron at the beginning of act 4:

> Liver of blaspheming Jew,
> Gall of goat and slips of yew
> Slivered in the moon's eclipse,
> Nose of Turk and Tartar's lips,
> Finger of birth-strangled babe
> Ditch-delivered by a drab,
> Make the gruel thick and slab.
> Add thereto a tiger's chawdron,
> For th' ingredience of our cauldron.

(4.1.26–34)

For the Weird Sisters, what the dismembered body parts of the "birth-strangled babe" and the Jew, the Turk, and the Tartar all have in common, of course, is that they are all forms of life unbaptized by the church—and so all are lives unsaved, unredeemed, even damned. They are each consigned to a kind of spiritual bare life—or even unbearable life—because they have not been theologically reborn into the kingdom of God. If this primal biopolitical scene around the Sisters' cauldron undoubtedly speaks to a very particular Early Modern Christian imaginary, it is also tempting to place it in a Benjaminian historical constellation with that other defining biopolitical scene of modernity: the camp. What if the unbearable "child" of Shakespeare's Jew, Turk, and Tartar (whose bodies are indiscriminately consigned to an infernal furnace) is that other abject Jewish Turk or Turkish Jew—the *Muselmänn*?[45]

4

UNCOMMON

Hobbes's Martyrs

As for example, upon the occasion of some strange and deformed
birth, it shall not be decided by Aristotle, or the philosophers,
whether the same be a man or no, but by the laws.

—Thomas Hobbes, *The Elements of Law Natural and Politic*

I n *Leviathan,* Thomas Hobbes takes seriously only one possible exception to the universal rule that governs his political philosophy. It is now commonplace (after Schmitt,
Agamben, and Esposito) to see Hobbes as one of the architects
of the modern biopolitical state because of his famous claim that
politics begins and ends with the common human desire to preserve its bare physical life. As the philosopher himself famously
narrates it, humanity's desire for self-preservation is not only the
basic condition of life in the state of nature but also the reason
why we take the decision to leave behind that perilous state and
enter the Commonwealth.[1] To recall the terms and conditions
of Hobbes's "social covenant," the human being wills the mighty
Leviathan into being precisely because it offers her what she most
craves—security of life and protection from death—in exchange
for her absolute obedience and subjection. If the philosopher

necessarily assumes this desire to survive to be universal—even to the point of regarding suicide and supposedly "heroic" acts of self-sacrifice not merely as irrational but unnatural—it is rarely observed that he also recognizes at least the theoretical possibility that there exists a category of human who does *not* desire the preservation of her life and postponement of her death over and above all values. For the Hobbes of the *Elements of Law Natural and Politic* (1640) and *De Cive* (1642), we can find precisely such an uncommon human being in the figure of the religious martyr who is apparently all too willing to disobey her worldly sovereign and lay down her life for her god: "But what? Must we resist princes, when we cannot obey them?" he asks. "Truly no; for this is contrary to our civil covenant. What must we do then? Go to Christ by martyrdom."[2] In what follows, I trace the fate of the Hobbesian martyr from Catholic and Protestant dissenters in the seventeenth century up to the contemporary Islamist *shahid*. This chapter argues that the radically "uncommon" figure of the religious martyr—a figure who stands outwith the biopolitical calculus of life and death—returns to the very heart of the "common" in the Hobbesian Commonwealth. Why does *Leviathan* (1651) come to the conclusion that, in the modern epoch, religious martyrdom is not merely undesirable and unnecessary but actually impossible?

In chapter 6 of part 2 of *The Elements of Law* (1640)—"That Subjects Are Not Bound to Follow Their Private Judgements in Controversies of Religion"—Hobbes asks why a religious subject (such as a Roman Catholic or a member of one of the new proliferation of Protestant sects in an increasingly unstable English body politic) should obey her civil sovereign rather than her own private beliefs. For the early Hobbes, the answer to this question is very clear: "obedience to God and man stand well together."[3] If the very idea of martyrdom is predicated upon the necessity of choosing between competing and irreconcilable political and religious loyalties—God or Man, Christ or Caesar, private conscience or public duty—Hobbes seeks to demonstrate that (whether considered historically, politically, or religiously) this is almost always a false choice: a Christian subject, in particular, must pledge their allegiance to a Christian sovereign. In his three major works—*Elements of Law*, *De Cive*, and *Leviathan*—he thus deploys a range of ingenious, intricate, and occasionally tortuous arguments to neutralize the existential threat posed to his Commonwealth by martyrdom. What, then, is Hobbes's solution to the problem of the religious martyr?

To start with, Hobbes observes that the allegedly ancient "choice" of the martyr—between religious belief or political obligation—is actually a very modern Christian phenomenon. It is impossible to find any conflict between religious freedom and civil obedience in Greek, Roman, or Mosaic Law, or even (at least according to his own selective quotations) in the New Testament.[4] As he goes on to make clear, the question of martyrdom really only emerges with the Reformation and the new weight Luther and Calvin place upon freedom of conscience over questions of scriptural interpretation. However, in a strategic move that will have huge implications for his later reputation as a "proto-liberal" thinker, Hobbes sees the martyr's dilemma as a pseudo-problem: we can find no contradiction between private freedom of conscience and public obedience of the law because "no human law is intended to oblige the conscience of a man, but the actions only."[5] If Christian subjects are free to believe whatever they like in private, the question only remains of whether there are any grounds on which they can still publicly disobey their civil sovereign—and the answer is "no." For Hobbes, a Christian only has one undeniable and fundamental belief that is essential to her salvation, and it is a mantra that is repeated incessantly throughout his work: "Jesus is the Messiah, that is, the Christ."[6] In a Commonwealth ruled by a Christian sovereign, we can be certain that no subject will ever be compelled to renounce this fundamental belief—and so there are no legitimate grounds for becoming a martyr.

It is obviously in the case of a non-Christian Commonwealth—a Commonwealth presided over by what Hobbes calls an "infidel" sovereign—that the real problem of religious martyrdom arises, because here there would seem to be a clear contradiction between the subject's civil and religious loyalties that may ultimately force them to choose one way or the other. As a matter of fact, though, *The Elements of Law* is still remarkably circumspect about the subject's right to disobey even an infidel sovereign on religious grounds. For Hobbes, a Christian subject who has "subjected himself to the authority of an infidel" would be "discharged of his obedience" in matters of religion if—and only if—he is commanded to deny what we have seen to be the one and only belief that he deems fundamental to Christian salvation: Jesus is the Messiah.[7] If a subject is thus theoretically entitled to disobey their sovereign on religious matters, Hobbes is insistent that this is not a license for civil disobedience more generally: the infidel sovereign's right to govern over his Commonwealth—which the subject has already given to him in exchange for protecting her life—remains absolute and unbound. This is why Hobbes concludes that, if the true Christian subject really is forced to choose between her religious and her political allegiances, she has only one legitimate course of action left open to her. In choosing to disobey her sovereign, the Christian relinquishes the right to self-preservation that she receives from her sovereign in return for her obedience and can become a martyr: "In which case it seemeth reasonable to think, that since all covenants of obedience are entered into for the preservation of a man's life, if a man be content, without resistance to lay down his life, rather than to obey the commands of an infidel; in so hard a case he hath sufficiently discharged himself thereof."[8]

In chapter 18 of *De Cive* (1642), "Concerning Those Things Which Are Necessary for Our Entrance into the Kingdom of Heaven," Hobbes again carves out a special niche for the religious martyr within his social contract theory. To start with, he once again insists that in a Christian Commonwealth "obedience is due to the sovereign in all things, as well *spiritual* as *temporal*."[9] However, if commanded to renounce their fundamental belief in Christ by an infidel sovereign, the Christian subject is again entitled to disobey on religious grounds. For Hobbes, who is all too aware that religious disobedience is often merely a precursor to political disobedience, this spiritual liberty comes with the usual command to obey the sovereign on all civil matters: "the same obedience, even from a Christian subject, is due in all *temporal matters* to those Princes who are no Christians."[10] If the Christian subject decides that she can no longer obey her prince, then she can surrender the natural and civil right to self-preservation that she has entrusted to the care of her sovereign and take the only option left open to her: death. In *De Cive*, the Christian martyr's willingness to choose death even becomes a kind of existential litmus test that distinguishes the genuine believer—who believes that she will not die but live eternally in Christ—from a hypocrite who merely uses religion as a pretext for civil dissidence:

> But what? Must we resist princes, when we cannot obey them? Truly no; for this is contrary to our civil covenant. What must we do then? Go to Christ by martyrdom; which if it seem to any

man to be a hard saying, most certain it is that he believes not with his whole heart, *that Jesus is the Christ, the Son of the living God*; for he would then desire to be dissolved, and to be with Christ; but he would by a feigned Christian faith elude that obedience, which he hath contracted to yield unto the city.[11]

What, to pause momentarily, is at stake in Hobbes's somewhat obscure early discussions of the question of religious martyrdom? To the vast majority of scholars, Hobbes's interest in martyrdom is so marginal or exceptional that it is barely worthy of detailed discussion,[12] but I want to argue that it actually goes to the heart of his political project of establishing and preserving sovereign power. It is his overriding objective, of course, to monopolize all authority in the figure of the civil sovereign by greatly reducing—if not eliminating altogether—the grounds on which any subject can legitimately disobey. Accordingly, his willingness to grant religious subjects "freedom of conscience"—which is, as we have already hinted, a cornerstone of the "liberal" reading of Hobbes—is transparently also a device to render such a freedom politically impotent. For Hobbes, his apparently innocent decision to restrict the basis of potential Christian dissent to the most fundamental belief of all—"Jesus is the Messiah"—is clearly central to this overall strategy of neutralizing Christianity politically.[13] By limiting Christian confession to the general claim that "Jesus is the Christ," Hobbes not only forbids the religious subject from dissenting on more narrow doctrinal grounds (such as transubstantiation or predestination) but also ensures that, even when it is permissible, such disobedience must remain politically contentless: any believer who claims the right to confess something more than this bare truth is using a religious pretext to infringe upon civil authority and thus becoming a de facto political dissenter. If Hobbes is at pains to vastly diminish the possibility of religious martyrdom, though, it is important to note that his earlier work does not quite eradicate it completely: a Christian who finds that she cannot obey an infidel prince's command to deny that Jesus is the Messiah is granted the final "freedom" of breaking her civil covenant and returning to the state of nature by laying down her life for her god. In this sense, Hobbes effectively concedes that the religious martyr constitutes a real (though vanishingly rare) exception to the *lex naturalis* of self-preservation that lies at the basis of his cherished Commonwealth.

In the ten years that lead up to *Leviathan* (1651)—which is of course one of the most momentous decades in English political history—Hobbes's view of the meaning of the religious martyr seems to undergo a dramatic transformation: what was once deemed to be a (rare) exception to the rule of self-preservation— the Christian willingly laying down her life for her beliefs—is now no longer even possible within Hobbesian natural or civil law.[14] It is not merely that Hobbes changes his mind on the right of the religious martyr to disobey their sovereign (even if that sovereign is an infidel) but something more radical still: religious martyrs can no longer be said to even *exist* in the Commonwealth. As we will see, it is against the backdrop of the philosopher's famous distinction between public and private worship that this remarkable shift must be seen.[15] To recall Hobbes's argument here, the sovereign alone has the right to control what is called "Publique Worship"—all the visible words and actions of religious expression. They have the power to appoint religious authorities, for example, to license their activities, and to decide whether interpretations of scripture are faithful or heretical, and so on. If such a state monopoly upon the forms of public worship would seem to set the Commonwealth on a collision course with religious groups who profess allegiance to another worldly sovereign (like Roman Catholics) or who reject a civil sovereign altogether (like some of the more radical Protestant sects such as the Anabaptists), Hobbes again inserts his usual caveat about freedom of conscience: public worship in no way infringes upon the freedom of the individual to confess her faith privately. For Hobbes, the individual's religious faith (or lack thereof) is a private matter that simply cannot be subject to political coercion: "Faith is a gift of God, which Man can neither give, nor take away by promise of rewards, or menaces of torture."[16] What, then, should a Christian living under an infidel sovereign who commands her to publicly deny her sworn belief that Jesus is the Messiah now do—if not kill herself?

For Hobbes, the answer is very simple: obey. It is the Christian subject's civil duty to participate in any acts of public worship demanded by her infidel sovereign. According to the crucial distinction between public and private worship, though, her civil duty to the sovereign in no way contradicts her religious duty to God: any private belief that Jesus is the Messiah remains uncompromised even when she is publicly forced to deny it. To reinforce this point, Hobbes goes on (as we will see he often does at potentially fraught moments of argumentation) to give a biblical example: Naaman the Syrian in the Book of Kings, who secretly converted to the God of Israel, but who continued to worship outwardly at the pagan House of Rimmon (2 Kings 5:17). If a Christian is commanded by their sovereign to worship publicly in a way that contravenes their private faith, Hobbes insists they have the same freedom that Naaman had, because, in the end, their words and actions are not properly to be regarded as their own, but those of their ruler. By commanding a citizen to utter the heretical words "Jesus is not the Messiah," in other words, the sovereign becomes the real author of the heresy and the citizen is absolved of any responsibility for their actions. In a significant departure from his earlier work, then, Hobbes now refuses the right of the religious citizen to martyr themselves even when living under an infidel sovereign:

> What if wee bee commanded by our lawfull Prince, to say with our tongue, what wee beleeve not; must we obey such command? Profession with the tongue is but an externall thing, and no more than any other gesture whereby we signifie our obedience; and wherein a Christian, holding firmly in his heart the Faith of Christ, hath the same liberty which the Prophet Elisha allowed to Naaman the Syrian.[17]

In his insistence upon the freedom to worship privately, Hobbes cuts the ground out from underneath the would-be martyr in a manner that anticipates the famous Kantian distinction between public and private reason: why do you need to lay down your life for your god, he asks, when you have the freedom to believe whatever you like so long as you obey? It is revealing, though, that *Leviathan* is not content to rest on the claim that martyrdom is unnecessary, because Hobbes goes on to play what he evidently regards as his trump card: martyrdom is quite simply *impossible*. According to the Greek etymology of the term, he recalls, a "martyr" (μάρτυς) is someone who "bears witness," and this definition leads Hobbes to conclude that, strictly speaking, a true Christian martyr can only be someone who physically witnessed the Resurrection of Jesus, whether that person died under persecution or not. To be clear, Hobbes is philologically quite correct in his interpretation here, but this fact should not obscure what is arguably his most blatant power grab yet on behalf of the civil sovereign. By telescoping the category of "martyr" to include only the original witnesses to the Resurrection, Hobbes not only brackets off the contemporary sense of the term (and the very sense in which he himself has used it up to this point in his work) as naming someone who is willing to die for their religious beliefs, but effectively excludes every Christian martyr after the first century from being called a "martyr" to Christ. They are, at most, only martyrs to the *original* martyrs, witnesses to the original act of bearing witness, no matter whether they die or not.[18] If every act of bearing witness to a revealed religious truth can safely be confined to either the remote past (the time of the Resurrection) or the distant future (the time of the Second Coming), then Hobbes is free to claim the present as the sole preserve of the civil sovereign.[19] For the author of *Leviathan*, the religious martyr is thus an extinct species and anyone who claims to be willing to die for their religious beliefs today should be added to the long list of public enemies enumerated in chapter 29, "Of Those Things That Weaken, or Tend to the Dissolution of a Common-wealth."[20] In the later Hobbes, the martyr's terrible existential decision is turned into something closer to a chilling sovereign ultimatum: why—if you really believe everything you say—aren't you *already* dead?

> They [modern religious martyrs] have the license that Naaman had, and need not put themselves into danger for it. But if they do, they ought to expect their reward in Heaven, and not complain of their Lawfull Soveraign; much lesse make warre upon him. For he that is not glad of any just occasion of Martyrdome, has not the faith he professeth, but pretends it onely, to set some color upon his own contumacy.[21]

Why, then, does Hobbes ultimately find the modern Christian martyr to be a species of unbearable life, almost as if it were
one of the strange or deformed births described in the epigraph
to this chapter? It seems clear that the very idea of the religious
martyr—which is to say, of a human being who does not possess the overwhelming love of life and fear of death that are the
natural foundation of the social order—has no place within
Hobbes's natural law theory or philosophical anthropology. At
the same time, the martyr's defining belief that there is a private
sovereign who should be obeyed over the public one—even or
especially to the death—constitutes a real and present political
danger to the Hobbesian Commonwealth that threatens it with
dissolution. To put it in a word, the Hobbesian martyr would
seem to be a figure of the radically *uncommon*: a point of wholly
unnatural and uncivil excrescence that can never be absorbed
into the political ontological "we" of the Commonwealth—and
so Hobbes has no choice but to consign it to ancient history. Yet,
there is still something genuinely curious about the act of logic
chopping by which the philosopher finally dispatches the martyr from his political universe. If Hobbes can be seen to progressively insist that (1) martyrs only rarely exist; (2) martyrs need
never exist; and, finally (3) martyrs *cannot* exist, then we might
begin to see him as an early practitioner of what Freud will
famously call "kettle logic" in the *Interpretation of Dreams:* "No,
I didn't borrow your kettle, I didn't break it either and, anyway,
it was already broken when you lent it to me."[22] For Freud, of
course, this triangulation of mutually contradictory explanations
only serves to confirm the truth they try so hard to deny—"Yes,
I broke your kettle!"—and we may start to wonder whether
Hobbes's multiple attempts to expel the martyr conceals a
similar act of surreptitious political capture: "Yes, martyrs exist

in my Commonwealth." In what follows, I argue that the uncommon figure of the religious martyr returns to the very heart of the common in Hobbes's account of absolute sovereign power.

In order to test this hypothesis, I now want to place Hobbes's discussion of the problem of religious martyrdom in a different (and apparently totally unrelated) context: the philosopher's defense of the sovereign right to punish. To begin with, Hobbes argues that the supreme sign of the sovereign's absolute power over life and death in the Commonwealth is, of course, his right to punish and, if necessary, put to death any of his subjects.[23] It is important to stress here that the political theorist is not just making the self-evident claim that the sovereign has the right to wield the public sword against a subject who breaks the civil law by inflicting capital punishment. As we will see, he is actually making a much more radical claim about the sovereign's absolute power of life and death, which problematizes the quid pro quo of protection and obedience on which his social contract famously rests. For the author of *Leviathan*, as chapter 21, "Of the Liberty of Subjects," shows, the sovereign ultimately possesses the right to punish or kill *anyone*—guilty or innocent—in the name of preserving the greater peace of the Commonwealth:

> And therefore it may, and doth often happen in Common-wealths, that a Subject may be put to death, by the command of the Soveraign Power; and yet neither doe the other wrong: As when *Jeptha* caused his daughter to be sacrificed: In which, and the like cases, he that so dieth, had Liberty to doe the action, for which he is neverthelesse, without Injury put to death. And the

same holdeth also in a Soveraign Prince, that putteth to death an innocent Subject.[24]

If Hobbes does argue that the sovereign remains bound by both divine and natural law to pursue what is "good" for the Commonwealth, and equally affirms that the subject possesses certain rights and liberties—the right to a public trial in a court of law, the right to a punishment commensurate to their crime, and, of course, the famous natural right to physically resist any violence inflicted upon them—this does not in any way disqualify or delimit the absolute right of the sovereign to inflict punishment or death with legal impunity: a sovereign who punishes or kills an innocent subject does not commit any crime.[25] What exactly, though, gives Leviathan the right to kill any one of its subjects, innocent or guilty?

It is notoriously difficult to find a definitive answer to this crucial question in Hobbes's own thought.[26] As we saw in chapter 1, the philosopher famously insists that the sovereign right to punish and kill is not a product of the social contract but has a "natural foundation" in the right to self-preservation. To reconstruct Hobbes's somewhat controversial argument here, we all possess the right to do whatever it takes to preserve our existence in the state of nature—including "subduing, hurting, or killing any man"[27]—and this right is the natural foundation of what will become sovereign punishment in society. For Hobbes, we do not so much give the sovereign our natural right to punish us when we enter society as give up—or relinquish—our own natural right to punish others in order to strengthen the sovereign's own such right. In *Leviathan*, the sovereign is thus the only person in the Commonwealth who effectively retains his original natural right to use violence to preserve not only his own life, but all life, in the form of the right to punish.[28]

Yet, Hobbes's attempt to locate the origin of the sovereign right to punish in the state of nature encounters significant opposition—even, indeed, from within his own political theory. To read him against himself in this way, the philosopher's naturalist account of punishment clearly sits uneasily within his more general theory of "authorization" that consistently maintains (as we will see momentarily) that the subject is the "author" of all sovereign acts.[29] It is thus incumbent upon him to explain where exactly this "natural foundation" of punishment can be found in a world (lest we forget) before the existence of sovereigns and subjects, law and crime—and his attempt to smuggle it through the back door of self-preservation does not get around the problem. After all, we need only return to Samuel von Pufendorf's classic demolition of Hobbes's sleight-of-hand here: "the right to exact punishment differs from that of self-preservation," he argues, and "since the former is exercised over subjects, it is impossible to conceive how it already exists in a state of nature, where no man is subject to another."[30] If a contemporary scholar like Giorgio Agamben relies heavily on the naturalist reading of Hobbesian sovereign punishment to legitimize his own theory of sovereignty as the politicization of bare life by a sovereign "wolf-man," this account arguably also falls victim to Pufendorf's charge of confusing natural and civil right: what is supposedly retained by the civil sovereign—the natural right of self-preservation—is actually entirely the product of civil sovereignty. For Agamben, recall, sovereign power's origin is to be found in "the sovereign's preservation of his natural right to do anything to anyone, which now appears as the right to punish"[31]— but this argument becomes untenable if the sovereign never possessed any such natural right that could be "preserved" in the first place. In reply to Agamben's typically dramatic claim that the sovereign is the *homo lupus* who dwells "permanently"[32] in the city, we might thus ask whether a bona fide, natural wolf-man would be capable of dwelling "permanently" anywhere, of living but apparently not dying, of loving life but not fearing the sudden and violent death that makes men wolves in the first place.

For other contemporary readers of Hobbes like Roberto Esposito, we can only fully explain the sovereign right to punish not by returning to the state of nature but by placing it within *Leviathan*'s larger theory of authorization.[33] It is with the subject's decision to authorize the sovereign to act on her behalf in the Commonwealth (expounded in the famous chapter 16, "Of Persons, Authors and Things Personated") that the right to punish begins, because this decision also includes the authorization to punish and even kill that very subject if it proves necessary to the preservation of the state. As we have already seen, Hobbes explicitly rejects this interpretation in chapter 28 of *Leviathan*—but elsewhere in the text (chapters 18, "Of the Rights of Soveraignes by Institution," and 21, "Of the Liberty of Subjects") he repeatedly grounds the sovereign right to violence in the subject herself: "every particular man is Author of all the Soveraigne doth; and consequently he that complaineth of injury from his Soveraigne, complaineth of that whereof he himselfe is Author."[34] To take this logic to its extremity, the subject also a priori becomes the author of her own potential future death in the form of capital punishment: what appears to be a sovereign act of natural killing in chapter 28 is here actually an act of artificial self-killing performed by the subject.[35] Yet, as Jonathan Sheehan recognizes in an excellent article, this new civil account of the right to punish also gives rise to an aporia that goes to the heart of the Hobbesian Commonwealth's raison d'être.[36] If Hobbes is still insistent that every subject possesses the natural right to defend themselves against sovereign punishment or death—because no one can alienate their right to preserve their own lives—it is now clear that they are defending themselves not against some sovereign *homo lupus* but against their own selves: they are both sovereign and subject, punisher and punished, killer and victim. This decision to become author of everything the sovereign does, even to the point of authorizing their own potential deaths, means that the subject paradoxically both creates the Commonwealth and destroys its principal reason for existing, namely, to protect the lives of its members. In Sheehan's analysis, sovereign punishment thus becomes, legally and civilly speaking, something that Hobbes himself had hitherto regarded as wholly irrational and unnatural: suicide or self-murder.[37]

What is Hobbes's own solution to the aporia at the heart of self-authorizing sovereign killing? To prove his case, Hobbes does not give an argument but (as we saw in his invocation of Naaman the Syrian in the reading of martyrdom) resorts to another intriguing biblical example—this time from the Book of Judges.[38] It is the story of Jephthah the Gileadite, a famous warrior, who pledges to God that, if he is victorious in his battle against the Ammonites, he will offer up the first person who comes to his door after the battle as a burnt offering (Judges 11:31). After winning a great victory, Jephthah returns home only to find that the first person to welcome him is his own daughter—and so he is faced with the awful choice of breaking his vow or killing his only child. Yet, Jephthah's daughter herself has the solution to her father's horrible dilemma: she willingly submits to being sacrificed, and so Jephthah proceeds to kill her in fulfillment of his promise to God (Judges 11:36). For Hobbes, Jephthah's daughter thus becomes a paradigm for the subject's authorship of every sovereign act, including her own guiltless putting to death: "A Subject may be put to death, by the command of the Soveraign Power; and yet neither doe the other wrong: As when *Jeptha* caused his daughter to be sacrificed: In which, and the like cases, he that so dieth, had Liberty to doe the action, for which he is neverthelesse, without Injury put to death. And the same holdeth also in a Soveraign Prince, that putteth to death an innocent Subject."[39] By freely submitting to die so that her father does not break his vow to God, Jephthah's daughter transforms her death from what would presumably be a simple murder into a legitimate act of sovereign violence. If the right to punish has a foundation, then, it would appear to lie neither in some natural desire for self-preservation nor quite in an act of unnatural self-murder but in something closer to a gesture of civil *self-sacrifice* carried out in order that the community as a whole may live: "as when *Jeptha* caused his daughter to be sacrificed." The social contract is thus dependent on what Esposito calls a "sacrificial dynamic,"[40] in which "life is sacrificed to the preservation of life."[41] This new account of the origin of the sovereign right to punish, which locates it in the subject's act of civil self-sacrifice, would seem to fill the lack in Hobbes's naturalist reading of punishment, but only at what the reader will immediately recognize to be a very singular price. In order to found his Commonwealth upon the rock of the subject's self-sacrifice, Hobbes is compelled to appeal to the very figure he has already excluded as radically uncommon: Jephthah's daughter is nothing other than a religious martyr.[42]

In order to understand exactly what is at stake in this curious gesture, we need to place Hobbes's particular reading of martyrdom within the larger and more controversial context of his political theology. To recall, Hobbes's somewhat sanitized reputation today as a proto-liberal rather than absolutist thinker is predicated, amongst other things, upon his alleged "great separation" of political and ecclesiastical authority into public and private realms.[43] It is *Leviathan*'s disaggregation of political and religious power via the distinction between public and private worship—and with the latter the emergence of individual conscience as a locus of liberty—that is taken to lay the groundwork for the modern liberal state. Yet, of course, a long countertradition of anti-liberal readers of Hobbes from Schmitt to Taubes have stressed that, far from decoupling politics and religion, *Leviathan* is a revolutionary articulation of the original *unity* of religion and the state. For Hans Barion, Abraham Bosse's famous original copper frontispiece to *Leviathan*, which was apparently designed according to Hobbes's own specifications, intriguingly depicts the figure of the sovereign holding a bishop's crozier in his left hand and the public sword in his right.[44] What if this reversal of the traditional hierarchy between the ancient polarities of *auctoritas* and *potestas*—spiritual and temporal power—in the medieval *societas christiana* signifies that Hobbes's political theory has not so much proto-liberally privatized spiritual authority as (quite literally) *taken hold of* the sacred?

To return to Hobbes's reading of martyrdom against this backdrop—public versus private worship, civil obedience versus individual conscience, liberalism *avant la lettre* versus the last gasp of political theological absolutism—we can perhaps begin to see that what seems to be a foundational moment in the emergence of the private liberal subject is also a gesture of political capture of spiritual power by the state. It may seem at face value, of course, that Hobbes's ingenious solution to the problem of the religious martyr is precisely the point at which liberalism enters his political theory. As Schmitt argues in his eulogy for the absolutist Hobbes, *The Leviathan in the State Theory of Thomas Hobbes* (1938), the philosopher's tactical concession that the religious subject has the liberty to pray to whatever God they want in private may well have seemed like a small price to pay to secure the greater prize of public obedience.[45] However, it is this barely visible "crack" in the edifice of the total state that liberalism will use to break the Leviathan in two. For Schmitt—whose anti-liberalism and anti-Semitism begin to coalesce at this point—Spinoza and later Jewish thinkers will turn individual freedom of thought from a mere private right into the authentic source of public sovereignty. In the hands of such "liberal Jews," what Hobbes had intended to be an "Artificiall Man" greater than the sum of the many individual men out of which it is made—the sovereign is not a member of the Commonwealth, he is not a party to the covenant that brought it into existence, and his power is unbound by its laws[46]—is emptied of all authority to the point where it becomes little more than a massive Weberian state bureaucracy administering for private men.[47]

For Schmitt, then, Hobbes's hard-won victory over the religious martyr ultimately turns out to be Pyrrhic. It is the English philosopher's tragic fate to become what the German jurist (as we will see in chapter 6) calls the *katechon* of liberalism—the one who delays, but can never completely arrest, the rise of the liberal state.[48] By giving every citizen the "liberty of Naaman"—who privately prayed to one God while paying public lip service to another—Hobbes saves his Commonwealth from the immediate risk of religious dissent, only to end up sacrificing it to the existential threat posed by the neutralization and depoliticization of the state apparatus itself.[49] Yet, Hobbes has more to say about martyrdom than Schmitt acknowledges (the latter focuses almost entirely on controversies over miracles), and what Hobbes does say significantly complicates the story of progressive disenchantment Schmitt wants to narrate. If Hobbes certainly seems to want to convert the religious martyr into something like the proto-liberal subject—by giving her freedom of thought—I want to propose that there is also a parallel, almost invisible, anti-liberal gesture taking place in his work: the so-called liberal subject will themselves be transformed into a kind of martyr who authorizes, by the very act of becoming a citizen, her own potential future death at the hands of her sovereign. This Hobbes is less the victim of liberalism's historic triumph over political theological absolutism, as Schmitt argues here, than the heroic defender of the ancient political theological unity of the state against all liberal depoliticization that the latter champions in his earlier work.[50] In *Leviathan*, recall, the paradigm of the civil subject is not the private, free-thinking individual at all but a public martyr: Jephthah's daughter.

Why, then, does the uncommon figure of the religious martyr return as something close to the self-sacrificing source of the Hobbesian civil Commonwealth itself? It is necessary to compare Hobbes's—apparently so different but paradoxically symmetrical—readings of religious martyrdom and sovereign punishment one last time to appreciate this remarkable *détournement* or hijacking of the right to die by the right to kill. To recall his specific argument against religious martyrdom in chapter 42 of *Leviathan*, Hobbes claims that choosing to martyr yourself when commanded to publicly contradict your beliefs is simply unnecessary because the *sovereign*, not the subject, is to be regarded as the real author of every act of public worship: "Profession with the tongue is but an externall thing, and no more than any other gesture whereby we signifie our obedience," he writes, "and wherein a Christian, holding firmly in his heart the Faith of Christ, hath the same liberty which the Prophet Elisha allowed to Naaman the Syrian."[51] However, what is remarkable here is that the very theory of authorization that Hobbes rejects in chapter 42, when it concerns the martyr's right to die, is the one he deploys in chapter 18, to justify the state's right to punish and kill. If Hobbes had earlier argued that the sovereign was the author of the subject's acts, he now contends that the *subject* is not only the author of every sovereign action but, crucially, they must even be regarded as authorizing the sovereign's decision to kill them. In the case of Jephthah's daughter, we find the logical conclusion of Hobbes's claim that "every particular man is Author of all the Soveraigne doth; and consequently he that complaineth of injury from his Soveraigne, complaineth of that whereof he himselfe is Author."[52]

In Hobbes's own preferred terms, then, Jephthah's daughter can never be Naaman the Syrian. It seems that she is the only religious martyr in the Hobbesian universe who seemingly must die in public for what she believes in private, namely, the absolute right of the sovereign. As the theological prototype of the civil subject, she also personifies the *détournement* of religious freedom by civil obligation, martyrdom by punishment, the right to die by the right to kill. To insist that Jephthah's daughter must be the author of her own sovereign punishment in this way— that all sovereign punishment has its basis in the subject's own free but necessary act of self-sacrifice—Hobbes's *Leviathan* thus does not so much abolish the subject position of the martyr, as capture it for the state: *the martyr's right to die is preserved as, and transformed into, the sovereign's right to kill.* If the martyr is the one who naturally kills herself to live in Christ, and the subject is the one who artificially kills herself in order to live in the Commonwealth, then it becomes possible to speak of the birth of civil society as an uncanny "becoming-martyr" of the subject. For Hobbes, then, political subjectivity is a civic species of martyrdom, and the social contract is more properly understood as a *mortgage*: a promise to the death. In the end, this might be the reason why the religious martyr, alone amongst all human beings, is consigned to the realm of unbearable life by Hobbes's Commonwealth—not because she is nothing but a deluded fanatic or enthusiast, because she is a political dissident in disguise, or because true martyrdom has safely been consigned to the distant past of the time of the Resurrection—but rather because she is everywhere and everyone.

In the video testimony he recorded before blowing himself up on a crowded London tube train on July 7, 2005, the self-proclaimed Islamic *shahid* (martyr, witness) Mohammed Siddique Khan had the following chilling message for his infidel sovereign: "We love death as you love life."[53] It is difficult to imagine a more perversely Hobbesian threat to the modern Commonwealth than this. After all, Hobbes is the author of that Commonwealth's sole biopolitical raison d'etre: "Life is of interest only insofar as it concerns the here and the now, the physical existence of the individual, of actual living beings," Schmitt presciently notes of *Leviathan*, "the most important and the highest goal is security and the possible prolongation of this kind of physical existence."[54] Yet, the English philosopher was also the first thinker to recognize the uncommon threat that the religious martyr poses to the community of we, the living. Not only does the martyr resist their sovereign on private grounds but—as Khan's message proclaims—she rejects the entire natural and civil foundation of self-preservation upon which the Commonwealth is organized. To be sure, Hobbes gives many (and often mutually contradictory) responses to this threat, but this chapter has tried to argue that perhaps his most profound and disturbing solution to the problem of the martyr is to *become* one—to capture the martyr's subject position for the state. If the religious martyr proclaims "We love death as you love life," the Hobbesian civil subject replies, "We love death *more*, we were martyrs first, we have already died for our love of life." For Hobbes, then, "life" in the modern Commonwealth is predicated upon a curious kind of a priori or virtual death that may or may not ever be actualized: we have always already artificially died for our sovereign, even or especially as we carry on physically living under his protection. Perhaps this is why the most significant biblical figure in the whole of *Leviathan* (as the legend on the original frontispiece again indicates) is another innocent victim of sovereign punishment compelled by his sovereign to endure a curious kind of posthumous existence: Job. This abject figure—who wishes that "as a hidden untimely birth I had not been; as infants which never saw light" (Job 3:16) but who carries on living regardless; who remains physically alive even though he feels "my breath is corrupt, my days are extinct" (Job 17:1)—uncannily describes the fate of the civil subject under the reign of Leviathan. In Hobbes's Commonwealth, we are all uncommon now.

5

INCORRUPTIBLE

Robespierre and the Already Dead

When the blade falls on Saint-Just and Robespierre, in a sense it executes no one.

—Maurice Blanchot, "Literature and the Right to Death"

I n his final speech to the National Convention on 8 Thermidor, Revolutionary Year 3—delivered less than forty-eight hours before his execution—Maximilien Robespierre declared that in a certain sense he was *already* dead: "I am a living martyr [*martyr vivant*]" of the Republic.[1] It was not the first time in his short public life that the Jacobin leader had pronounced his own death. As many historians have noted, his speeches were, from the very beginning of his political career, dominated by a rhetoric of self-sacrifice, martyrdom, suicide, annihilation, posterity, immortality.[2] To be sure, Robespierre's famous nom de guerre—the "Incorruptible"—was originally intended as a tribute to the purity of his revolutionary virtue,[3] but it also captures the uncanny sense in which his supporters saw him as someone not quite alive in the first place: a saint's body, at least according to the Roman Catholic and Orthodox belief in physical incorruptibility, does not, of course, decompose in the same way as an ordinary corpse. Yet, if anything, the sense of Robespierre as someone who was dead even when he was alive intensified following his actual putting to death in the coup of 9 Thermidor: the Incorruptible was memorably described by one of his enemies as a "living cadaver" (*cadavre vivant*) who presided over a republic of the dead.[4] For Chateaubriand, recalling the Reign of Terror in his posthumously published *Mémoires d'outre-tombe* (1848–1849), the living, breathing Robespierre resembled nothing so much as one of his countless victims: "His head looked like it had been cut off because of his pale skin, the sharpness of his teeth and his blood-streaked drool. A headless corpse presiding, in a spirit of equality, over the decapitations."[5] If Robespierre's reputation arguably continues to be seen through the prism of the Jacobin/Thermidorean power struggle even today—which turns him into either a proto-totalitarian fanatic (Schama, Israel) or a faithful subject to truth (Badiou, Žižek, Hallward) depending upon your political tastes—both sides agree that, for better or worse, his persona is predicated upon a certain moral, political, and even physical inhumanity: what the proper name "Robespierre" signifies in contemporary political discourse is still something more or less than "human"—saint or monster, martyr or machine—which has been ascetically subtracted from the realm of mere life or interest.[6] In this chapter, I explore Robespierre's politics of the "already dead," from the Revolutionary Terror up to contemporary revolutionary movements like the Zapatistas. This chapter argues that Robespierre's political philosophy offers a new conjugation of the politics of unbearable life, which transforms it from an apparently passive and abject fate to be endured into a new revolutionary subject position to be affirmed and mobilized. Why, to recall Maurice Blanchot's intriguing words from his famous essay "Literature and the Right to Death" (1949), does the guillotine that falls on Robespierre apparently kill no one?

In order to begin to understand Robespierre's claim to be already dead, I think we need to read it as the outworking of a certain biopolitics of retroactivity—of the "always already" (*toujours déjà*)—that is, as many commentators have noted, paradoxically intrinsic to the revolutionary moment. To recall Jacques Derrida's famous reflections upon the American Revolution, for example, the Declaration of Independence (1776) is, firstly, a performative speech act that serves to bring the American people into existence ex nihilo: the People "do *not* exist as an entity, the entity does not exist *before* this declaration, not *as such*."[7] Yet, at the same time, he notes, the declaration disguises itself as a constative description of a *preexisting* authority: it claims to speak in the name of, and by the authority of, the people themselves. If the declaration invents "the People," that is, it simultaneously claims to have been invented *by* them in what Derrida calls a gesture of "fabulous retroactivity."[8] The people are posited as always already there, preceding and authorizing their own announcement as such, in the form of natural law or even God. This political fiction retrofits the present into the past, performativity into constativity, contingency into necessity, via a kind of constructed fatalism. In one very literal sense, though, Derrida's genealogy of fabulous retroactivity is not quite retroactive enough—because the logic of the "already there" was itself already there more than a decade before Thomas Jefferson's text in one of the philosophical foundations of the French Revolution.

To turn to Jean-Jacques Rousseau's *Social Contract* (1762), we can find the same aporia at work: the general will (*volonté generale*) of the people (in at least some of its many ambiguous formulations) is paradoxically always already there before its declaration.[9] It preexists its own determination as such by any political metric or count, such as popular votes in elected assemblies. As Slavoj Žižek observes, this retroactive gesture is again made possible by a "short-circuit between the constative and the performative," which rewires contingency into necessity.[10] If a group of representatives vote upon a law in a political assembly, Rousseau argues in the chapter on "Suffrage," they do not so much decide upon what will become the general will, but rather discover what the will already was *before* any act of voting took place.[11] For Rousseau, the general will decides the political arithmetic, not the other way around: what appears to be a numerical accident or contingency is retrofitted into a supernumerary, even quasi-transcendental "fate" or predestination.[12] This is why he argues that the difference between the majority and the minority view in a vote is not just a question of number: what the minority discovers after the vote is not merely that it is outnumbered, but that it is *outwith* the will itself.[13] In Žižek's reading, as we will see in more detail later on, this retroactive substantialization of the general will into an entity that preexists and prejudges any particular individual will—deciding at the very outset who is in conformity with it and who is not—is the philosophical gesture that, more than any other, will enable the Terror.[14]

Who or what must the French Revolution retroactively declare to be unbearable life—never there—in order to produce the fable of a people who are already there? It is with *What Is the Third Estate?* (*Qu'est-ce que le Tiers Etat?*), the famous pamphlet written by Emmanuel-Joseph Sieyès at the beginning of the Revolution,

that we can begin to see the implicit violence of "fabulous retroactivity" coming out into the open. To recall the argument of
this seminal text, Abbé Sieyès declares that what is traditionally
called the "third estate" is in fact "everything" (*tout*): the entire
nation in itself.[15] Yet, it is only possible to elevate the third estate
to everything by reducing the other estates to nothing: "Nothing else exists except nonsensicalities, dangerous fancies, or per-
nicious institutions."[16] By retroactively sweeping away the old
vertical political theological hierarchy—and replacing it with a
radically monist, horizontal materialist continuum—Sieyès
leaves literally no place for the aristocracy.[17] If the people were
always there, the aristocracy were never there, and the Revolution is an almost-but-not-quite tautological demonstration of
their essential political nullity. For Sieyès, what we all too prematurely call "the aristocracy" is not a public or foreign enemy
to be fought and killed at all, but a parasite, disease, or cancer
upon the body politic that merely needs to be surgically removed:

> Do not ask what is the appropriate place for a privileged class in
> the social order. It is like deciding on the appropriate place in the
> body of a sick man for a malignant humor that torments him and
> drains his strength. It must be *neutralized* [*il faut la* neutraliser].
> The health and the order of the organs must be restored, so as to
> prevent the formation of noxious combinations that vitiate the
> essential principles of life itself.[18]

This act of what we might call retroactive ontological annihilation effectively declares the ancién regime outwith life and
death—always already dead, never really alive—long before the
empirical act of their political proscription and execution in the
Terror. In passing this a priori death sentence, Abbé Sieyes's

revolutionary manifesto ensured that the blade that fell on the aristocracy would kill no one.

In many ways, the king—that obscure entity variously named Louis XVI, Louis *le dernier, le ci-devant roi*, or just plain Citoyen Capet—was the first and most public example of Sieyes's "already dead." It is now well documented that the very idea of putting the king on trial for treason following the flight to Varennes gave rise to a set of intractable legal, political, and even theological questions that were exhaustively debated in the National Convention in the winter of Revolutionary Year 1 (1792). As Ernst Kantorowicz was arguably the first to observe, the people's representatives were forced to contemplate something utterly unprecedented within the history of sovereignty. To remember Kantorowicz's classic genealogy in *The King's Two Bodies* (1957), the French revolutionaries, even more than their English predecessors, presided over the final closure of the epoch of medieval political theology: they killed, for the first time in history, *both* the king's bodies. If earlier acts of regicide sought to replace the murdered king with another king, and even the English Revolution killed Charles I in the name of kingship more widely, the French Revolution, alone, destroyed both the physical body of the king and the kingly body politic.[19] This act of self-conscious physical and symbolic regicide could only be accomplished, as Michael Walzer observes in his classic study of the National Convention debates, after a long and tortuous premeditation on its meaning.[20] Who or what exactly was this thing called a "king" that the Convention sought to dispense with—a divinely ordained ruler (as the royalists believed), a citizen to be put on trial like any other (as the Girondins argued), or a public enemy to be killed according to military law (as the Jacobins contended)? Was Louis above the law (the royalists), subject to it like every other citizen (the Girondins), or utterly outwith it as a foreign body (the Jacobins)? What exactly was the king's crime—to expose the charade of victor's justice, to have broken the bonds of citizenship that bind the social contract together, or simply to have had the presumption to exist in the first place?

To begin with, the National Convention's attempt to even put the king on trial, let alone execute him, faced a number of formidable legal obstacles in its path. Its single biggest problem was self-inflicted: the 1791 Constitution that established post-Revolutionary France as a constitutional monarchy. As Walzer notes, this constitution not only preserved the ancient status of the king as "inviolable and sacred" (and thus immune from prosecution) but also stipulated that the sole legal penalty for any act of treason by the monarch should be impeachment—and Louis had already been subject to this punishment after the abolition of the monarchy and thus, constitutionally, should face no further action. Yet, at the same time, doing nothing to the *ci-devant* king was obviously not an option either: any republic that absolved such a public and self-confessed traitor would scarcely be worthy of the name. For Jean-Baptiste Mailhe, who the Convention appointed to lead a legislative committee to resolve the legal problem, the answer was simply to cut the Gordian knot: "Louis XVI can be judged" he bluntly declared.[21] If the king had ever been sovereign, Mailhe reported back, it was only because his sovereignty had been contracted to him by the nation, and the people—via the good offices of their representatives in the Convention—retained the right to judge their rulers. In other words, the 1791 contract between the king and the people was effectively null and void, and so Louis could be tried: "royal inviolability might never have been."[22]

For the Jacobin faction in the National Convention, though, Louis was not plain "Citoyen Capet" to be tried and punished under positive law, but a public enemy to be fought under the laws of war. It sought to destroy the fiction that the king was a fellow citizen who was equal under the law by insisting upon the very principle everyone else sought to finesse away: royal exceptionality. After Louis's own lawyers rejected the strategy adopted by Charles I—who, as we saw in chapter 3, refused to recognize the legitimacy of the proceedings against him—the Jacobins ironically became the last spokespersons for the ancient royalist doctrine of the divine right of kings: "Louis claimed that he had once not been a citizen," Walzer observes, "the Girondins claimed that he had always been a citizen; the Jacobins that he had never been and could not be a citizen."[23] However, where the ancient royalist doctrine of absolute sovereign power was obviously a means of protecting the king from the law, the Jacobins cunningly exploited the same absolutism to leave him utterly exposed to political violence. To recall the maiden speech of the young Louis-Antoine Saint-Just, which best articulated the logic of the Jacobin position, a "king" who possessed absolute power was merely a tyrant or usurper under another name, and there was only one thing to be done with him: "I say that the king should be judged as an enemy; that we must not so much judge him as combat him; that as he had no part in the contract which united the French people, the forms of judicial procedure here are not to be sought in positive law, but in the law of nations."[24] If Louis was always above the law, then the supposed contract between the king and the people was "of necessity void, since nothing is legitimate which is not sanctioned by ethics and nature."[25] The king must not be regarded as a fellow citizen who has breached that contract and judged according to civil law, he averred, but as what Rousseau in the *Social Contract* calls a "foreigner amongst the Citizens," which is to say a public enemy to be defeated and killed.[26] This is why Saint-Just could come to his famous conclusion that the very *existence* of the King, rather than his alleged acts, was the real crime: *"No man can reign innocently."*[27] In Saint-Just's speech, we can already detect the extrajudicial shadow of the coming Terror, but the Girondins (at least temporarily) held sway: Louis was tried and executed as a fellow citizen who had committed treason, not killed as a public enemy whose very being constituted a crime against humanity.[28]

In another sense, though, the "king" was already dead— politically, theologically, and philosophically—long before he ever went to the guillotine. It is tempting to read these arcane debates between the Girondins and the Jacobins over whether the king was really a citizen or a public enemy as a kind of fabulous retroactive death sentence pronounced, speech by speech, upon the very idea of kingship: Louis had never been inviolable; the throne had always been empty; when the blade fell, it killed no King. At opposing ends of the political spectrum, both Mailhe and Saint-Just invoke the paradoxical temporality of the null and void contract to describe the constitutional status of Louis: the king is to be treated as if he had simply never existed *ab initio* (from inception). Yet, according to many critics of the trial, of course, the decision to annul Louis was less the present correction of a historical anomaly than (to anticipate chapter 7 of this book) a flagrant and unjust attempt to change the past to make it fit the needs of the present. To royalist defenders of the king, for instance, the National Convention was guilty of a classic act of ex post facto (after the fact) justice that retroactively changed the legal status of past actions or conduct. By declaring that the king could be guilty of treason, the Convention retrospectively criminalized a set of actions that, for all of Mailhe's constitutional gymnastics, were certainly legal under the 1791 Constitution when Louis originally performed them. If the revolutionaries obviously did not invent the specific crime of treason—which has a very long history—what they did create was a new category of *criminal*, or better still, "the possible criminality of the King": a monarch could, albeit unbeknownst to him, commit treason like any other man.[29] For Saint-Just and the Jacobin faction, this possible criminality became an actual and necessary crime because of the very nature of kingship itself: a king could not reign legitimately according to the laws of ethics and nature and so he is always already a tyrant. The king is thus no longer the living embodiment of the body politic itself but an unnatural excrescence within that body that can be surgically removed. This is why Robespierre's own contribution to the debates famously argues that the existence of the king and the republic are mutually incompatible: "Louis must die because the nation must live" he claims.[30] In Robespierre's speech to the Convention, though, what is most remarkable is that Louis XVI's execution is again described less as the physical killing of the king than as a reassertion of his original and essential nullity that simply returns him to the void from whence he came: "A people does not judge as does a court of law," Robespierre declares, "it does not hand down sentences, it hurls down thunderbolts; it does not condemn kings, *it drops them back into the void* [*ils les replongent dans le néant*]."[31]

In the Reign of Terror of 1793–1794—beginning with the establishment of the Committee of Public Safety (Comité de salut public), the implementation of the notorious Law of 22 Prairial, and culminating in the summary execution of around 40,000 people—we confront the definitive political theatre of the already dead. To quickly summarize the battle lines of its critical reception, the Terror divides scholars from the very beginning (recall Kant and Hegel's seminal readings) into those who see it as essential or inessential to the progress of the Revolution, and it continues to do so even today: was it the inevitable out-working of a certain proto-totalitarianism that was present from the very start (Schama), a deviation from, or betrayal of, the radical Enlightenment values of 1789 (Israel), or a logical working through of the truth of the revolutionary event itself (Badiou, Žižek)? If the question of whether the Terror really was "already there" or not is clearly never going to go away (and there is still something about the French Revolution, more than any other historical event, that compels scholars to take sides and symbolically refight it), it is perhaps because this debate ironically repeats or reproduces a certain politics of retroactivity—of the already there—which we have seen to be intrinsic to the revolutionary event itself. For Walter Benjamin, writing in his "Theses on the Philosophy of History" (1940), recall, "the French Revolution viewed itself as Rome reincarnate."[32] In Robespierre's imaginary, the Terror becomes less a state of emergency instituted in response to—lest we forget—a very real and present set of dangers than a kind of virtual war waged over the existence (or nonexistence) of a certain *past*.

To return to the philosophical backdrop to the Revolution we explored earlier, Robespierre's very idea of "the people" completes the retroactive entification or substantialization of the general will begun in Rousseau. It subtracts popular sovereignty from any political metric or count and retrofits it into a preexisting state of virtue. According to Rousseau, recall, the general will still emanates into the view of the majority—thus allowing us to safely ignore the minority as "mistaken."[33] Yet, Robespierre completes the *détournement* of number by virtue in his second speech on the trial of Louis when—seeking to prevent a popular referendum on the king's fate that he knew could well end up sparing his life—he famously declares that "virtue was always in the minority on the earth" (*la vertu fut toujours en minorité sur la terre*).[34] If Robespierre consistently invokes the figure of the "people" in all his public speeches, it is thus a people that clearly preexists or postdates the empirical or countable people of France themselves.[35] In a speech to the Convention on 27 Brumaire, Year 2, Robespierre explicitly defines "the people" as what Jon Cowans nicely calls a revolutionary "vanguard of the virtuous"[36] who transcend the mass of empirical humanity and prepare the ground for a people-to-come: "Which of us does not feel all his faculties enlarged, which of us does not feel raised above humanity itself, on reflecting that we are not just fighting for one people, but for the universe; for the men who are alive today, but also for all those who will exist [*pour tous ceux qui existeront*]."[37]

If Robespierre's ideal "people" radically precede and exceed the body of people who are alive today, then it is not difficult to see why the people's Terror descends from a more or less justifiable monopoly upon state power in a time of genuine emergency to an exercise in mass political killing: the enemy is really or potentially everywhere. It is no longer the minority who are deemed to be outwith the general will but the majority and—via the judicial short-circuit of 22 Prairial—they become almost inherently untrustworthy, suspicious, guilty. Accordingly, the list of public enemies grows ever longer to include not merely Louis XVI, the Girondins, and the Hébertists but even former heroes of the Revolution like Danton. For Saint-Just, whose speech of the 19 Vendémiaire, Year 2, is characteristically the most remorseless extension of this paranoiac logic, the people themselves, in all their empirical particularity or individuality, effectively become the real enemy of the people:

Purge the nation [*la patrie*] of its enemies: You can hope for no prosperity as long as the last enemy of freedom breathes. You have to punish not only the traitors but even those who are neutral; you have to punish whoever is inactive in the Republic and does nothing for it: because, since the French People has declared its will, everyone who is opposed to it is outside the sovereign body; and everyone who is outside the sovereign body is an enemy.[38]

This threat becomes retroactively self-fulfilling with the implementation of notorious legislation like the Law of Suspects, which invented the crime not simply of actively opposing the revolution but of demonstrating insufficient commitment to it. In the words of the Dantonist Camille Desmoulins, who published a devastating (and, as it turned out, suicidal) attack on this law in his journal *Le Vieux Cordelier* in December 1793, the logical conclusion of such legislation was ultimately to criminalize all the vital signs of human existence itself: "Once words had become crimes against the state, from there it was only one step to turn into crimes mere looks, sadness, compassion, sighs, even silence."[39]

In terms of the logic we have been unpacking, however, the Terror's victims were, again, strictly speaking never quite alive enough to be killed in the first place: they were the living decapitated who had always already died transcendentally long before the event of their empirical executions. It is only necessary to recall the (perhaps apocryphal) fates of those who sought to cheat death by committing suicide in their prison cells to recognize that the Terror was always something more—or less—than a simple exercise in political killing: they (or rather their corpses) were guillotined anyway in a practically redundant, but somehow still symbolically necessary, confirmation that they were already dead.[40] As Rebecca Comay has compellingly argued, it was Hegel who first recognized that the guillotine was essentially a retroactive killing machine engaging in what we might almost call ex post facto judicial executions: the Terror produced "the coldest and meanest of all deaths," he famously claims in the "Absolute Freedom and Terror" chapter of the *Phenomenology*, "with no more significance than cutting off a head of cabbage or swallowing a mouthful of water."[41] For Hegel, Robespierre and his fellow Terrorists had already sent their victims to the philosophical guillotine that was subsumption without remainder into absolute freedom long before they deigned to cut off their cabbage-like heads: "The guillotine provides the practical confirmation of the object's essential nonexistence in that it strips even death itself of its singularity and intensity: the machine retroactively retracts the minimal recognition it simultaneously concedes its victim (as worthy of suspicion) in that it directs itself in the first instance against the already nullified nonentity of the lost object."[42] This moment of retroactive annihilation is why the guillotine is perhaps best seen not as the first modern killing machine—preempting by some 150 years or so the mass industrialization of death in the Nazi concentration camps—than as a curious kind of automated undertaker disposing of the always already virtually dead. What machine, after all, could kill a king who was *himself* never anything but a machine in the first place—the "crowned automaton" (*l'automate couronné*), as Robespierre memorably calls him?[43] In this sense, Blanchot's claim about Robespierre actually holds true, not merely for Louis XVI, but for all the victims of the Terror: when the blade fell on the 40,000, it executed no one.

In closing, I want to return to our original figure of the already dead: the Incorruptible, the living cadaver, the headless corpse presiding over the decapitations, Maximilien Robespierre himself. It is one of the many paradoxes of the Terror that this mass retroactive production of the dead was not carried out from the sovereign biopolitical perspective of "life"—or even of eternal life, immortality, or posterity—but from the thanatopolitical subject position of "death" itself. As we suggested at the beginning, Robespierre does not just mobilize thanatopolitics as a critique of the state of "living death" occupied by the enemies of the revolution but as a positive descriptor of the revolutionary subject himself. To be a true revolutionary, Robespierre repeatedly argues in his public performances, it is necessary to have always already given your life to the revolution—to live your life as if it were already over, as if your eventual death has already happened, as if the blade that will kill you executes no one. If the figure of the "already dead" is starting to acquire a certain currency in biopolitical debates,[44] I thus want to argue that it has a much longer political history or genealogy that has still to be written. Why does Robespierre speak of himself as always already dead? How does this figure persist within a certain archive of revolutionary politics? To what extent can this gesture of preemptive self-annihilation—which turns the Revolution's principal actors into its very first "victims"—philosophically save (or at the very least make it possible to mount a defense of) the Terror?

To be sure, Robespierre's revolutionary death drive has complex origins in Greek civic heroism and Christian martyrdom and serves diverse and contradictory ends throughout his public career.[45] It becomes everything from a profession of total revolutionary virtue by someone with nothing to gain or lose, an appeal to vindication by posterity when confronted by increasing opposition, and, most pathetically, even a simple desire for self-annihilation in the face of seemingly certain defeat. After the flight of Louis to Varennes in June 1791, he declared to the Jacobin club that, at the very beginning of the Revolution, when he was nothing more than an obscure deputy, "I sacrificed my life to truth, to liberty, to my country."[46] For Robespierre, this declaration that he is willing to sacrifice everything—name, interest, but above all life itself—for the Revolution becomes the basis for his own *parrhesia* against the enemies of the people. "If I must cease declaiming against the scheming of the country's enemies," he tells the Jacobin Club in a September 29, 1791, speech rallying against the National Assembly's attempts to limit the political activities of the clubs, "let me perish before liberty is lost."[47] This rhetoric of self-sacrifice also persists all the way through to his own physical or empirical end. In a speech after the arrest of Danton on 11 Germinal, Year 2, he declares: "What do I care about danger! My life is *la patrie*; my heart is free from fear; and if I died, I would do so without reproach and without ignominy."[48]

For *l'Incorruptible*, though, it is not enough to declare that he is willing to die, or that he does not fear future death, because he goes on to proclaim that he is, in every sense except the purely physical, *already* dead. It seems that the ideal revolutionary subject occupies a kind of postmortem body long before the event of his execution. As he puts it in a speech to the Convention on 15 Frimaire, Year 2—adding a strangely literal twist to the famous Socratic formulation—"your representatives know how to die" (*vos représentans savent mourir*).[49] Yet, of course, the reverse logic also applies: anyone who wants to live, to survive, to cling to their animal existence, becomes suspect. To give just one brutal example here, Robespierre is able to condemn Deputy Philippe Briez—a survivor of the Siege of Valenciennes who returned to criticize the Committee of Public Safety—in front of the National Convention precisely *because* he survived the siege rather than giving his life: "The member will never answer this question: 'Are you dead?' [*Êtes-vous mort?*] [*Repeated applause*] If I had been at Valenciennes in those circumstances, I would never have been able to give you a report on the events of the siege, I would have wanted to share the fate of those brave defenders who preferred an honourable [*honorable*] death to a shameful [*honteuse*] capitulation."[50] If Robespierre can apparently answer "yes" to his own question—"Are you dead?"—it is because his own physical death, whenever it occurs, will be merely the contingent, empirical outworking, or actualization of an older transcendental death that has already taken place: "I am already in the state to which my assassins want to consign me," he declared after a series of assassination attempts in 1793, "I am more independent than ever of the wickedness of men."[51] In a speech given after the assassination of Marat, Robespierre even declares that revolutionary virtue is not merely in the minority on earth but no longer exists among the living at all: "providence" has reserved the only "sure and precious refuge" for virtue in "the tomb."[52]

If Robespierre's desire for political self-annihilation is present from the beginning of his political career, as we have seen, it reaches something of a (literal and philosophical) conclusion in his long and almost hysterical final address to the National Convention on 8 Thermidor, Year 3. To defend himself against the charge of "dictatorship" increasingly being levelled by internal opponents, the Jacobin leader characteristically responds by turning the charge on its head: the proper name "Robespierre" is an empty signifier. It is only those counterrevolutionaries who seek to deny the popular legitimacy of the National Convention itself that accuse him, alone, of exercising absolute power: "So the National Convention does not exist! So the French People is annihilated [*anéanti*]!"[53] After all, why else accord such "gigantic and ridiculous importance" to a mere "weak individual" like himself—if not "to debase you by denying your very existence, in the same way that an impious man denies the existence of the Divinity he fears?"[54] For Robespierre, this final speech thus becomes a performance of what we might almost call retroactive self-annihilation that seeks to divest or strip its author of any suspicion of subjective agency, private will or interest, and ultimately even of "life" itself: "Who am I, that stands accused? A slave of liberty [*esclave de la liberté*], a living martyr [*martyr vivant*] of the Republic; the victim as much as the enemy of crime."[55] In almost the last words of his last speech to the National Convention, this living martyr once again proclaims that he has already endured the fate that awaits him: "what objection can they make against a man who is right and who knows how to die for his country [*un homme qui a raison et qui sait mourir pour son pays*]?"[56]

Why must the revolutionary assume the sovereign position of a dead man? Is it a "totalitarian" reversal of means and ends, the sacrifice of human life to the absolute idea, the pathos-laden dream of world-purifying divine violence? Or can we offer a more "positive" (or at least less clichéd, complacent, or triumphantly moralizing) reading of this thanatopolitical imaginary? To piece together the larger philosophical agenda out of what may well seem like contingent rhetorical fragments, I want to conclude that we should read Robespierre's collected political speeches as a kind of extended thought experiment on political subjectivity that produces a new figure of the revolutionary subject: the already dead. It is in this sense that Blanchot's elliptical remarks about the "real meaning" of the Reign of Terror contain an unexpected historical purchase. According to a logic first articulated in Hegel's discussion of the dialectic of master and slave, and then made explicit by Alexandre Kojève,[57] Blanchot locates sovereignty in the capacity of the master to face—and transcend—bare biological existence: "When the blade falls on Saint-Just and Robespierre, in a sense it executes no one. Robespierre's virtue, Saint-Just's relentlessness, are simply their existences already suppressed, the anticipated presence of their deaths, the decision to allow freedom to assert itself completely in them and through its universality to negate the particular reality of their lives."[58] By passing straight through "the instant of my death" (to recall that very strange late text by Blanchot that is, in its own way, also a reflection on Hegel and the legacy of the Terror) and out the other side, Robespierre achieves what the narrator of Blanchot's essay mysteriously calls a moment of "sovereign elation": "He was perhaps suddenly invincible. Dead—immortal."[59] Yet, Blanchot is not the only critic to observe what we might call the empty throne—or empty guillotine?—on which revolutionary sovereignty sits in Robespierre's political philosophy. For Žižek, whose recent defense of the Terror does not refer to Blanchot but comes to a strikingly similar conclusion some sixty years after the fact, what the signature "Robespierre" comes to name is a revolutionary equivalent to the classic Kantian subject who exists entirely independently of any empirical being as a kind of pure or empty transcendental point of reference: "Every authentic revolutionary has to assume this attitude of thoroughly abstracting from, despising even, the imbecilic particularity of one's immediate existence."[60] In Žižek's account, revolutionary subjectivity comes perilously close to a kind of philosophical scorched-earth policy that preemptively destroys its empirical self in order to better preserve this ideal transcendental self.

In spite (or because) of such attempts to philosophically dignify them, many other thinkers deem Robespierre's politics of the already dead to remain basically indefensible. It is hardly surprising that both Blanchot's and Žižek's readings of this revolutionary moment have been accused of ratifying a kind of absolute state violence—whether of the right or the left. According to Derrida, Blanchot's essay belongs to a long tradition of "right-wing" philosophy in support of the death penalty,[61] whereas Martin McQuillan has accused Žižek's reclamation of Robespierre for the radical left of promulgating a Maoist "onto-thanato-theology."[62] Yet, in his defense, Žižek is clear that he is not simply endorsing the Terror so much as trying to recover a virtual core—what it could or should have been or might still be—from its appalling horrific actuality. Not only does he specifically deny that Robespierre makes any kind of Stalinist or Maoist appeal to a transcendental "Last Judgment"—a future ethical horizon that legitimizes violence in the here and now as somehow necessary or fated—but he also claims that true revolutionary subjectivity must consist in precisely the annihilation of every symbolic "Big Other."[63] To the charge that Robespierre's politics are politically "indefensible," Žižek would thus presumably reply that this is precisely the (Hegelian) point: Robespierre is less a political fatalist than a solitary, even quasi-Schmittean, sovereign whose utterly contingent—even mad or senseless—decisions rather seek to *invent* the political conditions according to which, retrospectively, they might eventually be seen as "necessary."[64] If we are seeking a theoretical precursor to Žižek's attempt to release Robespierre's Terror from its fatalist straitjacket here, then it is no coincidence to find him appealing to another famous or notorious defense of a popular revolution from thirty years earlier: Michel Foucault's reportage on the beginnings of the Islamic Revolution in Iran in 1978–1979. In his account of the Iranian uprisings against the shah—a reading that was also routinely accused of legitimizing totalitarian political violence as the expression of a thanatological political spirituality of martyrdom—Foucault likewise rejects any political, historical, or ethical calculus by affirming the absolutely evental status of the revolutionary *kairos*: "The man in revolt is ultimately inexplicable. There must be an uprooting that interrupts the unfolding of history, and its long series of reasons 'why,' for a man 'really' to prefer the risk of death over the certainty of having to obey."[65] What if the absent cause—the missing "why"—that enables the man in revolt to prefer the risk of death to life in servitude is that he is already dead?

In a 1994 communiqué issued to mark the anniversary of the assassination of Emiliano Zapata, the mythical collective subject named Subcomandante Marcos declares: "Everything for everyone, nothing for us. We the nameless, the always dead. We, the Zapatista National Liberation Army."[66] It might be possible to argue that the massively overdetermined proper name "Maximilien Robespierre" marks something close to the beginning of the process that leads to the creation of the empty signifier "Subcomandante Marcos." As Žižek argues, the revolutionary army of "we, the dead" inaugurated by Robespierre stretches from Mao Zedong through Che Guevara up to the Iranian Revolution.[67] To add to this (ever-growing) list, Howard Caygill's recent study of modern resistance groups like the Black Panthers, the Palestinian Liberation Organization, and the Zapatista National Liberation Army goes so far as to propose that "resistant subjectivity is in a sense already dead, a posthumous subjectivity."[68] For Caygill, the ZNLA and other movements regard themselves as already dead not only because they have no choice *but* to resist—they have no life worth living in the first place—but because this becoming-posthumous also gives them the dignity to resist without fear: "By affirming death, by saying 'enough', the resistant is no longer hostage to the useless death in life and assumes the dignity of a resistant life without fear of death."[69] If the bullet that kills a Zapatista kills no one, in other words, it is because they have turned their very weakness into a new locus of political strength: they become unkillable, indestructible, incorruptible precisely because they have nothing to live for, because they have already lost everything, because they are already dead. In the struggle of the nonexistent Subcomandante Marcos, Robespierre's politics of the already dead still live—and die.

6

UNLEASHED

Schmitt and the *Katechon*

The darkness drops again; but now I know
That twenty centuries of stony sleep
Were vexed to nightmare by a rocking cradle,
And what rough beast, its hour come round at last,
Slouches towards Bethlehem to be born?

—W. B. Yeats, "The Second Coming"

I
n recent decades, Carl Schmitt's *katechon*—the mysterious
Pauline "restrainer" who holds back the appearance of the
lawless one or Antichrist until the appointed hour—has
emerged as one of the most important concepts in his political
theory.[1] It first appears in his work during the decisive wartime
winter of 1941–1942, when the failure of the Russian invasion and
the entry of America into the war threw the Wehrmacht onto the
defensive for the first time and changed the whole course of
World War II. After Germany's defeat, the figure of the
restrainer briefly becomes central to his postwar reflections on
the nature of sovereignty, rule, *nomos*, and history itself. For the
later Schmitt, writing in a 1947 entry in his posthumously published *Glossarium*, the *katechon* is neither simply a historical fact
nor a normative concept but, as Marc de Wilde rightly observes,

something close to a personal article of faith: "I believe in the *katechon*: it is for me the only possibility as a Christian to understand history and find it meaningful [*er ist für mich die einzige Möglichkeit, als Christ Geschichte zu verstehen und sinnvoll zu finden*]."[2] Yet, Schmitt's notorious reputation within modern political theory—supposed "crown jurist" of the Third Reich, political and religious anti-Semite, apologist for a quasi-divine sovereign decisionism, master theorist of the *polemos* of friend and enemy as the condition of the political—has understandably led many influential critics to view this appeal to the *katechon* with suspicion. If Schmitt often seems to appeal to the *katechon* as the only genuine theological ground for political action, Jacob Taubes and other critical commentators have interpreted this gesture as a crude *politicization* of theology in the interests of preserving state power in perpetuity as a bulwark against an alleged anarchy—a Christian political theology of order that reaches its nadir, according to Taubes, in the German legal theorist's alliance with National Socialism as the Weimar Republic disintegrated into chaos in the early 1930s.[3] In what follows, I seek to offer a new reading of Schmitt's political theology of the *katechon*, from its first appearance in the obscure early essay "Beschleuniger wider Willen" (Accelerator despite itself) (1942) to its paradoxical reemergence in the discourse of neoliberal biopolitics of security. This chapter argues that Schmitt's *katechon* is less a sovereign "delayer" or "restrainer" of history—which seeks to preserve state power in the face of anarchy—than, paradoxically, a kind of sovereign *accelerator* of anomia or anarchy. What if the sovereign is himself the Yeatsian "rough beast" he is seeking to prevent from ever being born?

In his First Letter to the Christian Community at Thessalonica, the Apostle Paul famously compares the time that remains to giving birth.[4] It seems that our time is pregnant with another time, or rather our time is already in the process of giving birth to that messianic time, if we could but realize it. To anyone tempted to presume that the current order will endure indefinitely, Paul thus issues a dire warning: "When they say 'There is peace and security' then sudden destruction will come upon them, as labor pains come upon a pregnant woman, and there will be no escape!" (1 Thessalonians 5:2–4). However, in his Second Letter to the Thessalonians, Paul (or whoever authors the letter in that name) gives an intriguingly different account of the relation between the time that remains and the time of the Messiah. If the purpose of the earlier letter seems to be to warn his readers that they must prepare themselves for the imminent end, Paul's second letter to the Thessalonian community (whose apocalyptic enthusiasm had apparently led them to abandon worldly authority altogether and embrace hedonistic excess) not only seems to suggest that the existing order might endure a little longer than he earlier implied but also offers a (qualified) defense of this order. For Paul, it now seems that historical forms of power—the very demand for "peace and security" that he scorned in his earlier letter as futile—possess eschatological value in their own right. What has changed in the balance of power between history and eschatology?

To answer this question, the Paul of the Second Letter to the Thessalonians speaks of a mysterious new figure who stands between historical and eschatological time—the time that remains and the time of the end—and this figure is the *katechon*. It seems that a complex sequence of events—a kind of eschatological domino theory—must now unfold before the return of the Messiah, which was so confidently declared to be imminent in the First Letter. Firstly, Paul asserts that a "lawless one" (*anomos*) (who the early Church identified to be the Antichrist mentioned in John's letters) will be revealed, and he will go on to oppose himself to God and declare himself to be God. Yet, the letter also goes on to assert that, in fact, "the mystery of lawlessness is already at work," and the only reason why the lawless one has not fully revealed himself is because someone or something is temporarily restraining him. For Paul, this mysterious figure holding back the appearance of the lawless one until the appointed time is the *katechon*:

> Do you not remember that I told you these things when I was still with you? And you know what is now restraining [*to katechon*] him, so that he may be revealed [*apokaluphthēnai*] when his time comes. For the mystery of the lawlessness is already at work [*to gar mystērion ēdē energeitai tēs anomias*], but only [*monon*] until the one who now restrains [*ho katechon*] it is removed. And then the lawless one will be revealed, whom the lord Jesus will destroy with the breath of his mouth, annihilating him by the manifestation of his coming [*tē epiphaneia tēs parousias autou*].

(2 THESSALONIANS 2:6–8)

If the sudden appearance of the *katechon* remains one of the most opaque moments within Pauline theology—and even as eminent an authority as Augustine of Hippo confesses, as we will see in a moment, that he has no idea what Paul is talking about at this point in the Second Letter—it does provide some kind of answer to one of the most persistent aporias in the former's thought, namely, the competing claims of historical and eschatological sovereignty upon the Christian community in the time that remains. Why should a Christian obey a worldly sovereign like the Roman emperor when (as the First Letter to the Thessalonians reminds us) destruction will be visited upon that authority at any moment, like labor pains upon a pregnant woman? In his appeal to the figure of the *katechon*, Paul seems to give his response: a form of worldly power or sovereignty is necessary to hold back, if only temporarily, what we might call the birth before the birth, the chaos before the chaos that will be the full revelation of the lawless one.

In the early centuries of the Christian church, the mysterious figure of the *katechon* evidently grew in significance, as the time between the first and second comings of the Messiah became more and more protracted.[5] To begin with, Hippolytus and Tertullian began to appeal to the figure of the Pauline restrainer in the second century to legitimize the post-Eusebian Church's political accommodation with its erstwhile enemy, the Roman Empire. It was Tertullian's audacious claim, for example, that Christians should pray for the safety of the emperor because he is the *katechon* who is holding back the rising tide of anarchy that would sweep Christians and pagans alike away: "We know that the great force which threatens the whole world, the end of the age itself with its menace of hideous suffering, is delayed by the respite which the Roman Empire means for us."[6] After the fall of the Roman Empire in the Middle Ages, we find similar katechontic claims being made for the Byzantine, Carolingian, and Holy Roman Empires: they are all, in their different ways, politico-eschatological restrainers of the end of the world. However, as many scholars have observed, the essentially finite status of the original Pauline figure of the *katechon* becomes increasingly obscured as the time that remains begins to extend indefinitely into the future. If Paul's Second Letter clearly depicts the restrainer as a temporary stopgap in a larger eschatological story that will conclude with the return of the Messiah, Christian political theology subtly transforms it into a permanent fixture in an interregnum that now seemingly stretches outward toward infinity. For Augustine of Hippo—whose own political theology, of course, decisively breaks with the post-Eusebian rapprochement between Jerusalem and Rome—the Pauline *katechon* is, revealingly, inexplicable: "I must admit that the meaning of this [2 Thessalonians 2:6–7] completely escapes me."[7] In the view of Taubes, as we will see later on, Christianity's katechontic complicity with state power betrays its Jewish messianic origins altogether and turns it into something close to an eschatologized Caesarism.[8]

What, if anything, can we add to the wealth of exegesis on the relationship between the *katechon* and the Antichrist in Paul's Second Letter to the Thessalonians? It is 2 Thessalonians 7 that unpacks the precise chronological sequence of events that leads to the return of the Messiah: "the mystery of the lawlessness is already at work, but only [*monon*] until the one who now restrains it is removed." As we have seen, the orthodox reading of this verse is that the *katechon* is simply holding back the full revelation of the Antichrist. Yet, arguably, this account condenses the complex temporal logic ("already . . . but only until") at work here. Not only has the state of lawlessness already arrived in spite of the attempt to restrain it, but the gesture of restraint itself takes the form of a certain qualified *liberation* of that lawlessness. To turn the orthodox reading upside down, the *katechon* does not just restrain the mystery of lawlessness but rather enables it to operate freely, albeit under its own jurisdiction: "only until the one who now restrains it is removed." For Roberto Esposito, who offers a compelling reading of this eschatological dynamic in *Immunitas* (2002), the Pauline restrainer thus becomes a kind of theological precursor to what he famously calls the biopolitics of immunization, in which a political body seeks to protect itself against external threats by incorporating its own negation with it:

The *katechon* restrains evil by containing it, by keeping it, by holding it within itself. It confronts evil, but from within, by hosting
it and welcoming it, to the point of binding its own necessity to
the presence of evil. It limits evil, defers it, but does not eradicate
it, because if it did, it would also eliminate itself. We could go so
far as to say that the *katechon*—its constitutive juridical principle—
opposes the absence of law by taking it up inside itself, and
thereby, in some way, giving it form, rule, and norm. The *katechon* antinomically assigns a *nomos* to anomie, thus restraining its
catastrophic unfolding.[9]

If Esposito is correct that Paul's *katechon* can only uphold the
law by immunologically incorporating something of this chaos
within itself—and thereby transforming it into a kind of restricted
or contained chaos that prevents a total or absolute chaos from
unfolding—then we move beyond any simple political theological opposition between *nomos* and anomia, the restrainer and the
restrained, the *katechon* and the Antichrist. This alleged political theological Caesarism thus risks becoming the harbinger of
what we might, on the contrary, call a kind of sovereign anomia
or anarchy. In order to prevent Yeats's "rough beast" from reach-
ing its gates, the city of Bethlehem must paradoxically permit
it entry—or even (if we recall our discussion of Augustine in
chapter 2) *become* the beast itself.

In many ways, Carl Schmitt's reflections on the *katechon* are
themselves somewhat katechontic: a burst of writings that occupy
a kind of interregnum between the major works of the 1920s and
1930s on political theology, sovereignty, and decisionism and the

great texts of the 1940s, 1950s, and 1960s on *nomos*, space, and political theology again. It seems he became interested in the Pauline figure as early as 1932, but it first explicitly appears in "Beschleuniger wider Willen" (1942) and recurs through his magnum opus, *The Nomos of the Earth* (1950), only to disappear more or less completely after "Die andere Hegel-Linie" (The other Hegel tradition) (1957). As Felix Grossheutchi has shown, Schmitt's reading of the restrainer also evolves over his career: what begins as a negative term—used to signify the futile attempts of ageing imperial powers like Britain or the United States to arrest the march of world history—increasingly becomes a positive conceptual descriptor. To recall Schmitt's words in *The Nomos of the Earth*, for instance, the *katechon* plays what we have seen to be its classic political theological role, from Paul to Tertullian and beyond, of squaring the circle between worldly power (*potestas*) and sacred power (*auctoritas*), Rome and Jerusalem, empire and kingdom:

> I do not believe that any historical concept other than *katechon* would have been possible for the original Christian faith. The belief that a restrainer holds back the end of the world provides the only bridge between the notion of an eschatological paralysis of all human events and a tremendous historical monolith [*Geschichtsmächtigkeit*] like that of the Christian empire of the Germanic Kings.[10]

If Schmitt reads the *katechon* as a "bridge" between history and eschatology, though, many of his subsequent critics suspect that the German jurist really saw the Pauline restrainer as a way of burning that bridge down once and for all. For Taubes, of course, Schmitt's reading of the *katechon* effectively replaces the "eschatological paralysis" that afflicts all human events in the time that remains with a *political* paralysis that extends this interregnum infinitely:

> This is what [Schmitt] later calls the *Katechon*: The restrainer [*der Aufhalter*] that holds down the chaos that pushes up from below. That isn't my worldview, that isn't my experience. I can imagine as an apocalyptic: let it go down. I have no spiritual investment in the world as it is. But I understand that someone else is invested in this world and sees in the apocalypse, whatever its form, the adversary and does everything to keep it subjugated and suppressed, because from there forces can be unleashed that we are in no position to control.[11]

In this *contretemps* with Schmitt, Taubes pinpoints a classic paradox at the heart of the theology of the *katechon*: any attempt to delay the Antichrist also delays the advent of the Messiah himself (whose own return is contingent upon the reign of anarchy instituted by the Antichrist) and thus ends up upholding the prevailing historical order more or less permanently.[12] What if the Schmittean *katechon* is less a harbinger of the imminent return of the Messiah than an anti-messianic signifier of the indefinite *postponement* of the end of the world?[13]

To try to resolve the ambiguity at the heart of the Schmittean *katechon*, I want to focus on the (almost totally unread) 1942 text in which he appeals to the figure of the Pauline restrainer for the very first time: "Beschleuniger wider Willen, oder: Problematik der westlichen Hemisphare" (Accelerator despite itself: The problem with the Western Hemisphere).[14] It is Schmitt's ambition in this article, which was first published in the bestselling Nazi Party weekly newspaper *Das Reich* on April 19, 1942, to offer a historical and political assessment of Germany's new Western enemy following the attack on Pearl Harbor in

December 1941: the United States.[15] As we have already suggested, Schmitt's first reference to the *katechon* takes the form of
an attack on imperial decadence: people in antiquity believed
that "a mysterious delaying power" existed called "kat-*echon*
(from the Greek for 'to hold down')," he recalls, which "prevented
the long-overdue apocalyptic end of times from happening
now."[16] For Schmitt, the United States has succumbed to the
political fate of all great empires, from Rome to the British
Empire: they all end up as "restrainers and delayers" (*Aufhalter
und Verzogerer*) of history. If America is a delayer of history, then
there is little doubt who or what it is delaying: the Third Reich
is the new "great mover" (*grosse Beweger*) on the world stage,
which the old imperial powers like Britain and the United States
are vainly seeking to hold back. In this essay, then, Schmitt
begins by emphatically placing himself on the side of the "great
mover" rather than the "restrainers and delayers"—even at
the expense of casting the Third Reich in the role of secular
Antichrist—but, intriguingly, he then goes on to complicate this
simple opposition between the delayers and the accelerators of
history by arguing that the American *katechon* has turned from
a delayer into an "accelerator despite itself."[17]

For Schmitt, as he makes clear in in a set of contemporaneous political reflections on his geopolitical moment,[18] the United
States finds itself caught in a contradiction between two incompatible roles at this critical juncture in its history. It must now
choose between the great Schmittean polarities of land and sea,
between being a territorial power and an oceanic power, or, more
widely, between remaining just one continental actor (alongside
Germany) in an essentially multipolar world or seeking to become
a transcontinental, universal actor in a unipolar world. At the
level of both base political calculation and larger political

philosophy, Schmitt's own preference is very clear: the United States should embrace a limited territorial identity—and by implication come to some kind of political accommodation with the Third Reich—instead of pursuing a spurious liberal depoliticization and neutralization that would merely unleash a new and unpredictable set of conflicts.[19] Yet, as William Hooker notes, the biggest danger of all in Schmitt's account is not that the United States will take the right or wrong decision, but that it will not take a decision at all: rather, it will be overcome by "a lack of decision" (*Entscheidungslosigkeit*) that leaves it adrift in the "maelstrom of history" (*Mahlstrom der Geschichte*).[20] If the United States seeks to restrain the forces of history by not taking a decision—by avoiding decisionism at all—then Schmitt argues that it will become "neither a great mover [*grosse Beweger*], nor a great restrainer [*grosse Verzogerer*], but can only end up, against its will, as an accelerator [*Beschleuniger wider Willen*]."[21] In order to live up to its historical role as a *katechon*, and arrest the dangerous process of acceleration it has inadvertently set in motion, the United States must paradoxically *stop* delaying—and act.

In rereading the essay today, "Beschleuniger wider Willen" seems less interesting as a reflection upon contemporary geopolitics than as an insight into Schmitt's own political theological imaginary. It had already been overtaken by events by the time it was written, and its bellicosity toward the United States now reads more like anxious bravado: America had, as Hooker observes, already taken its world-historical "decision"—and ended any chance of a negotiated peace—when it entered the war months earlier. As a matter of fact, it was the Third Reich—whose armies were already floundering on the eastern front and now faced a formidable new western enemy as well—that ironically now found itself in the position of an imperial *katechon*, vainly holding back the "great movers" of history. However, what is remarkable about Schmitt's early essay is how it preemptively challenges the binary terms—order and chaos, delay and acceleration, holding back the end of the world and letting all go down—in which the debate on the *katechon* has since been conducted. To recall the aporia we located in Paul's original discussion, Schmitt's ideal *katechon* is by no means a simple restrainer: it maintains order through chaos, paralyzes by catalyzing, preserves by accelerating change. By taking a world-transforming decision—land or sea—the United States can live up to its destiny and become a genuine *katechon* rather than a mere "involuntary" accelerator of history. If Schmitt also seeks to secure an eschatological mission for other imperial projects like the Holy Roman Empire in contemporaneous interwar works like *Land and Sea* (1942), I find it significant that, once again, becoming a *katechon* is not simply a question of preserving the past as it was, but of determining the future on its own terms: the German emperor Rudolf II and other historical "delayers" are not merely reactive figures who seek to preserve the status quo but dynamic actors who plunge into the becoming of world history.[22] In Schmitt's "Beschleuniger wider Willen" we thus reencounter the very sovereign "beastliness" we first found in Paul's letter: Schmitt's *katechon* does not merely restrain lawlessness but seeks to incorporate or internalize a kind of anomia—"acceleration"—into itself as its own sovereign principle.

What if the real scandal of the Pauline *katechon*, then, is that it may only be possible to delay the apocalypse by accelerating it, to preserve the world by destroying it, by letting it all go down (Taubes), but from above (Schmitt)? It is my hypothesis that the figure of the restrainer is not the site of a simple opposition between order and chaos—nor of a choice or decision one way or the other, depending upon one's particular orientation—but of a more complex and variegated field of political theological force. As we will see momentarily, Schmitt's belated diagnosis of the United States' historical fate in essays like "Beschleuniger wider Willen" is (albeit radically divested of its Christo-Hegelian teleology) also uncannily prescient of what we might call the constitutive aporia of contemporary neoliberal politics of "security." To briefly foreshadow the conclusion of this chapter, Schmitt's restrainer arguably finds something close to its late modern or postmodern successor in the familiar figure of the (political, military, or financial) *securer* of the present political dispensation, who today finds herself equally caught in the position of being a—voluntary or involuntary—accelerator. If the Pauline *katechon* is not a simple delayer or restrainer of the end of history—because "acceleration" is ultimately unavoidable—then the modern katechontic question thus becomes *what* to accelerate, how, and why, and this is the question to which we will now turn. For contemporary politics of security, the *katechon* is less the name of an attempt to impose *nomos* on anomia—order upon chaos, law upon lawlessness—than to make anomia itself into a new kind of *nomos*, to unleash a kind of state anarchy or lawlessness. In Schmitt's later work, I will argue that the essential political question posed by the *katechon* is whether it is possible to transform the necessary contingency or finitude of state power into a principle of enduring political formation—whether, to borrow Samuel Beckett's famous phrase, it is possible for a failed state to "fail again. Fail better."[23]

In order to understand Schmitt's appeal to the *katechon*, we need to see it not only in its original theological context but also in the much more contemporary political context of the conservative revolution in (post–) Weimar Republic Germany. It is now becoming clear, for example, that the attempt to defend state power by appealing to a mysterious "restrainer" was no mere personal theological eccentricity of Schmitt's but a wider intellectual phenomenon in Germany in the 1920s and 1930s. As Marc de Wilde has argued in a recent essay exploring the political and theological genesis of the concept, Schmitt's reading of the *katechon* overlaps significantly with that of his friend and contemporary, Hans Freyer (1887–1969). To recall the argument of Freyer's monumental *World History of Europe* (1949), for instance, European history is consistently depicted as the history of a very familiar "restraining force" (*haltende Mächte*), which holds back social and historical acceleration and which assumes many of the same concrete forms as Schmitt's own restrainers: Rome, Byzantium, the church, and the German Reich. Yet, as Freyer goes on to make clear in his essay "Progress and Restraining Forces" (1952), the *katechon* is not designed only to hold back the forces of change: "what merely delays and prevents change no longer plays a role in history; brakes will wear out, and then the wagon will really thunder on." If the restraining force does not simply hold back progress, it is because its real task is something close to accelerating the progress of history, albeit on its own terms. For Freyer, we should not seek "to slow down the progressive course," but "to appropriate it and to communicate to it osmotically that which can never emerge autogenously in secondary systems: vitality, human sense, human fullness and fruitfulness."[24] This theory of the *katechon* as a creative and revolutionary as much as a conservative force is cited approvingly by Schmitt in his last major text on the Pauline restrainer "Die andere Hegel-Linie" (1957). What does it mean, then, to reconcile enduring state power with historical change so that the state can become a kind of accelerator?

To catch a glimpse of how future *katechon*s might avoid the fate of their predecessors—how they might fail again but better—I now turn to the text that offers Schmitt's definitive account of the figure: *The* Nomos *of the Earth*. It seems that he wrote much of this magnum opus between 1942 and 1945—as it was becoming increasingly clear that Germany would lose the war—and the book is often read today as an exercise in partial self-exculpation. As Zarmanian observes, Schmitt's text is remarkable for the absence of any discussion of contemporary events: a text on the new world order never mentions the Nazi occupation of Europe.[25] Yet, this work also remains deeply invested in the question of why political empires fail and, more crucially, of how imperial projects can survive their own finitude. For Schmitt, it is again the *katechon* that holds the key to understanding the life and death—or the life *after* death—of the Christian empire of the Middle Ages:

> This Christian empire was not eternal. It always had its own end and that of the present eon in view. Nevertheless, it was capable of being a historical power. The decisive historical concept of this continuity was that of the restrainer: *katechon*. "Empire" in this sense meant the historical power to restrain the appearance of the Antichrist and the end of the present eon; it was a power that withholds (*qui tenet*) as the Apostle Paul said in his Second Letter to the Thessalonians.[26]

In a curious sense, the Christian Empire's power lies in its capacity to occupy a simultaneously historical and eschatological sovereign position at the same time: it is both (eschatologically) weak and (historically) strong, both (eschatologically) finite and (historically) enduring, both (eschatologically) able to keep its own end in view and, nevertheless, (historically) able to thrive as an imperial project.

If Schmitt self-consciously places his own thinking within a specifically Christian archive, Julia Hell had recently sought to situate the Schmittean *katechon* within an older and distinctly pagan genealogy of end-time thinking that stretches from Spengler, Volney, and Gibbon back to the Greco-Roman historian Polybius: ruin-gazing. It is this classic trope of imperial decline and fall—in which historians imagine themselves gazing melancholically upon the future ruins of a seemingly invincible empire like Rome—that is remobilized in Schmitt's own reflections on the finitude of every imperial project. At the same time, imperial ruin-gazing also offers an intriguingly pagan equivalent to the Christian eschatological perspective of the *katechon*. To quickly unpack Hell's argument, imperial ruin-gazing is paradoxically a means not of mourning the demise of the imperial project but of *perpetuating* it: a ruin-gazer is not merely a passive or impotent observer but a political actor who subtly serves to recapitulate the power of colonizer over colonized even at the moment of her defeat. For Hell, what is significant is that this imperial subject consistently remains in a position of "(scopic) mastery" throughout the ruin-gazing scenario: the European subject is always the one who is "doing the looking," in other words, even when what they are looking at is the ruins of Europe itself.[27] By giving the imperial subject *herself* the power to bear witness to the ruins of empire—rather than conferring that privilege on some notional postimperial observer like the Goths or the Turks—the classical trope of the ruin-gazer ironically perpetuates and aesthetically reintegrates empire. In the end, empire survives—in order to serenely contemplate empire's own end.

For Schmitt, I want to propose that the *katechon* embodies precisely this power to aesthetically transform the *end* of empire into *empire's* very own end. Its time is not messianic time, the time that remains, or even what Giorgio Agamben calls "*the time that time takes to come to an end*,"[28] but something closer to what Jean-François Lyotard calls the time of the future perfect (*futur antérieur*): the time of the *will have been*.[29] As Hell observes, the imperial ruin-gazer keeps empire's end in view by granting herself the imperial privilege of bearing future witness to her own demise through the eyes of her conquerors: the Goths, the Turks, and so on. To perpetuate its own power, Schmitt's imperial *katechon* similarly adopts the victorious perspective not of the Goth, the Turk, or the Muslim in this case but of its own ultimate nemesis: the rough beast slouching toward Bethlehem to be born that is the Antichrist. If the aesthetic perspective of the ruin-gazer thus enables Schmitt to square the historico-eschatological circle of power—to transform the end of empire into empire's own end—we must always remember that the Schmittean restrainer is not just a kind of conservative, anti-messianic equivalent to what Taubes scathingly calls the "aesthetic messianisms" of utopian thinkers like Ernst Bloch.[30] In Schmitt's *katechon*, we do not confront a kind of aesthetico-political thought experiment—one that merely seeks to imagine what a future in which it no longer existed would look like—but a real political actor that seeks to capture that future and put it to work, here and now, in the interests of its own continuing survival.

To what extent can we pursue this new theory of the *katechon* as the protagonist of a kind of sovereign anarchy into the wider field of Schmitt's political theology? It goes without saying, of course, that Schmittean political theology is a vast and complex field whose perimeters far exceed the scope of this chapter, but I want to argue that not only does the *katechon* make possible a counter-reading of some of its familiar conceptual operators—sovereign decisionism, the state of emergency, and so on—but it may also help to explain its (tragic or culpable) historical fate. To recall Walter Benjamin's famous claim in the "Theses on the Philosophy of History" (1940), which Giorgio Agamben claims was written in secret dialogue with Schmitt's *Political Theology*, the political state of exception (*Ausnahmezustand*) undergoes something close to the same permanent extension as the *katechon* in Christian theology: the "'state of emergency' in which we live is not the exception but the rule."[31] Yet, the Pauline figure of the restrainer—whose constitutive juridical principle, as Esposito puts it, is to give form, rule, and law to the very absence of law—arguably clarifies why this state of permanent exceptionality is no accident. If Schmitt argues that sovereignty and anarchy exist in a "clear antithesis" in the conclusion to *Political Theology*, he also recognizes that they share an uncanny symmetry that renders them mirror images of each other: "Bakunin, the greatest anarchist of the nineteenth century, had to become in theory the antitheologian of theology and in practice the dictator of an antidictatorship."[32] For me, the Pauline *katechon* occupies precisely this permanent state of sovereign anarchy where above and below, *nomos* and antinomianism, dictatorship and anti-dictatorship, Schmitt and Bakunin coincide. What if the state of emergency is not the restraint but the *acceleration* of anomia within its own limited jurisdiction? What if the becoming-rule of the state of exception famously imagined by Benjamin is the katechontic taking up of anomia as its own enduring sovereign principle? What if the real tragedy of Schmitt's *katechon* is that *katechon* and Antichrist, sovereignty and anarchy, Bethlehem and the beast become impossible to tell apart from one another?

In "Security Unleashed," a 2006 marketing campaign designed to promote its security products both to national governments and to multinational corporations, the American information technology company Unisys Corporation poses a series of intriguing questions: "What if security wasn't a cage? What if, instead of keeping things out, it let amazing things in? What if it made you bolder, more ambitious, and enabled you to accomplish more than you ever thought possible? What if security unleashed your full potential?"[33] It is now surely impossible to deny that something called "security"—whether cyber, civil, financial, or military—has become the dominant political ontology of our epoch, to which all other ends or goods must be subordinated. As the Unisys Corporation's self-promotion eloquently testifies, though, the philosophy of security in the contemporary epoch has undergone something of a paradigm shift. To recall the work of the political theorist Michael Dillon, security today is less in the business of securing persons, property, and states prophylactically against a set of contingencies that may befall them from without than of exposing them to, participating in, and seeking to master a radical contingency now revealed to be the basic ontological condition of life itself. For Dillon, this securitization of the living is accomplished via the "regulation of life's exposure to, and its productive and profitable exploitation of, contingent happenings and effects, including not only those occurring in nature, but also those that follow from the independent actions and interventions of biological being itself."[34] While Dillon largely dates this transformation in the field of security to the modern epoch—or, more precisely, to the complex aesthetic, political, and philosophical field of formation he names the Baroque—I want to conclude this chapter by hypothesizing that it can also be seen as the outworking of an ancient aporetic logic that can be traced all the way back to that protopolitics of security called Paul's Second Letter to the Thessalonians. What is the *katechon* we have been describing here, after all, if not the embodiment of "security unleashed"?

To reiterate the thesis of this chapter—the Pauline figure of the restrainer is an accelerator despite (or today perhaps even *because* of) itself: it does not seek to simply hold back the end of the world so much as to accelerate it, preemptively, and on its own terms.[35] It is this messianic vocation—bodily lifted out of its original Judeo-Christian eschatological context and newly transplanted into an ontology of radical anti-teleological contingency—that paradoxically survives unscathed in our contemporary biopolitics of security. As the radical messianic voluntarism of the Unisys manifesto makes abundantly clear, risk is no longer conceived as an external threat to a stable or self-identical body, but an opportunity for unlocking a seemingly infinite potential within that very body: "Security is no longer a defensive measure. It's an enabling catalyst for achievement."[36] If contemporary politics of security so often seem to be presiding over the destruction of everything they seek to secure—civil rights, national, international, and military law, sovereignty—this is not a performative self-contradiction, in other words, but the realization of their own project of maximizing life's own inherently productive (and destructive) properties. In our contemporary Bethlehem, the rough beast already reigns: any political solution to the "chaos" of market crashes, cyber crime, terrorist attacks, and so on necessarily entails *more* chaos—the apocalypse from above—all unleashed under the sign of security, resilience, disaster preparedness, stress-testing, future-proofing, and the Schumpeterian creative destruction that is neoliberal capitalism itself.

In its status as (voluntary or involuntary) accelerator of history, then, the modern security state still perversely embraces the historic political-theological vocation of the *katechon*. It is this state of permanent crises—which cannot be resolved but only technocratically managed—that Massimo Cacciari's recent study of 2 Thessalonians intriguingly calls the "Age of Epimetheus."[37] After all, Epimetheus—the mythical brother of Prometheus whose name literally means "afterthought," whose idiotic impetuousness sets in motion the course of events that will lead to the opening of Pandora's Box, and whose tragic fate Carl Schmitt would, in his postwar internment, assume as his own—is perhaps the original accelerator despite himself.[38] However, there is one more *katechon* I want to consider before closing—one more rough beast at the heart of the city—and this is the figure of the modern neoliberal sovereign himself. To be sure, our contemporary sovereign immediately grasps the defining eschatological challenge of the modern epoch: "how do we secure the future for our party and for our country" in a "world fast forwarding to the future at unprecedented speed?" If we are to secure this future, it cannot be by seeking to preserve the way things are, but only by embracing the ever-accelerating force of change itself: "The pace of change can either overwhelm us, or make our lives better and our country stronger. What we can't do is pretend it is not happening," he argues. "It is replete with opportunities, but they only go to those swift to adapt, slow to complain, open, willing and able to change." For British prime minister Tony

Blair, speaking at the apogee of his own power and arguably of the neoliberal order itself in September 2005, such a messianic politics can only be accomplished through what he revealingly calls the "patient courage of the change-maker": "Unless we 'own' the future, unless our values are matched by a completely honest understanding of the reality now upon us and the next about to hit us, we will fail."[39] In the figure of the modern neoliberal sovereign—who seeks to secure the future by becoming the change-maker—the Pauline *katechon* completes its transformation from a restrainer into an unleashed accelerator of history.

7

UNDEAD

Benjamin and the Past to Come

*Of this alone even a God is deprived—to make what is all done
to have never happened.*

—Aristotle, *Nichomachean Ethics*

I n a 1927 article in *Die Literarische Welt*, Walter Benjamin
indulges himself in an "arabesque of a joke." Its subject was
the famous American aviator, Charles Lindbergh, who had
recently arrived in Paris following his historic solo flight across
the Atlantic. As Benjamin recalls, someone telephoned all the
city newspapers with the "news" that the École Normale Supéri-
eure had decided to bestow upon the great man the honor of
being "a former student," and the newspapers were taken in by
the hoax: a Lindbergh lookalike was paraded outside the École
Normale in front of photographers, the fake announcement was
written up as fact in the press, and the American aviator became,
briefly, a Normalien. Yet, this arabesque of a joke (an "arabesque"
is a pose in ballet in which one leg is extended backward at
right angles, the torso bent forwards, and the arms outstretched,
one forward and one backward) was not just a joke, because it,
too, extends forward and backward in time. To jump to the

punchline, Benjamin concludes that this early twentieth-century experiment in what we would today call fake news, alternative facts, or post-truth was actually the secular bureaucratic conclusion of a much older theological project: "Among the medieval Scholastics, there was a school that described God's omnipotence by saying: He could alter even the past, unmake what had really happened, and make real what had never happened. As we can see, in the case of enlightened newspaper editors, God is not needed for this task; a bureaucrat is all that is required."[1] If Benjamin's article does not expand on this historical allusion, he is clearly recalling a specific medieval theological debate about divine power: does God have the power to do whatever he wills whenever he wills it or is that power in some way limited by his prior will or decisions? For Pietro Damiani (1007–1072), who is the most famous or notorious spokesperson for the doctrine of divine omnipotence in the Christian tradition, God's absolute power over his creation finds its highest expression in the apparently fixed and immutable field of the *past*: God does indeed have the capacity to change the past, undoing what has been done and doing what was never done.[2] This concluding chapter seeks to construct a speculative constellation between Damiani's theory of divine omnipotence over the past in his letter "On Divine Omnipotence" and Benjamin's own theory of a messianic power to redeem the past in the "Theses on the Philosophy of History" (*Über den Begriff der Geschichte*) (1940). In Benjamin's famous claim that we still possess a "*weak* Messianic power [*messianische kraft*]" to redeem the past,[3] I propose that we encounter a weak, profane, and immanent rewriting of Damiani's own idea of the past as a theater for the exercise of divine power: Benjamin offers what we might (rewriting Taubes's own famous rewriting of Schmitt) call a divine power "from below."[4] What happens if we take absolutely seriously—indeed, quite literally—the strange proposition that it is possible to undo what has been done?

In a discussion with Desiderius, rector of the Abbey of Monte Cassino, sometime around 1065, the Benedictine monk Pietro Damiani was asked whether he thought God could restore the virginity of a fallen woman so that she never lost it in the first place. It was no idle speculation, of course, but a question that brought back to life a long theological debate about the limits of divine omnipotence. As Damiani well knew, it had already been answered centuries earlier by a distinguished theologian: "I dare say although God can do all things," Jerome argued to Eustochium, "he cannot raise up a virgin after her fall" (*cum omnia Deus possit suscitare virginem non potest post ruinam*).[5] However, if Jerome was willing to place limits upon divine power—and undoing what has been done is something even God cannot do—Damiani staunchly defended the theory of divine omnipotence. To unpack the complex and at times contradictory argument of his letter to Desiderius, "On the Divine Omnipotence in the Restoration of What Is Destroyed and in Rendering What Is Done Undone"—Damiani's God has the power to act outside of the laws of nature despite—or rather precisely because of—the fact that he himself has created those laws: "he who brought nature into being, at will easily abrogates the necessity of nature."[6] For Damiani, at least according to the maximalist reading of his work, God's omnipotence even or especially extends into what is apparently the most irrevocable order of all: the past. If God is not subject to time, if he exists in an eternal now (*sempiternam*

praesens) outside past, present, and future, if his power cannot diminish or increase with the passage of time, then "God could have caused things that have happened, not to have happened."[7] This is why we can say without absurdity that he can unmake what has been made: "God has the power after Rome was founded that it be non-founded."[8] In this way, Damiani concludes that Desiderius's question could be answered with an emphatic "yes": "I state and affirm this without fear of abuse or captious arguments to the contrary, the omnipotent God has power to restore virginity to any woman, no matter how many times she has been married, and to renew in her the seal of integrity, just as she was when taken from her mother's womb."[9] What exactly is at stake—theologically, philosophically, and above all politically—in the debate around divine omnipotence?

To be sure, Pietro Damiani's hyperbolic apology for God's absolute power is—for all its audacity—a kind of perverse extension, or rather inversion, of the classic Christian doctrine of *creatio ex nihilo*. It seems almost logical to assume that, in addition to the power to create something out of nothing, God possesses the equal and opposite power of what John D. Caputo nicely calls *reductio ad nihilum*—to return something to nothing, to annihilate.[10] At the same time, though, Damiani's God also constitutes the beginning of a famous debate within medieval theology between the competing demands of necessity and contingency that will persist for more than two hundred years. For Damiani, God's absolute power over his creation is purchased at the (exorbitantly high) cost of divesting the created order of any necessary rational or natural structure of its own and consigning it to a state of total contingency: this is a deity who could potentially lie or deceive, suddenly change his mind, or intervene in creation at any point according to his own whim. If Damiani's theology clearly anticipates the God of the nominalist revolution here—sovereign, voluntarist, omnipotent—it arguably even fore-shadows contemporary materialist philosophies of radical contingency: Damiani's God could even be said to preside over an anti-philosophical parallel universe to Quentin Meillassoux's hyperchaos.[11] In "On Divine Omnipotence," Damiani thus confronts us with an ontotheological state of exception in which the natural, rational, and logical order are subject to the seemingly arbitrary will of a God who may interrupt, reconstitute, or annihilate it at any given moment: "he who created nature has power to change the natural order at his pleasure; and while ordaining that all created things should be subject to the dominion of nature, reserved to the dominion of his power the obedience of a compliant nature."[12]

In the eyes of twelfth-century Christian Aristotelian philosophy, of course, Damiani's disturbingly radical solution to the ancient aporia of necessity and contingency—that God is not obliged to, or constrained by, the world he has created but can change it any point—was tantamount to an intolerable kind of divine anarchism or even gnosticism. It thus sought to reassert a measure of control over divine omnipotence over the past by binding the divine will to its own prior decisions. Accordingly, Scholastic theology devised the famous distinction between God's absolute power (*de potentia absoluta*) and his ordained power (*de potentia ordinata*): God has the power to do whatever he wills but he freely limits himself to act in accordance with what he has already ordained.[13] To rehearse the basic argument here, God could have created any world he wanted—or not created it all—but he chose to create the world as it is, and so he will not change it. If Scholastic theology obviously does not return to the pagan universe of Aristotelian necessitarianism—creation remains the product of an original, arbitrary, and contingent divine decision—it just as clearly does seek to contain

God's absolute power within the realm of what Mika Ojakan-gas calls hypothetical "divine possibility" alone: divine omnipotence refers only to what *could* have happened, but did not, because he decided otherwise.[14] This attempt to bind God to his prior decisions also restores a certain immanent, rational, even "economic"[15] order to creation as the product of divine ordination. In his discussion of the "Power of God" in the *Summa Theologica*, for instance, Thomas Aquinas revealingly argues that it is not in God's power to "make the past not to have been," and so Damiani's hypothetical fallen woman must remain forever fallen: "God can remove all corruption of the mind and body from a woman who has fallen; but the fact that she had been corrupt cannot be removed from her."[16]

In the nominalist revolution of the later Middle Ages, though, we witness a curious rehabilitation of Damiani's God. It is not necessary to rehearse the general implications of nominalism for the Christian Aristotelianism promulgated by Thomist theology—the move from realism to empiricism, from universals to singularities, and so on—in order to appreciate the extent to which the nominalists sought to liberate God's absolute power from the chains of his ordained power.[17] As Michael Gillespie observes, Duns Scotus and William of Ockham restore God to his original sovereign power after Thomism's attempt to bind him to his prior decisions: "omnipotence means the supremacy of God's *potentia absoluta* over His *potentia ordinata*."[18] However, revealingly, it is once again the past—as the supposed last refuge of necessity in being—that becomes the arena in which the theological battle over divine power is joined. To recall Duns

Scotus's lectures on contingency and freedom, for instance, God's absolute power does not describe a merely hypothetical realm of possibility—which could have been realized in the past, but was not, and now never will be—but a real capacity that he can still actualize at any given moment.[19] If the original Scholastic distinction between absolute and ordained power was never intended to describe a field of divine action—God chose to create this world, and once he made that choice, as we have seen, he would never reverse it—Scotus's so-called theory of synchronic contingency reinscribes divine *potentia absoluta* as a field of present agency: God retains the power to make things otherwise than he ordered them to be made at any point whatsoever. In this radical operationalization of God's absolute power, Scotus renders creation itself absolutely contingent for both divine and human alike: any given state of affairs is accompanied—not merely at an earlier or later moment but at every moment—by the simultaneously logical and real possibility that it could be otherwise.

To solve the classic problem of human freedom versus divine fatalism—how can humans be free agents if God already knows everything that is going to happen to them?—William of Ockham's classic treatise *Predestination, God's Foreknowledge, and Future Contingents* also summons up the ghost of divine omnipotence over the past.[20] Its attempt to square the circle between freedom and determinacy turns upon a distinction between what Nelson Pike famously calls "hard" and "soft" facts about the past. As Pike relates, a hard fact about the past is one that solely concerns events in the past (for example, "John went to London yesterday") whereas a soft fact about the past is one whose factuality is still conditional upon some future event taking place (for example, "Jane will go to Paris tomorrow").[21] If God's foreknowledge of the future must be considered a "soft" fact—insofar as it obviously concerns things that have not happened yet—this

means that its factuality does not necessarily exclude the operation of human agency or natural contingency before the event
takes place: Jane may well decide to go to Berlin instead tomorrow, not Paris, or something completely unforeseen could happen that means she cannot go anywhere at all. For Ockham, at
least according to this line of argument, God's past foreknowledge (as soft fact) would not be negated or contradicted by this
future contingency—as if God had somehow been proved
"wrong" or had changed his mind—but, rather, this contingency
retroactively transforms what God's foreknowledge always
already was: we now know what God *really* knew all along. In
positing this new theory of the past—open, soft, and future ori-
ented rather than closed, hard, and past dependent—Ockham
thus bestows upon human beings the power, if not exactly to
"change" the past, then to fix or determine what it really was,
anew, through their present actions.

In many ways, though, Pietro Damiani's thought experiment—
and the debate around divine omnipotence more generally,
from Thomism to nominalism—was never purely a theological,
or even philosophical, matter, because it quickly assumed political significance in the Middle Ages. It is now widely documented that this new activist paradigm of God's absolute power
as entirely unbound by and irreducible to ordained power was,
rightly or wrongly, translated into a paradigm of political power
within both the medieval ecclesiastical and civil orders. As William Courtenay observes, the pope famously possessed "plenitude of power [*plenitudo potestatis*] through which he could, on
an individual basis, temporarily suspend or alter particular, lesser
laws through dispensations or privileges for the common good
of the church at large [the *ratio ecclesiae*]."[22] Yet, it is less commonly recognized that even attempts to delimit papal *plenitudo
potestatis*—such as the Franciscan Order's famous "poverty"

dispute with Pope John XXII—were not, as we might imagine, legitimized by the doctrine of *potentia ordinata*, but by an even more powerful assertion of God's *potentia absoluta*.[23] To track this theological genealogy of the political into modernity, Carl Schmitt's *Political Theology* (1922) also famously compares the "omnipotent" God to the "omnipotent" lawgiver—and divine omnipotence clearly has a precise theological meaning and history here that has rarely been remarked upon by commentators— whereas, as Ojakangas observes, his *Constitutional Theory* (1928) specifically draws an analogy between the medieval theological concept of God's *potentia absoluta* and political constitution- making power (*verfassunggebende Gewalt*).[24] If Damiani's divine power thus arguably constitutes a possible and neglected origin for what we now call "sovereign exceptionality," I want to argue that this power to render lives unlived—cities unfounded, worlds uncreated—may also represent something close to the meta- physical foundation of one particular privileged manifestation of the state of exception, namely, what Banu Bargu has recently called "sovereignty as erasure."[25] For Bargu, modern sovereignty no longer finds its paradigm in the visual spectacle of public power—symbolized in the public torture and execution of the regicide Damiens memorably invoked by Foucault[26]—but rather in the de-corporealization, privatization, or invisiblization of violence symptomized by what are now called the politics of enforced or involuntary "disappearance": "the arrest, deten- tion, abduction or any other form of deprivation of liberty by agents of the State or groups of persons acting with the autho- rization, support or acquiescence of the State, followed by a refusal to acknowledge the deprivation of liberty or by conceal- ment of the fate or whereabouts of the disappeared person, which place such a person outside the protection of the law."[27] In order to introduce this reading of Damiani's theology of divine omnipotence as a kind of political theology of enforced disappearance, I want to consider one final disturbing counterfactual possibility arising from his thought experiment about the fallen woman restored to virginity that (to my knowledge) has never been entertained by any of the theologian's ancient or modern commentators. What if the woman who lost her virginity had gotten pregnant? What if she already has a child at the moment God decides to restore her virginity? What will happen to that child after God decides she never lost her virginity in the first place—will it continue to exist as the result of a miraculous virgin birth or will it simply disappear into the void of unbearable life?

In Benjamin's philosophy of history—if we can use such a monolithic or systematic term to describe what emerges out of, and between, such singular textual events as the "Theologico-Political Fragment" (c. 1921) and the "Theses on the Philosophy of History" (1940)—I want to argue that we encounter a curious recapitulation (*Wieder-holung*, "bringing back") of this medieval theological debate about divine power. It may be relevant here that the writing of the "Theologico-Political Fragment"—which Gershom Scholem dates to 1920–1921—coincides with the period of its author's deepest immersion in scholastic theology: Benjamin's (later abandoned) plan for a *Habilitationsschrift* in 1920 focused on a reading of Duns Scotus on language. To be sure, Benjamin's theory of the redemption of history has many more plausible origins—whether in the Jewish kabbalistic idea of *tikkun* ("mending the world"), Christian *apokatastasis*, Blanqui and Nietzsche's eternal recurrence, Proust's involuntary memory, or

Baudelaire's theory of modernity[28]—but my hypothesis will be that it can also be read as a radically profane or immanent rewriting of the concept of divine omnipotence over the past, or what I have called a divine power "from below." If Pietro Damiani and his theological successors insist upon God's power to change the past—to unmake what really happened, and make real what never happened—Benjamin famously assigns to the present generation what we will see to be an equivalent messianic capacity to short-circuit the teleological progression of time from past to present—as well as the ontological progression of being from the potential to the actual—by synchronically actualizing real but virtual alternative potentialities that lie unrealized in history. In reading Benjamin's new political theological project in this ancient context, I argue we can also begin to make sense of one of its defining—yet still enigmatic, oversimplified, or simply ignored—tasks.[29] Why does Benjamin insist that what must be redeemed from the past is not simply the dead, the forgotten, or the oppressed, but rather what was *never* lived?

To answer this question, I want to begin by recalling Benjamin's first formulation of the redemption of history in the seminal critique of historicism that Theodor Adorno retrospectively entitled the "Theologico-Political Fragment."[30] It is clear from the opening sentence of this fragment that what is at stake in the Benjaminian "theologico-political" is very different from any Christo-Hegelian "political theology" that posits the messianic kingdom as a historical goal or *telos* to be realized. As this fragment insists, the Messiah is a *deus absconditus* who has radically subtracted himself from the profane order—and so he cannot form the basis of any politics whatsoever. For Benjamin, what he calls the "profane order" thus cannot be built upon the theocratic "idea of the Divine Kingdom" but, rather, on an altogether more crucial term of art in his philosophy: "happiness" (*Glück*).[31]

If the profane search for happiness runs directly counter to the messianic pursuit of the kingdom, Benjamin goes on to insist (via a possible allusion to Newton's third law of motion) that the profane can—through its very action—produce the opposing reaction that is the messianic order: "the order of the profane assists, through being profane, the coming of the Messianic Kingdom."[32] In the notoriously elliptical conclusion of the fragment, Benjamin goes on to define "happiness" as the rhythm of what we might paradoxically call a "profane messianism": "To the spiritual *restitutio in integrum*, which introduces immortality, corresponds a worldly restitution that leads to the eternity of downfall, and the rhythm of this eternally transient worldly existence, transient in its totality, in its spatial but also in its temporal totality, the rhythm of Messianic nature, is happiness."[33]

In order to gain entry to Benjamin's cryptic messianism, I would like to use one small hermeneutic key from this passage: "*restitutio in integrum*." It is worth recalling that, in addition to its theological meaning, this term has a precise legal history and significance. As Miguel Vatter recalls, *restitutio in integrum* is the general rule used in common law to decide the award of damages in cases of criminal negligence: what it dictates is that the sum awarded is not designed to punish the defendant for any injury inflicted, but rather to restore the plaintiff to the position they would have been in had the injurious contract not been entered into in the first place. To translate this juridical principle into a theological vocabulary, Vatter argues that Benjamin's messianic restitution could thus be said to rescind the terms of man's Mosaic and Christian covenants with God—and the attendant nexus of sin, guilt, and punishment they produce that is diagnosed in the "Capitalism as Religion" fragment—and to return us to the pagan state of original innocence ("happiness") that is participation in the eternal creation and destruction of immanent life.[34] Yet, one might argue that the juridical principle suggests an even more radical act of divine omnipotence here: a *restitutio in integrum* does not merely release the plaintiff from a tortious existing contract, but compels us to act as if that contract simply never existed *ad initio*. If we can begin to see the antinomies of Benjamin's messianism emerging in this context— the profane versus the messianic, eternal recurrence of the same versus historical progress toward the end, happiness versus guilt history—it is perhaps also now possible to observe the extent to which they may be a reanimation of the theological antinomies around which the debate on divine omnipotence revolved: contingency versus necessity, freedom versus fatalism, and—more precisely—absolute power versus ordained power over the past. For Benjamin, this profane redemption of history is made possible by a gesture of weak messianic sovereignty over the past, which frees the human from the burden of its obligations: a worldly *restitutio in integrum* changes the past by returning humanity to the original, precontractual, position we occupied before our fatal covenant with God was agreed. In restoring to us the capacity to begin life anew—the totality of possibilities natural life promises but cannot in its finitude deliver— Benjamin's messianism also reactivates the idea of the past as a contingent field of force for the operation of (human rather than divine) power.

In Benjamin's philosophical itinerary, this messianic power to rescue what we might call the originary contingency or potentiality of the past—its permanent excess over its own determined actualization as historical past—reaches its most powerful

formulation in the opaque series of late aphorisms called "Theses on the Philosophy of History" (1940). To overcome the fatalism of the vulgar naturalist theory of historicism and the social
democratic idea of progress—which remain in thrall to the idea
of the linear progression of "homogeneous, empty time" from
past to future[35]—the "Theses" famously propose that the true
task of the historical materialist is not to recuperate the past
"the way it really was"[36] but rather just the opposite: what must
be redeemed from the past is not what once existed for us, so
that it may exist again in the present, but rather what never
existed in the first place. Yet, if this exorbitant claim is the point
at which many commentators part company with Benjamin, as
we will see momentarily, what is taking place here can be read
as a logical extension of the worldly *restitutio in integrum* imagined in the "Theologico-Political Fragment." If the historical
materialist's vocation is to restore what we have called the original potentiality of our past—to rescue it from the determinism of fate or obligation—then the true litmus test of this *restitutio* is logically the power to relive a past that was wholly
unlived: unbearable life. In the second thesis, for example, Benjamin makes absolutely clear that his *restitutio* seeks to return us
to an original state of happiness that *never was*:

> Reflection shows us that our image of happiness is thoroughly col-
> ored by the time to which the course of our own existence has
> assigned us. The kind of happiness that could arouse envy in us
> exists only in the air we have breathed, among people we could
> have talked to, women who could have given themselves to us. In
> other words, our image of happiness is indissolubly bound up with
> the image of redemption. The same applies to our view of the past,
> which is the concern of history. The past carries with it a temporal

index by which it is referred to redemption. There is a secret agreement between past generations and the present one. Our coming was expected on earth. Like every generation that preceded us, we have been endowed with a *weak* Messianic power, a power to which the past has a claim.[37]

To try to unpack this remarkable claim as simply as possible, Benjamin's "happiness" (*Glück*) (and we should perhaps hear the alternative translation of "chance" or "happenstance" here too) refers not to a past that once was really present and now is not, but to an absolute past of contingent possibilities that were never, in reality, lived by us. It is a political affect or *stimmung* that envies not just lost causes or failed hopes—a past that happened albeit imperfectly or incompletely—but a past that quite simply never happened at all: "the air we have breathed," "people we could have talked to," and "women who could have given themselves to us," but did not. However, as Benjamin makes clear, it is only from the naturalist perspective of historicism—which persists in its stubborn belief that it can recapture the past "the way it really was"—that this unlived past is consigned to the realm of past hypothetical possibility or "what might have been." If what Benjamin calls the unlived past never literally took place—because our hypothetical friendships or love affairs were never, in reality, consummated—what is crucial here is that this past is emphatically not beyond redemption (*Erlösung*) in the present or future by us: "we have been endowed with a *weak* Messianic power [*messianische kraft*]," he famously observes, "a power to which the past has a claim." For Benjamin, we in the present generation are the inheritors of this unlived past and are bestowed with the power to somehow or somewhere reactualize its lost or unrealized potentiality—to breathe the air, to talk to the

people, to love the women. In the sense that we *are* the past—
because its totality of possibilities continue to exist in, and as,
us—we also have the power to change it.

In the vast majority of Benjamin scholarship, from Horkheimer to Žižek, of course, Benjamin's challenge to redeem the
past is either dismissed as an unfortunate relapse into theological dogmatism and/or reduced to a merely figurative description
of an immanent process of radical political emancipation. It is
worth remembering here Horkheimer's famous claim, repro-
duced in the *Arcades Project* (1927–1940), that Benjamin's messianism prevented him from recognizing the essentially
irrevocable—and thus irredeemable—status of history: "Past
injustice has occurred and is completed. The slain are really
slain . . . If one takes the lack of closure entirely seriously, one
must believe in the Last Judgment."[38] According to Terry
Eagleton, Benjamin's messianic attempt to redeem the past can
thus only be taken metaphorically: "Benjamin had the curious
notion that we could change the past. For most of us, the past is
fixed while the future is open. Benjamin thought that the past
could be transformed by what we do in the present. Not literally
transformed, of course, since the one sure thing about the past
is that it does not exist."[39] To answer the question of what form
this transformation of the past might take—if not a literal
change—Slavoj Žižek argues that Benjaminian historical
materialism consists in nothing more remarkable than the
"redemption-through-repetition" of lost causes like the French
Revolution: "the task of a true Marxist historiography," Žižek
writes, "is to unearth the hidden potentialities (the utopian
emancipatory potentials) which were betrayed in the actuality
of revolution and in its final outcome (the rise of utilitarian market capitalism)."[40] Yet, against such normalizing interpretations,
I read the "Theses" as something more complex than a simple

invitation to do better in the future what was done badly in the past—or even to "fail again, fail better" in the words of Žižek"s neo-Beckettian call to arms. For Benjamin, what is at stake in the "Theses" is not the figurative redemption of the past by the future but, to recall Agamben's pointed formulation from *The Time That Remains* (2000), nothing less than the literal "redemption of what has been":[41] the historical materialist's struggle has a genuinely "retroactive force and will constantly call into question every victory, past and present of the rulers."[42] If we reduce Benjamin's philosophy of history to a project of radical future emancipation—one that seeks to redeem the virtual content of the past from its historical actualizations by repeating them in the present and future—I worry that we risk emptying the "*weak* Messianic power" we possess over the past of this realist or ontological dimension in which even the fate of the long dead still somehow remains a "live" political question: "Only that historian will have the gift of fanning the spark of hope in the past who is firmly convinced that *even the dead* will not be safe from the enemy if he wins."[43] In the sense that it seeks to quite literally render the dead undead—or, better, to recognize that their life and death have not been definitively decided once and for all—Benjamin's messianism ironically out-materializes even his more orthodox materialist readers: the redemption of history becomes a real ontological event rather than just a mere figure of speech.

In his philosophy of history, then, Benjamin ends up making the same claim about the past that Marx famously makes about the world in his eleventh thesis on Feuerbach: "The point, however, is to change it."[44] To reiterate my guiding hypothesis, Benjamin's weak messianic power to transform the past can be read as an immanent, profane re-constellation of Damiani's theology of divine omnipotence. For Benjamin, the "Theses on the Philosophy of History" arguably also constitute an attempt to change political theology's own past by actualizing a virtual capacity within the very idea of divine omnipotence *itself* to take place otherwise. If Damiani and his successors give God alone the prerogative to change the past, Benjamin bestows this divine power upon human beings as the inheritors of history's unfulfilled promise. In the same way, Benjamin's immanent messianism also renders inoperative or workless the Schmittean political theology of absolute sovereign power to which (as we have seen) the theory of divine omnipotence gives rise: this new political theology is human, not divine; weak, not omnipotent; given to us, not willed by us; experienced by us without ever fully becoming an object of experience to be grasped, equally capable of producing suffering as well as happiness—and even of missing its appointment with the past altogether and deferring it yet again to a future generation. What happens then, to remember the question with which we started, if we take absolutely seriously— indeed literally—the curious idea that we can change the past?

To reread the classic debates of Benjamin's reception history— between Scholem, Adorno, and Brecht, between Judaeo-Christian messianism and historical materialism, between precritical theological dogmatism and Marxist critique—in this ancient but new context, we can also now begin to see the extent to which they (whether consciously or unconsciously) still circle around the question of the possible redemption of the past. It is important to observe here that Horkheimer's original charge of "theology" against Benjamin in *The Arcades Project* can only really refer to the theology of divine omnipotence, because not even belief in the universal resurrection of the Last Judgement—"there shall be a resurrection of the dead, both of the just and the unjust" (Acts 24:15)—is enough to make the dead never actually die in the first place, to unslay the slain. As Benjamin's famous reply makes clear, historical materialism does not simply seek to remember a past that is fixed and irrevocable but to change it *as* past by the very act of remembering it:

> history is not simply a science but also and not least a form of remembrance [*Eingedenken*]. What science has "determined," remembrance can modify. Such mindfulness can make the incomplete (happiness) into something complete, and the complete (suffering) into something incomplete. This is theology; but in remembrance we have an experience that forbids us to conceive of history as fundamentally atheological, little as it may be granted to us to try to write it with immediately theological terms.[45]

Yet, arguably the only contemporary Benjamin scholar who seems to be even aware of the theology of divine omnipotence over the past is Giorgio Agamben, who briefly alludes to Damiani's thought experiment on the fallen woman in his own theory of potentiality.[46] If Leibniz famously claims that actuality precedes possibility—that every possibility demands to exist in actuality—Agamben famously reverses this formula to claim that it is *possibility* that precedes and exceeds actuality: "each existent demands [*esige*] its proper possibility, it demands that it become possible."[47] For Agamben, as Jelica Šumič correctly observes, this (highly Benjaminian) redemption of possibility from actuality does not take place futurally but retroactively by transforming the apparent "actuality"—the very pastness—of the past itself: redemption, she writes, consists in "nothing less than the restoration, after the fact, retroactively, as it were, of the possibility, not of that which will take place but, paradoxically, of that which has taken place."[48] In restoring this originary contingency or potentiality of the past—its inherent potential to be otherwise than it is or was—Benjamin's philosophy of history returns us to a past that is every bit as open as the future.

In drawing this chapter to a close, I want to consider what is at stake in this curious political theological constellation between Walter Benjamin and Pietro Damiani, between weak and strong divine power, between (if you prefer) the redemption of the women who could have given themselves to us and of the fallen woman, married many times. To return to where we started in this book, I propose that what is taking place here—amongst many other things—is a (quite literal) *contretemps* between two competing versions of the political theology of unbearable life: the godlike power to render worlds uncreated, cities unfounded, and lives unlived by political means. It was Benjamin's 1927 joke, recall, that Damiani's God is no longer needed to change the past—"a bureaucrat is all that is required"—and perhaps we might see the politics of enforced or involuntary disappearance from the Stalinist purges through the Holocaust to extraordinary rendition as an exercise in political Damianism on an industrial scale.[49] As Banu Bargu compellingly observes, the politics of enforced disappearance do not merely exhibit a microphysics of power over its victims—whether it be through the falsification of records, papers, or photographs or the process of secret internment and torture—but a macro-political metaphysics or "worldview" that renders this disappearance possible in the first place. For Bargu, as we have already seen in the introduction, sovereignty as erasure is "a kind of violence that seeks not only to eradicate the person who is the target of enforced disappearance but also to erase the fact that the person ever existed," to the extent that "it is not only about the destruction of the individual but also the elimination of the individual's prior presence."[50] If this politics of retroactive disappearance has a political theological precursor, it arguably lies in Damiani's metaphysics of radical contingency, in which the past can be changed as easily as the future by an act of arbitrary will or voluntarism: "he who created nature has power to change the natural order at his pleasure; and while ordaining that all created things should be subject to the dominion of nature, reserved to the dominion of his power the obedience of a compliant nature."[51] In Benjamin's theory of a weak messianic power that gives us back the women who could have given themselves to us in the past but did not, we can perhaps also find a kind of affirmative counter-writing—a counter-metaphysics as well as a counter-politics—of Damiani's thought experiment of the fallen women, married many times, who can be restored to virginity. What if the woman who could have given herself to us could still give herself? What if she, too, could have a child? What if Benjamin offers a means of rendering that unbearable life bearable once more?

In January 1941, following his surprise victory over Franklin Delano Roosevelt in the previous November's election, Charles Augustus Lindbergh was inaugurated as the thirty-third president of the United States. To fulfil his one and only campaign pledge—keeping America out of the war in Europe—the new president quickly signed nonaggression pacts with Nazi Germany and Imperial Japan. By officially recognizing German and Japanese sovereignty over Europe and Asia in return for recognition of the United States' own territorial rights over North

America, Lindbergh effectively turned the United States into one of the Axis powers and he also strongly supported Germany's subsequent invasion of the state he evidently saw as the real enemy of world peace—Soviet Russia. Yet, in addition to allying itself with the Third Reich on the international stage, the Lindbergh administration—under the auspices of its secretary of the interior, former industrialist Henry Ford—also instituted a new Kulturkampf against the Jews at home. Ford's so-called Office of American Absorption (OAA) attempted nothing on the scale of the Nazi pogroms, of course, but it had the same origin in paranoid anti-Semitic fantasies about a cultural and racial enemy within: Jewish families on the East Coast were forcibly relocated to Christian communities in the Midwest, and non-Jews were introduced into predominantly Jewish neighborhoods in the cities with the clear but unstated objective of ethnically and culturally cleansing Jewish America. In Philip Roth's *The Plot Against America* (2004)—whose chilling counterfactual history of wartime America is, of course, what I am recounting here—Lindbergh's democratic Nazification of the United States is carried out with the consent and, indeed, overwhelming support of the vast majority of American citizens: "It can't happen here? My friends, it *is* happening here."[52]

To be sure, Roth's provocative counter-history can be read in many ways, but I want to conclude this chapter (and this book) by proposing it as a somber attempt to write what Benjamin calls a "history against the grain."[53] It is possible to suspect that the real "plot against America" in this *Trauerspiel* about courtly intrigue is Roth's own—this is a book that seeks both to interrupt the official narrative of American history and to re-narrate that history differently. As Roth's postscript to the book reminds us, his virtual history is no exercise in pure fantasy but an authentically counterfactual thought experiment. If the "real" historical Charles Lindbergh preferred private citizenship to running for public office, of course, he was by no means just a neutral observer of the great debates on American interventionism in the late 1930s and early 1940s. This popular American hero was, after all, a supporter of the strongly isolationist "America First" movement; he had given a speech publicly blaming American Jews for disloyally inciting the United States to enter the war, which led to him being denounced as a both a Nazi sympathizer and an anti-Semite by Roosevelt's secretary of the interior, Harold Ickes, and he had been talked up by Republican senators like William E. Borah as the ideal candidate to run against Roosevelt in 1940.[54] In actualizing this virtual—but at the same time real—President Lindbergh, Roth seeks to rescue what (in a strikingly Benjaminian formulation) his young narrator calls "unforeseen" history from the fatalist purview of historiography:

> And as Lindbergh's election couldn't have made clearer to me, the unfolding of the unforeseen was everything. Turned wrong way round, the relentless unforeseen was what schoolchildren studied as "History," harmless history, where everything unexpected in its own time is chronicled on the page as inevitable. The terror of the unforeseen is what the science of history hides, turning a disaster into an epic.[55]

In turning history the "right" way round again, Roth's novel thus exposes the essential wrongness of reading the past as an epic plot or narrative of inevitable events and turns it back into a site of pure and unpredictable possibility—the "terror of the unforeseen." Its true horror does not, I think, lie in the specific counterfactual possibility it presents—what if a fascist really had become president?—but rather in this revelation of a generalized state of radical contingency where everything necessary becomes possible once more. To see history itself as something radically "unforeseen," we must perform a Benjaminian *restitutio in integrum* that returns us to a past every bit as open, contingent, and unknowable as the future itself: the unlived past, the missed, unseized, or deferred past, the past that never was. If Benjamin's profane messianism insists that the past that never happened continues to exist as a possibility to be actualized by the future in a time of danger, Roth's novel similarly establishes an uncanny historical constellation between the state of emergency of 1940 and that of 2004: Roth's President Lindbergh—a plainspoken, populist demagogue who reassures the public that every sovereign decision he makes is taken solely to increase their security—is a *doppelgänger* for President George W. Bush, and Lindbergh's America, with its steady erosion of civil liberties and creeping atmosphere of authoritarianism, is strangely reminiscent of the America of Bush's War on Terror. For critics in the United States of 2018, of course, Roth's President Lindbergh also prefigures the unforeseen rise of another strongly isolationist—indeed, "America First"—celebrity president: "It is easier to comprehend the election of an imaginary President like Charles Lindbergh than an actual President like Donald Trump," Roth said in an interview with the *New Yorker* shortly before his death. "I would say that, like the anxious and fear-ridden families in my book, what is most terrifying is that [Trump] makes *any and everything possible*."[56] In Roth's alternative history of the American present, Benjamin's "arabesque of a joke" continues to echo backward and forward in time, making anything and everything possible once again. What if the great aviator Charles Lindbergh, whose flight over history reveals to us the accumulating "disaster" unfolding beneath his wings, is the secular avatar of that other tragic political theological flying machine famously imagined in Benjamin's ninth thesis?

This is how one pictures the angel of history. His face is turned toward the past. Where we perceive a chain of events, he sees one single catastrophe which keeps piling wreckage upon wreckage and hurls it in front of his feet. The angel would like to stay, awaken the dead, and make whole what has been smashed. But a storm is blowing from Paradise; it has got caught in his wings with such violence that the angel can no longer close them. The storm irresistibly propels him into the future to which his back is turned, while the pile of debris before him grows skyward. This storm is what we call progress.[57]

CONCLUSION

I n the aftermath of the 9/11 attacks, President George W.
Bush signed an executive order authorizing the detention
of so-called high-value terror suspects in a set of secret pris-
ons operated by the CIA around the world. It set in motion a
program that effectively outsourced the War on Terror by placing terrorists not only outside U.S. territory but beyond its legal
jurisdiction, in what have become known as "black sites." As
many journalists have subsequently observed, the so-called ghost
detainees imprisoned in these offshore black sites were deprived
of any legal or human rights except for those given to them by
their captors—and thus could be subjected to treatment and
conditions that would likely be deemed illegal on U.S. soil. To
take only the most notorious case, Khaled Sheikh Mohammed
(the alleged main organizer of the 9/11 attacks) was subject to
extraordinary rendition and held indefinitely without registra-
tion, without charge, without access to family, legal representation, or local authorities in a black site in Poland, where he was
subjected to so-called enhanced interrogation techniques like
waterboarding on dozens of occasions.[1] While Amnesty International estimated that around one hundred suspects were being

detained in black sites in 2005, the CIA detention and interrogation program still remains shrouded in remarkable secrecy today—despite, or arguably because of, the recent investigation of the Senate Select Committee on Intelligence. In 2018, as I write this, many states continue to deny sustained and credible allegations that they have ever hosted, or facilitated the operation of, a secret detention center. What, to bring this book to a close, are the—political, philosophical, and even theological— origins of the black site?

It is increasingly clear that there is nothing legally, historically, or politically "extraordinary" about such biopolitical *dispositifs* as extraordinary rendition. As Banu Bargu has observed, there is actually a disturbing historical, legal, and political precedent for the United States' policy in the politics of "enforced or involuntary disappearance" notoriously associated with Latin American states like Chile, Argentina, and Guatemala in the 1960s and 1970s.[2] To situate his case in this longer context, Khaled Sheikh Mohammed represents less a new kind of enemy—the "unlawful enemy combatant" deprived of the rights accorded enemy combatants under the Geneva Convention— than the latest member of the spectral community of *los Desaparecidos*. Although the United States has now officially ended its policy of extraordinary rendition, it goes without saying that the politics of enforced disappearance have themselves by no means "disappeared." For the United Nations Working Group on Enforced or Involuntary Disappearances, whose most recent annual report was issued in 2015, a total of 43,250 cases of enforced disappearance in some 88 states were identified as currently under active investigation.[3] This report almost certainly underestimates the true figure because, inevitably, the ongoing process of denial, intimidation, and concealment surrounding such cases has led to massive underreporting. In this context, we might begin to see the CIA's secret detention program less as an exception than as the becoming-rule—indeed becoming global *nomos*—of a sovereign *dispositif* of disappearance: the world as (virtual or real) black site.[4]

To recapitulate my argument one final time, I have sought in this book to offer a genealogy of the sovereign power to render life unbearable—neither alive nor dead—from Rome to the modern Republic, from *damnatio memoraie* to extraordinary rendition, from (if you prefer) Emperor Geta to Khaled Sheikh Mohammed. It has been my objective to lay bare not only some of the many *dispostifs* or apparatuses of power over unbearable life—torture, infanticide, assassination, and martyrdom, as well as proscription, eugenics, and disappearance—but, perhaps more importantly, what we might call its political ontology. As we saw in chapter 7, the politics of enforced disappearance arguably contain or exhibit their own peculiar "metaphysics" that renders all necessity radically contingent upon a political decision. For Bargu, recall, political disappearance does not only make its victims disappear, but also makes the very fact of their disappearance *itself* "disappear" in a political ontological act of (self-)erasure: this is "a kind of violence that seeks not only to eradicate the person who is the target of enforced disappearance but also to erase the fact that the person ever existed."[5] If we want to understand the politics of enforced disappearance, let alone attempt to resist, counter, or overcome it, I think we need to understand that this gesture of retroactive (self-)erasure or annihilation is not merely a monstrous fantasy of power but the symptom of a complex kind of political physics or metaphysics. In this book, I have thus tried to argue that the political will to render life unbearable—nonexistent, nothing, *nihil*—is not simply an "exceptional" modern phenomenon (in every sense of that word) but the outworking of a much older nihilopolitical imaginary that is operative in some of the primal scenes of the political theological archive.

For Michel Foucault in the Collège de France lectures, recall, the classical sovereign's power over the life and death of his subjects consists not merely in the ancient power to let them live or make them die but—more precisely—to position them in a kind of ontological or metaphysical "black site" where their very existence *qua* living subject is contingent upon a political decision: "the subject is neutral and it is thanks to the sovereign that the subject has the right to be alive or, possibly, the right to be dead."[6] It is Foucault's great insight here, as we saw in chapter 1, that sovereignty was never simply the power to kill or punish a subject whose prior life must be taken for granted, but rather the power to decide whether or not someone—whose originary status is a priori neutral from the perspective of the state—should be recognized as a living subject endowed with rights at all. To reread his work today, I think Foucault is arguably also the first "metaphysician" of disappearance insofar as his theory of biopolitics begins to lay bare the conceptual apparatuses that make the "physics" or politics of involuntary disappearance possible and inevitable. If Foucault is right that the first act of "extraordinary rendition" is performed by the sovereign upon life itself—because the subject neither appears nor disappears as subject until the sovereign decides they will—then it is no accident that the politics of enforced disappearance so often end up not merely removing its victims' supposedly inalienable rights or liberties but (as Bargu observes) returning those victims to that political void or "black site" of right, identity, and subjectivity in which they originally subsisted. In a gesture that will now be very familiar to us, political disappearance does not simply consist in making a set of naturally appearing subjects, bodies, or lives forcibly "disappear," so much as in revoking the original sovereign decision that forced them, equally involuntarily, to "appear" in the first place.

In closing, then, I would argue that this is the hyperbolic political ontological conclusion to which Foucault's thought experiment on the sovereign right of life and death inexorably leads us: what we call "sovereignty" conceives of itself from the very beginning as power not only over the production of life and death but of presence and absence—time and space, life and death, the natural and the political—in short, of the order of "being" itself. Its self-appointed task is to decide upon an ontology that has become (or is newly revealed to always have been) undecidable in any other terms but the "political." As we saw from chapter 2 onward, this sovereign must rule over a universe that properly belongs to Augustine's Cacus, Shakespeare's Macbeth, and the Schmittean *katechon*; a world that is radically anomic, atomistic, or lawless; a nature stripped of Greek or Christian natural law, providential order, or economy and a subject divested of any intrinsic natural or divine rights or properties. To fill this gap or lack in the real over which it must rule, modern sovereign power thus seeks (massively, voluntaristically, and hubristically) to become its *own* "real." By claiming to govern a preexisting constative or objective reality, sovereignty in fact presumes to produce and transform the ontological coordinates of the real itself: "We're an empire now," to recall the notorious words of an anonymous member of the Bush administration during the War on Terror, "and when we act, we create our own reality."[7] If this "empire of the real" takes many forms throughout history, I have argued that its privileged but invisible sign has always been acts of exorbitant annihilatory violence over those it deems to be somehow less than real, but whose nonreality must still, paradoxically, be confirmed again and again: the torture or punishment of a body that never possessed any rights (Augustine, Hobbes); the regicide of a king who was never a king (Shakespeare, the English Civil War, the French Revolution); the preemptive elimination of people who were never

supposed to be born (Nazism). This sovereign act of violence—
which retrospectively denies its victims even the bare recognition
of life that is being killed by presenting itself as nothing more
than the physical, indeed tautological, confirmation of the
victim's original metaphysical nullity—is thus curiously compelled to repeat its own gesture of nullification ad infinitum. For
Judith Butler, whose *Precarious Life* (2004) observes a similar "bad
infinity" at work in the endless War on Terror, political violence
wrought upon lives that have already been rendered politically
unreal or inhuman is thus caught in a logic of double negation
that ends up canceling itself out and paradoxically confirming
the inexhaustibility of its object: "they cannot be mourned because
they are always already lost or, rather, never 'were,' and they
must be killed, since they seem to live on, stubbornly, in this
state of deadness."[8] In being forced to negate its victims again and
again, even as it insists they never "were," what I have called
nihilopower ironically also ends up conferring upon those victims a certain spectral resistant power or immunity: they "live
on" in a state outside life and death.

What, in the end, may be done to resist this nihilopolitical
empire of the real? Is it possible to make the disappeared (literally or symbolically) "reappear," whether via due political or legal
process, cultural history, or aesthetic performance? Or might, as
I have proposed here, disappearance *itself* paradoxically become
a—black—site in which new forms of political subjectivity might
be produced? It is important to conclude this book by bearing
witness to the long and brave history of resistance to political
disappearance, which, from family protests outside secret pris-
ons in Latin America to the establishment of formal networks
like the International Coalition Against Enforced Disappearances (ICAED), has constantly insisted upon the stubbornly
ineradicable existence—the "thereness"—of those deemed to be

politically nonexistent.[9] At the same time, we have witnessed how biopolitical theory from Arendt to Esposito has constructed an affirmative counter-ontology to nihilopolitics that, again, posits an irreducible essence or moment within the living itself, which somehow escapes sovereign annihilation: natality, virtuality, potentiality, resistance, and so on. Yet, in contrast to such life-affirming appeals, this book's final claim has been that unbearable life produces its own radical conjugations of political subjectivity that cannot easily be made to live or die: monstrous birth (Augustine, Shakespeare); the never there (Hobbes, Benjamin); the already dead (Hobbes, Robespierre); the unlived past and the past to come (Benjamin). To give one final example that is perhaps particularly timely in the present context, I find it significant and hardly coincidental that the massive expansion of the "invisible" state over the past decade or so has found an exact and symmetrical parallel in the increasing proliferation of forms of what we might call "invisible" resistance or insurrection: Anonymous, Tiqqun, the Invisible Committee or Imaginary Party, the Luther Blissett project, hacktivism, non-state cyber attacks, the debate around the so-called right to be forgotten, and so on almost infinitely. For the anonymous political collective called the Invisible Committee, to take just one instance, our nihilopolitical condition becomes less another state of abjection than the productive site for a new resistant politics: it is a question of "learning to become imperceptible," they write in *The Coming Insurrection* (2009), of "regaining the taste for anonymity" and resisting the regime of the visible.[10] If the politics of enforced disappearance seek to eradicate its targets in both space and time, in other words, what seems to be taking place here is the dialectical transformation of "disappearance" *itself* into a new kind of collective political subject position that (rhetorically at least) claims to be both nowhere and everywhere, always already there and yet to come: Anonymous, the underground digital collective, famously declares, "We are Anonymous. We are Legion, We do not forget, We do not forgive, Expect us."[11] In this promise of invisible insurrection, we can perhaps begin to glimpse the future political children of unbearable life.

NOTES

INTRODUCTION

1. To be sure, scholars diverge upon the question of what precise relationship (if any) exists between Roman imperial apotheosis and political theological accounts of the king's two bodies, sovereign perpetuity, and so on. Firstly, Elias Bickerman asserts a genetic connection between the funeral ceremonies of Roman emperors and renaissance French kings in his essay "Roman Imperial Apotheosis." If Ernst Kantorowicz agrees that imperial apotheosis constitutes the historical origin of the royal funeral in *The King's Two Bodies*, he is skeptical that the link is anything more than historical: we cannot speak in any meaningful sense of the "emperor's two bodies" or of imperial sovereign perpetuity. Finally, Giorgio Agamben seeks to reestablish the political theological connection between Roman and Christian theories of sovereignty, albeit around the figure of the bare life of the sovereign. See Elias Bickerman, "Die römische Kaiserapotheose," *Archiv für Religionswissenschaft* 27 (1929), 1–34; Ernst Kantorowicz, *The King's Two Bodies: A Study in Medieval Political Theology* (Princeton, NJ: Princeton University Press, 1957), 427, 434; and Giorgio Agamben, *Homo Sacer: Sovereign Power and Bare Life*, trans. Daniel Heller-Roazen (Stanford, CA: Stanford University Press, 1998), 91–103.

2. Harriet I. Flower, *The Art of Forgetting: Disgrace and Oblivion in Roman Political Culture* (Chapel Hill: University of North Carolina Press, 2006).

3. Banu Bargu, "Sovereignty as Erasure: Rethinking Enforced Disappearances," *Qui Parle: Critical Humanities and Social Sciences* 23, no. 1
(Fall/Winter 2014): 35–75, 43.

4. Agamben, *Homo Sacer*; Judith Butler, *Precarious Life: The Power of
Mourning and Violence* (London: Verso, 2004); Eric L. Santner, *On
Creaturely Life: Rilke/Benjamin/Sebald* (Chicago: University of Chicago
Press, 2006); and Roberto Esposito, *Immunitas: The Protection and
Negation of Life*, trans. Zakiya Hanafi (London: Polity, 2011).

5. Hannah Arendt, *Origins of Totalitarianism*, 3rd. ed. (New York: Harcourt, Brace, and World, 1973), 442.

6. Michel Foucault, *"Society Must Be Defended": Lectures at the Collège
de France, 1975–76*, trans. David Macey (New York: Picador, 2003),
240.

7. Judith Butler, *Precarious Life*, 36. See also Judith Butler, *Frames of War:
When Is Life Grievable?* (London: Verso, 2009). In this text, Butler
beautifully underscores the retroactive gesture of annihilation that
silently attends non-grievable life: "Without grievability, there is no
life, or, rather, there is something living that is other than life. Instead,
'there is a life that will never have been lived,' sustained by no regard,
no testimony, and ungrieved when lost" (15).

8. Roberto Esposito, *Bios: Biopolitics and Philosophy*, trans. Timothy
Campbell (Minneapolis: University of Minnesota Press, 2008), 143–
45, 145.

9. Agamben, *Homo Sacer*, 88. Emphasis in original.

10. Butler, *Precarious Life*, 34.

11. Foucault, *"Society Must Be Defended,"* 256.

12. In the contemporary philosophical moment, the proper name "political theology" seems to encompass everything from an unashamed apology for a premodern Christian philosophy (John Milbank), through a
theological genealogy of the modern liberal order (Giorgio Agamben),
an irreducible transcendental remainder within the self-definition of
the secular (Hent de Vries), to a necessary fiction or fantasy through
which we must pass in order to enter a new radically materialist politics (Slavoj Žižek). If any self-professed political theology would seem
at the most minimal level to describe some kind of relationship *between*
the religious and the political, we can detect no clear consensus about
what form that relation might take: it seems to encompass everything
from a formal, structural, or homological analogy between the

religious and the political; a historical, genealogical, or sociological relation; a psychoanalytic lack, surplus, or work of mourning; to a much stronger ontological sense that the religious constitutes a permanent or necessary condition of the political. In what follows, I use "political theology" less to mark some undeclared religious or political commitment on my part (I have nothing to declare) and more as a kind of placeholder: an "X" that marks the spot where the ongoing interrogation of the—in my view clearly unfinished—relation between the religious and the political will take place.

13. See Claude Lefort, "The Permanence of the Theologico-Political?," in *Democracy and Political Theory*, trans. David Macey (Minneapolis: University of Minnesota Press, 1988), 213–55, 225. In Lefort's classic account, the "theologico-political" names an irreducibly "transcendental" outside that persists within the immanent liberal order: "Every religion *states* in its own way that human society can only open on to itself by being held in an opening it did not create. Philosophy says the same thing, but religion said it first, albeit in terms which philosophy cannot accept."

14. Eric Santner, *On the Pyschotheology of Everyday Life: Reflections on Freud and Rosenzweig* (Chicago: University of Chicago Press, 2001).

15. G. W. F. Hegel, "Absolute Freedom and Terror," in *Phenomenology of Spirit*, trans. A. V. Miller (Oxford: Oxford University Press, 1977), 355–64, 360.

16. Walter Benjamin, "Theses on the Philosophy of History," in *Illuminations*, trans. H. Zohn (New York: Schocken, 1968), 253–64, 254.

17. Eduardo Cadava, Peter Connor, and Jean-Luc Nancy, eds., *Who Comes After the Subject?* (London: Routledge, 1991).

18. See Horst Bredekamp, "Thomas Hobbes's Visual Strategies," in *The Cambridge Companion to Hobbes's 'Leviathan,'* ed. Patricia Springborg (Cambridge: Cambridge University Press, 2007), 29–60. In Bredekamp's analysis, Hobbes's Leviathan is a kind of a secular equivalent to the royal effigies displayed on tombs to symbolize the immortal body of the king in the Middle Ages.

19. See Michel Foucault, *Discipline and Punish: The Birth of the Prison*, trans. Alan Sheridan (Harmondsworth: Penguin, 1991); Agamben, *Homo Sacer*; and Jacques Derrida, *The Beast and the Sovereign*, vol. 1, trans. Geoffrey Bennington (Chicago: University of Chicago Press, 2010).

20. Jean-Luc Nancy, *The Truth of Democracy*, trans. Michael Naas and Pascale-Anne Brault (New York: Fordham University Press, 2010), 31. See also Peter Gratton, *The State of Sovereignty: Lessons from the Political Fictions of Modernity* (Albany: State University of New York Press, 2012), 205, for a helpful account of Nancy's theory of sovereignty.

1. UNBEARABLE: FOUCAULT AND THE BIRTH OF NIHILOPOLITICS

The epigraph to this chapter is taken from Michel Foucault, *"Society Must Be Defended": Lectures at the Collège de France, 1975–76*, trans. David Macey (New York: Picador, 2003), 240.

1. See Antonio Cerella, *Genealogies of Political Modernity* (London: Bloomsbury, 2019), for a compelling rereading of the origin of the sovereign right of life and death that significantly problematizes Foucault's account.

2. To be sure, Foucault is (albeit silently) tracking the passage from natural right to sovereign right here: human beings are no longer naturally endowed with rights by virtue of their reason but are given rights from without by their sovereign. See Brian Tierney, *The Idea of Natural Rights: Studies on Natural Rights, Natural Law, and Church Law, 1150–1625* (Cambridge: Eerdmans, 1997), for a now classic study of the natural right tradition.

3. Michel Foucault, *The Will to Knowledge*, vol. 1 of *The History of Sexuality*, trans. Robert Hurley (London: Penguin, 1978), 135.

4. Foucault, *The Will to Knowledge*, 136.

5. Foucault, *The Will to Knowledge*, 138.

6. Foucault, *The Will to Knowledge*, 136.

7. Foucault, *The Will to Knowledge*, 143.

8. Foucault, *"Society Must Be Defended,"* 240.

9. Foucault, *"Society Must Be Defended,"* 240.

10. Foucault, *The Will to Knowledge*, 135.

11. Foucault, *"Society Must Be Defended,"* 240.

12. Foucault, *"Society Must Be Defended,"* 241.

13. Michel Foucault, *Power/Knowledge: Selected Interviews and Other Writings, 1972–77*, ed. Colin Gordon (New York: Pantheon, 1980), 102.

14. Foucault, *Power/Knowledge*, 121.

15. Carl Schmitt, *The Leviathan in the State Theory of Thomas Hobbes: Meaning and Failure of a Political Symbol*, trans. George Schwab and Erna Hilfstein (Chicago: University of Chicago Press, 2008), 35. In one sense, Schmitt is the first critic to identify the "biopolitical" Hobbes some sixty years before the likes of Agamben or Esposito: "Life is of interest only insofar as it concerns the here and the now, the physical existence of the individual, of actual living beings," he presciently notes, and "the most important and the highest goal is security and the possible prolongation of this kind of physical existence."

16. Thomas Hobbes, *Leviathan or The Matter, Forme and Power of a Common Wealth Ecclesiasticall and Civil*, ed. Richard Tuck (Cambridge: Cambridge University Press, 1991), "Review and Conclusion," 17, 491.

17. Foucault, *"Society Must Be Defended,"* 241.

18. See also Foucault, *The Will to Knowledge*, 135, where the French philosopher claims that the Hobbesian subject simply transfers their natural right to kill and die to the sovereign, who assumes that right in the form of the civil right to punish: "Must we follow Hobbes in seeing it as the transfer to the prince of the natural right possessed by every individual to defend his life even if this meant the death of others?" In Hobbes's *Leviathan*, as we will see in chapter 4, the right to punish actually has its origin in the state of nature rather than the social contract and so is never "transferred" from subject to sovereign.

19. Thomas Hobbes, *De Cive*, in *Man and Citizen: "De Homine" and De Cive*," ed. Bernard Gert (Indianapolis, IN: Hackett, 1991), 2, XVII, 12, 345. See also Hobbes, *The Elements of Law Natural and Politic*, ed. Ferdinand Tönnies, 2nd ed. (London: Cass, 1969), II, 10, 8, 189.

20. Foucault, *"Society Must Be Defended,"* 248–49. Translation modified.

21. Foucault, *"Society Must Be Defended,"* 209.

22. Foucault, *"Society Must Be Defended,"* 35.

23. Foucault, *"Society Must Be Defended,"* 195–96.

24. Jean-Jacques Rousseau, *The Social Contract and Other Later Political Writings*, ed. Victor Gourevitch (Cambridge: Cambridge University Press, 1997), II, 7, 69. Emphasis mine.

25. Jean-Jacques Rousseau, "Discourse on the Origins and the Foundations of Inequality Amongst Men," in *The Discourses and Other Early Political Writings*, ed. Victor Gourevitch (Cambridge: Cambridge University Press, 1997), I, 134.

202 SO I. UNBEARABLE

26. Leo Strauss, *Natural Right and History* (Chicago: University of Chicago Press, 1953), 271.

27. Bernard Stiegler, *Philosopher par accident: Entretiens avec Elie During* (Paris: Galilée, 2004), 42. See Arthur Bradley, *Originary Technicity: The Theory of Technology from Marx to Derrida* (London: Palgrave, 2011), for a reading of Stiegler's philosophy of technology.

28. Rousseau, *The Social Contract*, II, 5, 64. See Peter Gratton, *The State of Sovereignty: Lessons from the Political Fictions of Modernity* (Albany: State University of New York Press, 2012), 27–63, for an important account of Rousseau's theory of the right of life and death to which my reading is indebted.

29. Rousseau, *The Social Contract*, II, 5, 64.

30. Foucault, *"Society Must Be Defended,"* 254–56.

31. Giorgio Agamben, *Homo Sacer: Sovereign Power and Bare Life*, trans. Daniel Heller-Roazen (Stanford, CA: Stanford University Press, 1998), 6. Emphasis in original.

32. Agamben, *Homo Sacer*, 88. Emphasis in original.

33. Roberto Esposito, *Communitas: The Origin and Destiny of Community*, trans. Timothy Campbell (Stanford, CA: Stanford University Press, 2010); *Immunitas: The Protection and Negation of Life*, trans. Zakiya Hanafi (London: Polity, 2011); and *Bios: Biopolitics and Philosophy*, trans. Timothy Campbell (Minneapolis: University of Minnesota Press, 2008).

34. Esposito, *Bios*, 143–45.

35. For Esposito, the Nazi suppression of birth begins with the Law for the Prevention of Genetically Diseased Offspring (*Gesetz zur Verhütung erbkranken Nachwuchses*). This law, which was passed soon after Hitler came to power in 1933, permitted the compulsory sterilization of any citizen who, in the opinion of a "Genetic Health Court" suffered from a list of alleged genetic disorders. In Esposito's account, this policy was extended to encompass compulsory abortion for "degenerate" parents (1934), castration for homosexuals (1935), and sterilization for women over the age of thirty-six (1936).

36. Quoted in Esposito, *Bios*, 145.

37. Esposito, *Bios*, 143.

38. Foucault, *The Will to Knowledge*, 143.

39. Foucault, *The Will to Knowledge*, 145.

40. See Peter Dews, "The Return of the Subject in the Late Foucault," *Radical Philosophy* 51 (1989): 37–41; Béatrice Han, *Foucault's Critical Project: Between the Transcendental and the Historical* (Stanford, CA: Stanford University Press, 2002); and Andrea Rossi, *The Labour of Subjectivity: Foucault on Biopolitics, Economy, Critique* (London: Rowman and Littlefield, 2015), for a range of critical responses to the question of Foucault, genealogy, and ontology.

41. Gilles Deleuze, *Negotiations, 1972–1990*, trans. Martin Joughin (New York: Columbia University Press, 1990), 108–11.

42. Foucault, *The Will to Knowledge*, 95.

43. Foucault, *The Will to Knowledge*, 143.

44. Esposito, *Bios*, 39.

45. Charles Dickens, *Our Mutual Friend* (Ware: Wordsworth Classics, 1997), 400.

46. Dickens, *Our Mutual Friend*, 443.

47. Gilles Deleuze, *Pure Immanence: Essays on a Life*, trans. Anne Boyman (New York, Zone, 2001), 29.

48. Esposito, *Bios*, 194.

49. See Gilbert Simondon, *L'individuation psychique et collective* (Paris, Aubier, 1989). In Esposito's account, Simondon's theory of psychic and collective individuation offers an affirmative theory of biopolitics by multiplying the singular event of the subject's birth into the constant production of new physical, psychic, biological, or political individuations: "The only way for life to defer death isn't to preserve it as such (perhaps in the immunitary form of negative protection), but rather to be reborn continually in different guises." Esposito, *Bios*, 181.

50. See Lorenzo Chiesa, "The Bio-Theo-Politics of Birth," *Angelaki: Journal of the Theoretical Humanities* 16, no. 11 (2011): 101–15, for a critique of Esposito's vitalism.

51. If Foucault and his successors seem to posit a certain neo-vitalist idea of life as the basis for an affirmative biopolitics, it is worth recalling that a new wave of biopolitical theory contends that, far from resisting power/knowledge, this theory of life as immanent, becoming, creative, and so on just *is* the dominant ontology of sovereign power over life today. In a classic recuperation of its own apparent "outside," contemporary financial, military, security, and medical discourse is frequently now predicated upon the very theory of life that "positive" biopolitical

theory has always claimed to be irreducible to political capture. See Melinda Cooper, *Life as Surplus: Biotechnology and Capitalism in the Neoliberal Era* (Seattle: University of Washington Press, 2008); Michael Dillon and Julian Reid, *The Liberal Way of War: Killing to Make Life Live* (London: Routledge, 2009); and Michael Dillon, *Biopolitics of Security: A Political Analytic of Finitude* (London: Routledge, 2015).

52. Dickens, *Our Mutual Friend*, 722.

53. Jean Hyppolite, *Genesis and Structure of Hegel's "Phenomenology of Spirit,"* trans. S. Cherniak and J. Heckman (Evanston, IL: Northwestern University Press, 1974), 172.

54. In recent biopolitical theory, the figure of the living dead, the already dead, or the zombie—all existing between life and death—has, of course, become a recurrent trope. See Achille Mbembe, "Necropolitics," *Public Culture* 15, no. 1 (2003): 11–40; Judith Butler, *Precarious Life: The Power of Mourning and Violence* (London: Verso, 2004); and Slavoj Žižek, *The Parallax View* (Cambridge, MA: MIT Press, 2006), for different variations on this theme.

55. Jacques Derrida, "The Rogue That I Am," in *Rogues: Two Essays on Reason*, trans. Pascale-Anne Brault and Michael Naas (Stanford, CA: Stanford University Press, 2005), 63–70.

2. UNGOOD: AUGUSTINE'S CITY OF CACUS

1. Augustine of Hippo, *City of God*, trans. Henry Bettenson (Harmondsworth: Penguin, 1972), 19.12.867.

2. Virgil, *Aeneid*, trans. David West, rev. ed. (Harmondsworth: Penguin Classics, 2003), 8.185–275. All further references will be given in the text by book and line number.

For Virgil's King Evander, Cacus lived in "a cave which the rays of the sun never reached . . . The floor of the cave was always warm with freshly shed blood, and the heads of men were nailed to his proud doors and hung there pale and rotting. The father of this monster was Vulcan, and it was his father's black fire he vomited from his mouth as he moved his massive bulk" (8.195–99). In addition to Virgil's account, variations of the story of Cacus appear in Livy, *History of Rome*, 1.7.3; Dionysius of Halicarnassus, *Roman Antiquities*, 1.39; Ovid, *Fasti*, 1.543–86, 1.643–52; and Propertius, *Elegies*, 4.9.1–20.

3. Augustine, *City of God*, 19.12.867.

4. Augustine, *City of God*, 11.23.454.

5. Augustine, *City of God*, 11.23.454.

6. See Gillian R. Evans, *Augustine on Evil* (Cambridge: Cambridge University Press, 1990), for a modern assessment of Augustine's privative theory of evil.

7. Augustine, *City of God*, 19.12.867–68.

8. Augustine, *City of God*, 19.12.868.

9. Augustine, *City of God*, 19.12.869.

10. To get an overview of Augustine's theory of monstrosity, see Lorraine J. Daston and Katherine Park's classic *Wonders and the Order of Nature* (Cambridge, MA: MIT Press, 2001). In fact, Cacus is beneath even the monster in Augustine's ontology: he simply does not exist at all.

11. Pindar, "The *Nomos-Basileus* Fragment (169)," in *Early Greek Thought from Homer to the Sophists*, ed. Michael Gagarin and Paul Woodruff (Cambridge: Cambridge University Press, 1995), 40.

12. Carl Schmitt, *The* Nomos *of the Earth in the International Law of the Jus Publicum Europaeum*, trans. G. L. Ulmen (New York: Telos, 2003), 342n19.

13. Carl Schmitt, *The* Nomos *of the Earth*, 342n19.

14. Mika Ojakangas, "Carl Schmitt and the Sacred Origins of Law," *Telos* 147 (Summer 2009): 34–54. In what follows, I am indebted to Ojakangas's analysis of Schmitt's interpretation of Hercules.

15. Carl Schmitt, *The* Nomos *of the Earth*, 48.

16. Giorgio Agamben, *"Nomos Basileus,"* in *Homo Sacer: Sovereign Power and Bare Life*, trans. Daniel Heller-Roazen (Stanford, CA: Stanford University Press, 1998), 30–38. In Agamben's account, the Pindar fragment (as cited in Plato's *Gorgias* 484b) does not equate violence and justice so much as absolutely distinguish between them: "here the 'justification of violence' is at the same time a 'doing violence to the most just.'" Agamben, *Homo Sacer*, 26.

17. Carl Schmitt, *Glossarium: Aufzeichnungen aus den Jahren 1947–51*, ed. Eberhard Freiherr von Medem (Berlin: Duncker & Humblot, 1991), 249.

18. K. W. Gransden, *Virgil: "Aeneid" Book VIII* (Cambridge: Cambridge University Press, 1976), 16.

19. R. O. A. M. Lyne, *Further Voices in Virgil's "Aeneid"* (Oxford: Oxford University Press, 1987).

20. Lyne, *Further Voices in Virgil's "Aeneid,"* 32.

21. Llewelyn Morgan, "Assimilation and Civil War: Hercules and Cacus," in *Virgil's "Aeneid": Augustan Epic and Political Context*, ed. Hans-Peter Stahl (London: Duckworth in association with the Classical Press of Wales, 1998), 175–98, 179.

22. Gransden, *Virgil*, 108.

23. Jacques Derrida, *The Beast and the Sovereign*, vol. 1, trans. Geoffrey Bennington (Chicago: University of Chicago Press, 2009), 14. In Derrida's account, we can detect an "irresistible and overloaded analogy" between the figures of the animal and the sovereign within the western political tradition running from Hobbes to Schmitt because both figures— beast and ruler—"share a space of some exteriority with respect to 'law' and 'right' (outside the law; above the law; origin and foundation of the law)."

24. Livy, *The Early History of Rome, Books I–V*, trans. Aubrey de Selincourt (London, Penguin, 2002), 1.7.9.

25. Michel Serres, *Rome: The Book of Foundations*, trans. Felicia McCarren (Stanford, CA: Stanford University Press, 1991).

26. Serres, *Rome*, 17.

27. Michel Serres, *The Parasite*, trans. Lawrence R. Schehr (Baltimore, MD: Johns Hopkins University Press, 1982), 24.

28. Serres, *The Parasite*, 253.

29. René Girard, *Violence and the Sacred*, trans. Patrick Gregory (Baltimore, MD: Johns Hopkins University Press, 1977).

30. Augustine, *City of God*, 19.12.868.

31. R. A. Markus, *Saeculum: History and Society in the Theology of Augustine* (Cambridge: Cambridge University Press, 1970), 72.

32. Markus, *Saeculum*, 167.

33. Markus, *Saeculum*, xi.

34. Markus, *Saeculum*, 167.

35. Markus, *Saeculum*, 95.

36. Markus, *Saeculum*, xi.

37. Oliver O'Donovan and Joan Lockwood O'Donovan, *Bonds of Imperfection: Christian Politics, Past and Present* (Grand Rapids, MI; Cambridge: Eerdmans, 2004).

38. Markus, *Saeculum*, 94–95.

39. See the following for a range of readings of Augustine's theology of punishment: Terrance C. McConnell, "Augustine on Torturing and Punishing an Innocent Person," *Southern Journal of Philosophy* 17 (1979): 481–92; Todd Breyfogle, "Punishment," in *Augustine Through the Ages*, ed. Allan D. Fitzgerald (Grand Rapids, MI: Eerdmans, 1999), 688–90; John von Heyking, "Augustine on Punishment and the Mystery of Human Freedom," in *The Philosophy of Punishment and the History of Political Thought*, ed. Peter Karl Koritansky (Columbia: University of Missouri Press, 2011), 54–73; and Peter Iver Kaufman, "Augustine"s Punishments," *Harvard Theological Review* 109, no. 4 (2016): 550–66.

40. Augustine, *City of God*, 19.6.860.

41. In Oliver O'Donovan and Joan Lockwood O'Donovan's account, it would be a mistake to see Augustine's critique of torture as merely an attack on the barbarous laws of evidence that prevailed in the later empire: "For him, it is a universal problem about all judicial processes everywhere. It is a guess as to which party is lying and which telling the truth, and any inquisitorial process adopted to reduce the element of hazard may backfire and defeat its own ends." *Bonds of Imperfection*, 70.

42. Augustine, *City of God*, 19.7.861–62.

43. Michael Dillon, "Lethal Freedom: Divine Violence and the Machiavellian Moment," *Theory and Event* 11, no. 2 (2008), https://muse.jhu .edu (accessed April 9, 2019).

44. O'Donovan and O'Donovan, *Bonds of Imperfection*, 70.

45. Jean Bethke Elshtain, "Augustine," in *The Blackwell Companion to Political Theology*, ed. Peter Scott and William T. Cavanaugh (Oxford: Blackwell, 2007), 35–47, 35. See the following for varying assessments of Augustine's realism: Reinhold Niebuhr, "Augustine's Political Realism," in *The Essential Reinhold Niebuhr—Selected Essays and Addresses*, ed. Robert McAfee Brown (New Haven, CT: Yale University Press. 1953), 123–41; Michael Loriaux, "The Realists and Saint Augustine: Skepticism, Psychology, and Moral Action in International Relations Thought," *International Studies Quarterly* 36 (1992): 401–20; and John von Heyking, *Augustine and Politics as Longing in the World* (Columbia: University of Missouri Press, 2001).

46. Janet Coleman, *A History of Political Thought: From the Middle Ages to the Renaissance* (Oxford: Blackwell, 2000), 339.

47. Elshtain, "Augustine," 45.

48. John Adams to Abigail Adams, August 14, 1776, in *Adams Family Correspondence*, vol. 2, ed. L. H. Butterfield (Cambridge, MA: Belknap Press of Harvard University Press, 1963).

49. Lynn Hunt, *Politics and Class in the French Revolution* (Berkeley: University of California Press, 1984), 87–119, 89–90. In the following paragraph, I draw extensively on Hunt's classic analysis of Herculean images during the French Revolution.

50. Hunt, *Politics and Class in the French Revolution*, 95.

51. Marc-René Jung, *Hercule dans la littérature française du XVIe siècle: De l'Hercule courtois à l'Hercule baroque* (Geneva: Droz, 1966), 129–31.

52. Maximilien Robespierre, *Œuvres de Maximilien Robespierre* (Paris: Société des études Robespierristes, 1912–2007), 10:182.

53. Jo Becker and Scott Shane, "Secret 'Kill List' Proves a Test of Obama's Principles and Will," *New York Times*, May 29, 2012, http://www.nytimes.com/2012/05/29/world/obamas-leadership-in-war-on-al-qaeda.html?pagewanted=all&_r=0 (accessed February 1, 2013). All quotations are taken from this article.

3. UNTIMELY RIPPED:
MACBETH'S CHILDREN

1. L. C. Knights, "How Many Children Had Lady Macbeth? An Essay in the Theory and Practice of Shakespeare Criticism," *Explorations* (London: Chatto & Windus, 1946), 1–39. In writing this opening paragraph, I am relying on Carol Chillington Rutter's very helpful reconstruction of the Bradley-Knights-Brooks debate in her "Remind Me: How Many Children Had Lady Macbeth?," in *Shakespeare Survey 57: Macbeth and Its Afterlives*, ed. Peter Holland (Cambridge: Cambridge University Press, 2004), 38–53.

2. William Shakespeare, *Macbeth*, The Arden Shakespeare, ed. Sandra Clark and Pamela Mason (London: Bloomsbury, 2015). References are given in the text by act, scene, and line number. Epigraph to this chapter is from 5.8.13–16.

3. Knights, "How Many Children Had Lady Macbeth?," 37.

4. Cleanth Brooks, "The Naked Babe and the Cloak of Manliness," in *The Well-Wrought Urn* (London: Dennis Dobson, 1949), 21–46, 31.

5. Brooks, "The Naked Babe and the Cloak of Manliness," 35.
6. See Carol Chillington Rutter, *Shakespeare and Child's Play: Performing Lost Boys on Stage and Screen* (London: Routledge, 2007); Chris Laoutaris, *Shakespearean Maternities: Crises of Conception in Early Modern England* (Edinburgh: Edinburgh University Press, 2008), 176–211; and Joseph Campana, "The Child's Two Bodies: Shakespeare, Sovereignty, and the End of Succession," *ELH* 81 (2014): 811–39, for important recent readings of the child in *Macbeth* that have influenced my own.
7. Rutter, *Shakespeare and Child's Play*, 169.
8. Frank Kermode, *Shakespeare's Language* (New York: Farrar, Straus & Giroux, 2000), 201–16.
9. Kathleen Davis, *Periodization and Sovereignty: How Ideas of Feudalism and Secularization Govern the Politics of Time* (Philadelphia: University of Pennsylvania Press, 2008). In many ways, I read Shakespeare's play as participating in, dramatizing, but also demystifying what Davis compellingly calls the sovereign gesture of periodization: *Macbeth* both seeks to retrofit James I into a patrilineal sovereign history and also exposes the violence that attends every sovereign attempt to reorder historical time to fit the demands of the present.
10. To be sure, Shakespeare critics have been exploring *Macbeth*'s relationship to the monarchy of James I for more than fifty years, and the play is commonly seen as an attempt to bestow political and theological legitimacy upon James by (variously) dramatizing his historic lineage, propagating his views on divine right kingship, paternal succession, or demonology, denouncing his attempted assassination in the Gunpowder Plot, or forging a symbolic "union" between England and Scotland. In the view of other critics, the play registers secret dissent from the Stuart monarchy in coded form. See the following for a range of different readings: David Norbrook, "Macbeth and the Politics of Historiography," in *The Politics of Discourse: The Literature and History of Seventeenth Century England*, ed. K. Sharpe and S. N. Zwicker (Berkeley: University of California Press, 1987), 78–116; Gary Wills, *Witches and Jesuits: Shakespeare's* Macbeth (New York: Oxford University Press, 1995); Richard Wilson, *Secret Shakespeare: Studies in Theatre, Religion and Resistance* (Manchester: Manchester University Press, 2004); and Sharon Alker and Holly Faith Nelson, "*Macbeth*, the Jacobean Scot, and the Politics of the Union," *Studies in English Literature, 1500–1900* 47, no. 2 (2007): 379–401.

11. See Campana, "The Child's Two Bodies," 828–30, for an alternative reading of this soliloquy.

12. See Johann P. Sommerville, ed., *King James VI and I: Political Writings*, (Cambridge: Cambridge University Press, 1994). In his attempt to legitimize his succession, as well as the union between England and Scotland, James draws extensively upon the medieval legal fiction of the king's two bodies.

13. Kristen Poole, "Physics Divined: The Science of Calvin, Hooker and Macbeth," *South Central Review* 26, nos. 1–2 (2009): 127–52.

14. See J. G. A. Pocock, *The Machiavellian Moment: Florentine Political Thought and the Atlantic Republican Tradition* (Princeton, NJ: Princeton University Press, 1975), Robert Kraynak, *History and Modernity in the Thought of Thomas Hobbes* (Ithaca, NY: Cornell University Press, 1990), and Ian Hunter, *Rival Enlightenments: Civil and Metaphysical Philosophy in Early Modern Germany* (Cambridge: Cambridge University Press, 2001) for now classic accounts of the emergence of this new and peculiarly modern political universe.

15. Rutter, *Shakespeare and Child's Play*, 165.

16. Ernst Kantorowicz, *The King's Two Bodies: A Study in Medieval Political Theology* (Princeton, NJ: Princeton University Press, 1957), 387.

17. Emmanuel Lévinas, *Totality and Infinity: An Essay on Exteriority*, trans. Alphonso Lingis (Pittsburgh, PA: Duquesne University Press, 1969), 231. See Jeremy Tambling, "Lévinas and *Macbeth*'s 'Strange Images of Death,'" *Essays in Criticism* 54, no. 4 (2004): 351–372, for a reading of *Macbeth* through the lens of Lévinas's ethics to which I am indebted.

18. Emmanuel Lévinas, *Existence and Existents*, trans. Alphonso Lingis (Pittsburgh, PA: Duquesne University Press, 2001), 52.

19. Lévinas, *Existence and Existents*, 56.

20. Lévinas, *Existence and Existents*, 56.

21. Lévinas, *Totality and Infinity*, 146.

22. Emmanuel Lévinas, *Otherwise Than Being*, trans. Alphonso Lingis (Pittsburgh, PA: Duquesne University Press, 2001), 1. Quoted in Tambling, "Lévinas and *Macbeth*'s 'Strange Images of Death,'" 367.

23. See David Kastan, *Shakespeare After Theory* (New York: Routledge, 1999); Richard Wilson, "'Blood Will Have Blood': Regime Change in *Macbeth*," in *Shakespeare Jahrbuch* 143 (2007): 11–35; and John Drakakis,

"*Macbeth* and Sovereign Process," in *Macbeth: A Critical Reader*, ed. John Drakakis and Dale Townsend (London: Bloomsbury, 2013), 123–53. I am grateful to John Drakakis for providing me with a pre-publication draft of this essay and for his insightful comments on an earlier version of this chapter.

24. Drakakis, "*Macbeth* and Sovereign Process," 136.

25. See Sandra Clark and Pamela Mason, "Introduction" to *Macbeth*, The Arden Shakespeare (London: Bloomsbury, 2015), 116–21, for a discussion of different theatrical and filmic renditions of the play's ending. In many modern stagings, the final scene is performed in anything but redemptive terms: Malcolm has been depicted as a potential tyrant like Macbeth, or a weak king who will be subject to the same fate as his father, and the Weird Sisters are often reintroduced at the end as well to reinforce this sense of vicious circularity.

26. Laoutaris, *Shakespearean Maternities*, 195.

27. Laoutaris, *Shakespearean Maternities*, 195.

28. Laoutaris, *Shakespearean Maternities*, 195.

29. Laoutaris, *Shakespearean Maternities*, 195.

30. Campana, "The Child's Two Bodies," 831–32.

31. Robert Appelbaum, *Terrorism Before the Letter: Mythography and Political Violence in England, Scotland, and France, 1559–1642* (Oxford: Oxford University Press, 2015). I am grateful to Robert Appelbaum for sharing his important work in this field.

32. See Graham Holderness and Bryan Loughrey, "Shakespeare and Terror," in D. A. Brooks, ed., *Shakespeare After 9/11: How a Social Trauma Reshapes Interpretation, Shakespeare Yearbook* 20 (2011): 23–56; Peter C. Herman, "'A Deed Without a Name': *Macbeth*, the Gunpowder Plot, and Terrorism," *Journal for Cultural Research* 18, no. 2 (2014): 114–31; and Robert Appelbaum, "Shakespeare and Terrorism," *Criticism* 57, no. 1 (2015): 23–45, for a range of different readings of *Macbeth*'s relation to terrorism.

33. H. F. Brown, ed., *Calendar of State Papers, Venice*, London Public Record Office (1900), 10:289.

34. Edward Coke, *A True and Perfect Relation of the Proceedings at the Severall Arraignments of the Late Most Barbarous Traitors* (London, 1606), sig. D3v. Emphasis mine.

35. Kantorowicz, *The King's Two Bodies*, 39. For Kantorowicz, Richard's description of his natural body as a traitor to his Kingly body politic foreshadows the Commons' charge against Charles: "high treason committed by the *k*ing against the *K*ing," emphasis in original. In Kantorowicz's view, the political theology of the King's two bodies thus survived the death of Charles and would not come to a definitive end until the trial and execution of Louis XVI in 1793.

36. See Michael Walzer, ed., *Regicide and Revolution: Speeches at the Trial of Louis XVI* (New York: Columbia University Press, 1992), 47, for a classic comparative assessment of the implications of trying and executing both Charles I and Louis XVI.

37. Quoted in Walzer, *Regicide and Revolution*, 47.

38. Walzer, *Regicide and Revolution*, 80. In Robespierre's speech to the National Convention arguing for the death of the king, he contended that the dauphin should be imprisoned in the temple "until peace and public liberty have a firmer hold upon us" (138), and Louis's son died there in 1795.

39. Leon Trotsky, *Trotsky's Diary in Exile: 1935*, trans. Elena Zarudnaya (Cambridge, MA: Harvard University Press, 1958), 82. Quoted in Walzer, *Regicide and Revolution*, 80.

40. Roberto Esposito, *Bios: Biopolitics and Philosophy*, trans. Timothy Campbell (Minneapolis: University of Minnesota Press, 2008), 121.

41. Esposito, *Bios*, 121. See also Gil Anidjar, *Blood: A Critique of Christianity* (New York: Columbia University Press, 2014), for a brilliant critique of the political theological fates of "blood" in the Western tradition.

42. Esposito, *Bios*, 143. Emphasis in original.

43. Hannah Arendt, *The Origins of Totalitarianism* (New York: Harcourt, Brace, and World 1951), 445.

44. Esposito, *Bios*, 143.

45. Primo Levi, *Survival in Auschwitz: The Nazi Assault on Humanity* (New York: Simon and Schuster, 1996), 90. In Levi's classic account, *der Muselmänn* (the "Muslim") was the ironic name of the "anonymous mass, continually renewed and always identical, of non-men who march and labor in silence, the divine spark dead within them, already too empty to really suffer. One hesitates to call them living: one hesitates to call their death death."

4. UNCOMMON: HOBBES'S MARTYRS

1. In *The Elements of Law*, we find the first substantial formulation of this proposition: "It is not against reason that a man doth all he can to preserve his own body and limbs, both from death and pain. And that which is not against reason, men call RIGHT, or *jus*, or blameless liberty of using our own natural power and ability. It is therefore a *right of nature*: that every man may preserve his own life and limbs, with all the power he hath." Thomas Hobbes, *The Elements of Law Natural and Politic*, ed. Ferdinand Tönnies, 2nd ed. (London: Cass, 1969), I, 14, 6, 71; chapter epigraph from II, 10, 8, 189. In both *De Cive* and *Leviathan*, the same natural law appears.

2. Thomas Hobbes, *De Cive*, in *Man and Citizen: "De Homine" and "De Cive*," ed. Bernard Gert (Indianapolis, IN: Hackett, 1991), 2, XVIII, 13, 384.

3. Hobbes, *Elements of Law*, II, 6, 144.

4. Hobbes, *Elements of Law*, II, 6, 2, 4–10, 146–57.

5. Hobbes, *Elements of Law*, II, 6, 3, 146.

6. Hobbes, *Elements of Law*, II, 6, 6, 148.

7. Hobbes, *Elements of Law*, II, 6, 14, 158.

8. Hobbes, *Elements of Law*, II, 6, 14.

9. Hobbes, *De Cive*, 2, XVIII, 13, 383. Emphasis in the original.

10. Hobbes, *De Cive*, 2, XVIII, 13, 383.

11. Hobbes, *De Cive*, 2, XVIII, 13, 384. Emphasis in the original.

12. See A. P. Martinich, *The Two Gods of Leviathan: Thomas Hobbes on Religion and Politics* (Cambridge: Cambridge University Press, 1992), 303–4; Gary Remer, *Humanism and the Rhetoric of Toleration* (Philadelphia: Pennsylvania State University Press, 1996), 169–202; and Eric Brandon, *The Coherence of Hobbes' "Leviathan": Civil and Religious Authority Combined* (London: Continuum, 2007), 89–90, for incidental discussions of Hobbes on religious martyrdom.

13. To be sure, Carl Schmitt, writing in his posthumously published *Glossarium*, declares that "Jesus is the Christ" is the "most important sentence of Hobbes." Its purpose is "to neutralize the effect of Christ in the social and political sphere; to de-anarchize Christianity, while leaving it at the same time as a kind of legitimating effect and in any case not to do without it." In echo of Schmitt, Jacob Taubes also

notes that the "cardinal sentence" in *Leviathan*, which is repeated over
forty times, is that *"Jesus is the Christ"* (emphasis in original). See Carl
Schmitt, May 23, 1949, *Glossarium: Aufzeichnungen aus den Jahren
1947–51*, ed. Eberhard Freiherr von Medem (Berlin: Duncker &
Humblot, 1991), and Jacob Taubes, "Leviathan als sterblicher Gott:
Zur Aktualität von Thomas Hobbes," *Evangelische Kommentare* 13
(1980), 571–74, 574.

14. Thomas Hobbes, *Leviathan or The Matter, Forme and Power of a Common Wealth Ecclesiasticall and Civil*, ed. Richard Tuck (Cambridge:
Cambridge University Press, 1991).

15. See Jeremy Waldron, "Hobbes on Public Worship," in *Nomos XLVIII:
Toleration and Its Limits*, ed. Melissa S. Williams and Jeremy Waldron
(New York: New York University Press, 2008), 31–53, for a recent dis-
cussion of Hobbes on public worship.

16. Hobbes, *Leviathan*, III, 42, 343.

17. Hobbes, *Leviathan*, III, 42, 343.

18. Hobbes, *Leviathan*, III, 42, 344–45.

19. J. G. A. Pocock, "Time, History and Eschatology in the Thought of
Thomas Hobbes," in *Politics, Language and Time: Essays on Political
Thought and History* (New York: Atheneum, 1971). In Pocock's words,
Hobbes renders any experience of God impossible in the present: it is
"conceivable only in the past and the future" (197).

20. See, in particular, Hobbes, *Leviathan*, II. 29, 221–30. In Hobbes's anal-
ysis, aspiring religious martyrs would undoubtedly be found guilty of
"Private Judgement of Good or Evill," "Erroneous Conscience," and
"Pretense of Inspiration," amongst other offenses.

21. Hobbes, *Leviathan*, III, 43, 414.

22. Sigmund Freud, *The Interpretation of Dreams*, in *Standard Edition of
the Complete Psychological Works of Sigmund Freud*, trans. A. A. Brill
(London: Vintage, 2001), 4:119–20.

23. Hobbes, *Leviathan*, III, 28, 214.

24. Hobbes, *Leviathan*, II, 21, 148.

25. Yet, of course, many scholars have detected a contradiction between
sovereign power and individual rights within Hobbes's contract theory here: Jean Hampton says it is impossible "for people to authorize
an absolute sovereign while at the same time reserving to themselves

the right to resist under certain circumstances." In any event, Hobbes's intention is clear even if his logic is flawed: the sovereign has the political right to inflict punishment on any subject, innocent or guilty, notwithstanding the subject's right to resist such punishment under the law of self-preservation. See Jean Hampton, *Hobbes and the Social Contract Tradition* (Cambridge: Cambridge University Press, 1986), 103.

26. See Alan Norrie, "Hobbes and the Philosophy of Punishment," *Law and Philosophy* 3, no. 2 (1984): 299–320; Thomas S. Schrock, "The Rights to Punish and Resist Punishment in Hobbes's *Leviathan*," *Western Political Quarterly* 44, no. 4 (December 1991): 853–90; and Dieter Hüning, "Hobbes on the Right to Punish," in *The Cambridge Companion to Hobbes' "Leviathan*," ed. Patricia Springborg (Cambridge: Cambridge University Press, 2007), 217–40, for different accounts of Hobbes on punishment.

27. Hobbes, *Leviathan*, II, 28, 214.

28. Hobbes, *Leviathan*, II, 28, 214.

29. See Hüning, "Hobbes on the Right to Punish." In Hüning's view, we can detect a "tension" (231) between Hobbes's theory of authorization—in which the subject gives the sovereign the right to act on their behalf—and his theory of the right to punish, which is explicitly not gifted in this way.

30. Samuel von Pufendorf, *De jure naturae et gentium*, ed. Frank Böhling, vol. 4 of *Gesammelte Werke*, ed. Wilhelm Schmidt-Biggemann (Berlin: Akademie-Verlag, 1998), viii, 3, para. 1. See Hüning, "Hobbes on the Right to Punish," 232–34, for an account of Pufendorf's critique.

31. Giorgio Agamben, *Homo Sacer: Sovereign Power and Bare Life*, trans. Daniel Heller-Roazen (Stanford, CA: Stanford University Press, 1998), 106.

32. Agamben, *Homo Sacer*, 107.

33. Roberto Esposito, *Bios: Biopolitics and Philosophy*, trans. Timothy Campbell (Minneapolis: University of Minnesota Press, 2008), 61–63.

34. Hobbes, *Leviathan*, II, 18, 124. See also II, 21, 148.

35. See Jonathan Sheehan, "Assenting to the Law: Sacrifice and Punishment at the Dawn of Secularism," in *After Secular Law*, ed.

Winnifred Fallers Sullivan, Robert A. Yelle, and Matteo Taussig-Rubbo (Stanford, CA: Stanford University Press, 2011), 62–79.

36. Jonathan Sheehan, "Assenting to the Law," 71. In my focus on Jephthah's daughter, I am greatly indebted to Sheehan's essay, notwithstanding any differences of interpretation.

37. Sheehan, "Assenting to the Law," 71.

38. For Hobbes, Jephthah's daughter is not the only biblical story that supports his theory of self authorized sovereign punishment. To strengthen his case, he also cites the story of David's killing of Uriah the Hittite in the Second Book of Samuel: David sleeps with Uriah's wife Bathsheba and, in order to get rid of his love rival, forges a note in Uriah's hand requesting that he, Uriah, be sent to the battlefield to die (2 Samuel 11:14–15). If David is thus responsible for the death of an entirely innocent man, Hobbes again reckons that he does Uriah no wrong because of the theory of authorization: "it was not an Injurie to *Uriah*; but to God. Not to *Uriah*, because the right to doe what he pleased, was given to him by *Uriah* himself" (*Leviathan*, II, 21, 148). This reading ignores the crucial point that, as Jonathan Sheehan notes, Uriah has *not* given his assent to his own death—he has been tricked by David—and thus sovereign punishment here is closer to murder than self-sacrifice. In this respect, Jephthah's daughter—who freely agrees to die—is the more powerful example.

39. Hobbes, *Leviathan*, II, 21, 148.

40. Esposito, *Bios*, 62.

41. Roberto Esposito, *Communitas; The Origin and Destiny of Community*, trans. Timothy Campbell (Stanford, CA: Stanford University Press, 2010), 14. In many ways, Esposito's reading of Hobbes across the three volumes of his triptych *Communitas*, *Immunitas*, and *Bios* comes closest to my own in its revelation of a sacrificial logic at the heart of Hobbesian thought, but my own argument is that this is more properly a martyrological logic, with all the problems for Hobbes's constitutive exclusion of the martyr this implies.

42. See John L. Thompson, *Writing the Wrongs: Women of the Old Testament among Biblical Commentators from Philo Through the Reformation* (New York: Oxford University Press, 2001), for an excellent survey of the complex reception of Jephthah's daughter in church history. In many

ways, Origen is the figure who inaugurates the reading of Jephthah's daughter's sacrifice as an anticipation of Christian martyrdom.

43. Mark Lilla, *The Still-Born God: Religion, Politics, and the Modern West* (London: Vintage, 2007). In fact, Lilla's account is only the most recent attempt to retrospectively claim Hobbes for liberalism.

44. Hans Barion, review of *Saggi storici intorno al Papato dei Professori della Facoltà di Storia Ecclesiastica*, in *Zeitschrift der Savigny- Stiftung für Rechtsgeschichte: Kanonistische Abteilung* 46 (1960): 481–501, 499–500.

45. Carl Schmitt, *The Leviathan in the State Theory of Thomas Hobbes: Meaning and Failure of a Political Symbol*, trans. George Schwab and Erna Hilfstein (Chicago: University of Chicago Press, 2008).

46. Hobbes, *Leviathan*, II, 18, 121–29.

47. Schmitt, *Leviathan in the State Theory of Thomas Hobbes*, 53–64.

48. See Felix Grossheutschi, *Carl Schmitt und die Lehre vom Katechon* (Berlin: Duncker & Humblot, 1996), for a comprehensive account of Schmitt's readings of the Pauline figure of the *katechon*.

49. Schmitt, *Leviathan in the State Theory of Thomas Hobbes*, 56–57.

50. Carl Schmitt, *Political Theology: Four Chapters on the Concept of Sovereignty*, trans. George Schwab (Chicago: University of Chicago Press, 2006). In the early Schmitt's reckoning, Hobbes is the last great hero of the philosophy of sovereign personalism or decisionism: "The classical representative of the decisionist type," he writes, "is Thomas Hobbes" (33).

51. Hobbes, *Leviathan*, III, 42, 343.

52. Hobbes, *Leviathan*, II, 18, 124. In A. P. Martinich's view, we can see this tension at work more generally within Hobbes's philosophy: "Hobbes has a theory of authorization and a theory of authority; and they are incompatible." *The Two Gods of Leviathan*, 170. This is not merely an innocent logical flaw or contradiction, in my view, but a bifocal strategy for maximizing sovereign power.

53. Raffaello Pantucci, *We Love Death as You Love Life: Britain's Suburban Mujahedeen* (New York: Columbia University Press, 2013). In fact, Khan's statement is a common rhetorical trope in Islamist rhetoric and has been used previously by such groups as Hamas and Al-Qaeda.

54. Schmitt, *Leviathan in the State Theory of Thomas Hobbes*, 35.

5. INCORRUPTIBLE: ROBESPIERRE AND
THE ALREADY DEAD

The epigraph to this chapter is taken from Maurice Blanchot, "Literature and the Right to Death," in *The Work of Fire*, trans. Charlotte Mandell (Stanford, CA: Stanford University Press, 1995), 319–20.

1. Maximilien Robespierre, *Œuvres de Maximilien Robespierre* (Paris: Société des études Robespierristes, 1912–2007), 10:556. Translations mine.

2. Annie Jourdain, "Robespierre and Revolutionary Heroism," in *Robespierre*, ed. Colin Haydon and William Doyle (Cambridge: Cambridge University Press, 1999), 54–74.

3. David P. Jordan, *The Revolutionary Career of Maximilien Robespierre* (New York: Macmillan, 1985), 8. In contrast to colorful contemporaries like Marat or Danton, Robespierre presented himself as a "pure political self": he apparently possessed no private life or interests; he was never accused of personal or financial impropriety, and, indeed, barely seems to have existed outside of his punishing regime of public appearances at the Jacobin Club, the Convention, and the Committee of Public Safety.

4. Antoine de Baecque, "Le tableau d'un cadavre: Les Récits de l'agonie de Robespierre: Du cadaver hideux au dernier héros," in *Robespierre: Figure-réputation (Yearbook of European Studies)*, ed. Annie Jourdain (Amsterdam: Rodopi, 1996), 169–203, 177. In other Thermidorean accounts, Robespierre is variously depicted as a wild animal (usually some kind of cat), a monster, a demon, a machine, and even a reanimated corpse.

5. François-René de Chateaubriand, *Mémoires d'outre-tombe* (Paris: Flammarion, 1949), 231. Translation mine.

6. See, for example, Simon Schama, *Citizens: A Chronicle of the French Revolution* (New York: Knopf, 1989); Jonathan Israel, *Revolutionary Ideas: An Intellectual History of the French Revolution from the Rights of Man to Robespierre* (Princeton, NJ: Princeton University Press, 2014); Alain Badiou, "What Is a Thermidorean?" in *Metapolitics*, trans. Jason Barker (London: Verso, 2005), 124–40; Slavoj Žižek, *In Defense of Lost*

Causes (London: Verso, 2008), 167–70; and Peter Hallward, "The Will of the People: Notes Towards a Dialectical Voluntarism," *Radical Philosophy* 155 (May/June 2009): 17–30.

7. Jacques Derrida, "Declarations," in *Negotiations: Interventions and Interviews, 1971–2001*, ed. Elizabeth Rottenberg (Stanford, CA: Stanford University Press, 2002), 46–54, 49.

8. Derrida, "Declarations," 49.

9. To be sure, the general will remains one of the most opaque and contested aspects of Rousseau's political philosophy. See Alain Badiou, "Meditation 32: Rousseau," in *Being and Event*, trans. Oliver Feltham (London: Continuum, 2006), 345–54; Bonnie Honig, *Emergency Politics: Paradox, Law, Democracy* (Princeton, NJ: Princeton University Press, 2009); and Simon Critchley, *Faith of the Faithless: Experiments in Political Theology* (London: Verso, 2012), for influential recent discussions.

10. Slavoj Žižek, "Introduction: Robespierre, or the 'Divine Violence' of Terror," in Maximilien Robespierre, *Virtue and Terror* (London: Verso, 2007), vii–xxxix, xxii.

11. Jean-Jacques Rousseau, *The Social Contract and Other Later Political Writings*, ed. Victor Gourevitch (Cambridge: Cambridge University Press, 1997), IV, 3, 124.

12. It is worth recalling here that Rousseau's account of the general will of the people has its origin in a seventeenth-century theological debate over the will of God: does God have a "general" will that all men will be saved—as Paul indicates in his letter to Timothy—or does he have a "particular" will that only some men will be saved and others consigned to hell? See Patrick Riley, *The General Will Before Rousseau: The Transformation of the Divine into the Civic* (Princeton, NJ: Princeton University Press, 1986).

13. See Rousseau, *The Social Contract*, IV, 3, 124. In Rousseau's words, "when the opinion contrary to my own prevails, it proves nothing more than that I made a mistake and that what I took to be the general will was not."

14. Žižek, "Introduction: Robespierre, or the 'Divine Violence' of Terror," xxii. In the period when I was writing this chapter, I regularly read headlines in British right-wing tabloid newspapers declaring that the

decision to leave the European Union following the Brexit referendum was the sovereign "will of the people" and that anyone who opposed this decision was therefore an "enemy of the people" or a "saboteur" who must be crushed.

15. Emmanuel-Joseph Sieyès, *Qu'est-ce que le Tiers Etat?*, critical ed. Roberto Zapperi (Geneva: Librairie Droz, 1970), 124.

16. Sieyès, *Qu'est-ce que le Tiers Etat?*, 124.

17. William H. Seward Jr., *A Rhetoric of Bourgeois Revolution: The Abbé Sieyès and "What Is the Third Estate?"* (Durham, NC: Duke University Press, 1994), 58–59.

18. Sieyès, *Qu'est-ce que le Tiers Etat?*, 218. Emphasis in original.

19. Ernst Kantorowicz, *The King's Two Bodies: A Study in Medieval Political Theology* (Princeton, NJ: Princeton University Press, 1957), 23. In Kantorowicz's words, Parliament succeeded "in executing solely the king's body natural without affecting seriously or doing irreparable harm to the king's body politic—in contradistinction with the events in France, in 1793."

20. Michael Walzer, ed., *Regicide and Revolution: Speeches at the Trial of Louis XVI* (New York: Columbia University Press, 1992).

21. Walzer, *Regicide and Revolution*, 109.

22. Walzer, *Regicide and Revolution*, 97.

23. Walzer, *Regicide and Revolution*, 58.

24. Walzer, *Regicide and Revolution*, 121.

25. Walzer, *Regicide and Revolution*, 123.

26. For Rousseau, any man who violates the social contract ceases to be a member of it and is to be regarded less as a citizen than as an enemy whose bare life can be disposed of according to the rules of war: "such an enemy is not a moral person, but a man, and in that case killing the vanquished is by right of war" (Rousseau, *The Social Contract*, II, 5, 65). However, as Walzer notes, Saint-Just does not simply rehearse Rousseau's own position in *The Social Contract* but significantly adapts it for his own purposes. In Rousseau's original account, he expressly states that a domestic enemy must be proved to be so by "trial and judgment" and cannot be subject to the laws of war—so he would not have agreed that Louis could simply be killed. Walzer, *Regicide and Revolution*, 72–73.

27. Walzer, *Regicide and Revolution*, 124. Emphasis in original.

28. Yet it is worth recalling that the Girondin faction were themselves tried and executed en masse by the Jacobins less than a year later, in a judicial purge that made the trial of the king seem like a model of due legal process.

29. Walzer, *Regicide and Revolution*, 76.

30. Walzer, *Regicide and Revolution*, 138. If Saint-Just's speech in the debate focused on the legal status of the king, Robespierre's subsequent contribution also examined the implications of a trial for the legality of the Revolution itself. It was inconceivable that the King should stand trial, he argued, for the very simple reason that a trial must presuppose the defendant's innocence. To entertain even the theoretical possibility of the king's innocence, Robespierre argued, would not only call into question the legitimacy of the August 10 Revolution that had overthrown Louis, but would also cast doubt upon that revolution's sole representative body—indeed the very body that now sought to judge him, namely, the National Convention itself. In order to fully expose the self-defeating logic of the Girondins, Robespierre thus invited his fellow deputies to imagine what would happen if Louis was actually found not guilty at trial: a verdict in favor of Louis would be a verdict against the people; the king would become a victim and the Revolution a crime. So Louis must be killed, not tried (*Regicide and Revolution*, 131–32).

31. Walzer, *Regicide and Revolution*, 133. Translation modified. Emphasis mine.

32. Walter Benjamin, "Theses on the Philosophy of History," in *Illuminations*, trans. H. Zohn (New York: Schocken, 1968), 253–64, 261.

33. Rousseau, *The Social Contract*, IV, 3, 124.

34. Walzer, *Regicide and Revolution*, 192. Translation modified.

35. See Jon Cowans, *To Speak for the People: Public Opinion and the Problem of Legitimacy in the French Revolution* (New York: Routledge, 2001), for an excellent survey of the competing meanings invested in "the people," and popular sovereignty more widely during the Revolution, which played themselves out remorselessly in the political field.

36. Cowans, *To Speak for the People*, 127.

37. Robespierre, *Œuvres*, X, 180. See also R. R. Palmer's classic *Twelve Who Ruled: The Year of the Terror in the French Revolution* (New York:

Atheneum, 1969), 277. In Palmer's words, "Robespierre's 'people' was the people of his mind's eye . . . the people as it was to be when felicity was established."

38. Paul Mautouchet, ed., *Le Gouvernement révolutionnaire (10 août 1792–4 Brumaire an IV)* (Paris: E. Cornely, 1912), 196–202.

39. Camille Desmoulins, *Le Vieux Cordelier*, ed. Henri Calvet (Paris: Armand Colin, 1936), 67–90.

40. See Daniel Arasse's *La Guillotine et l'Imaginaire de la terreur* (Paris: Flammarion, 1987) for a classic study of the guillotine.

41. G. W. F. Hegel, "Absolute Freedom and Terror," in *Phenomenology of Spirit*, trans. A. V. Miller (Oxford: Oxford University Press, 1977), 355–64, 360.

42. Rebecca Comay, "Dead Right: Hegel and the Terror," *South Atlantic Quarterly* 103, nos. 2–3 (2004): 375–95, 385.

43. Robespierre, *Œuvres*, X, 173.

44. See Eric Cazdyn, *The Already Dead: The New Time of Politics, Culture and Illness* (Durham, NC: Duke University Press, 2012), for an excellent recent discussion of the figure of the already dead in the context of contemporary medicine and biopolitics that has some parallels with my own.

45. Jourdain, "Robespierre and Revolutionary Heroism," 54–74.

46. Robespierre, *Œuvres*, VII, 523.

47. Robespierre, *Œuvres*, VII, 747.

48. Robespierre, *Œuvres*, X, 414.

49. Robespierre, *Œuvres*, X, 232.

50. Robespierre, *Œuvres*, X, 121.

51. Robespierre, *Œuvres*, X, 471.

52. Robespierre, *Œuvres*, IX, 623.

53. Robespierre, *Œuvres*, X, 553.

54. Robespierre, *Œuvres*, X, 553.

55. Robespierre, *Œuvres*, X, 556.

56. Robespierre, *Œuvres*, X, 576.

57. Alexandre Kojève, *Introduction to the Reading of Hegel: Lectures on the "Phenomenology of Spirit" Assembled by Raymond Queneau*, ed. A. Bloom, trans. J. H. Nichols Jr. (New York: Basic Books, 1969).

58. Blanchot, "Literature and the Right to Death," 319–20.

59. Maurice Blanchot, "The Instant of My Death," in Maurice Blanchot and Jacques Derrida, *The Instant of My Death/Demeure: Fiction and Testimony*, trans. Elizabeth Rottenberg (Stanford, CA: Stanford University Press, 2000), 1–12, 5. In Blanchot's enigmatic text, he observes that both the Russian and the German soldiers retain a perverse respect for the French nobility: the narrator's life is spared because he belongs to the nobility and the 1807 château is not burned down.

60. Slavoj Žižek, "Introduction: Robespierre, or the 'Divine Violence' of Terror," xviii.

61. Jacques Derrida, *The Death Penalty*, vol. 1, trans. Peggy Kamuf (Chicago: University of Chicago Press, 2014), 116. In Derrida's analysis, he makes a great deal of what he sees as Robespierre's shifting positions on the death penalty (he was an abolitionist who nonetheless went on to argue that Louis should be put to death), but, arguably, Robespierre was more consistent than Derrida suggests: he did not want Louis to be given the death penalty as a civil punishment but, as we have seen, to be killed as an enemy in wartime.

62. Martin McQuillan, "Extra Time and the Death Penalties: On a Newly Arisen Violent Tone in Philosophy," *Derrida Today* 2, no. 2 (2009), 133–50, 149.

63. Žižek, "Introduction: Robespierre, or the 'Divine Violence' of Terror," xxiv.

64. See Žižek, "Introduction: Robespierre, or the 'Divine Violence' of Terror," xi. In many ways, Žižek's account here is the product of his career-long rereading of the relationship between necessity and contingency in Hegel's dialectic where—far from predetermining all contingency—necessity itself is the effect of contingency: "'Dialectics' is ultimately a teaching on how necessity emerges out of contingency: on how a contingent *bricolage* produces a result which 'transcodes' its initial conditions into internal necessary moments of its self-production. It is therefore Necessity itself which depends on contingency." See Slavoj Žižek, *For They Know Not What They Do: Enjoyment as a Political Factor* (London: Verso, 1991), 129.

65. Michel Foucault, "Is It Useless to Revolt?" trans. Karen de Bruin and Kevin B. Anderson, in *Foucault and the Iranian Revolution: Gender and the Seductions of Islamism*, ed. Janet Afary and Kevin B. Anderson

(Chicago: University of Chicago Press, 2005), 263–667, 263. In his collected writings on Iran, Foucault continually (and problematically) views the unfolding events through the lens of the French Revolution as the expression of a quasi-Rousseauean general will. See Michael Dillon, "Afterlife: Living Death to Political Spirituality," *Millennium: Journal of International Studies* 14, no. 1 (2013): 114–34, for a critically acute reappraisal of Foucault's much-maligned and misunderstood concept of a "political spirituality."

66. Subcomandante Marcos, *Our Word Is Our Weapon: Selected Writings*, ed. J. Ponce de León (Toronto: Seven Stories, 2001), 20.

67. Žižek, "Introduction: Robespierre, or the 'Divine Violence' of Terror," xvii–xviii.

68. Howard Caygill, *On Resistance: A Philosophy of Defiance* (London: Bloomsbury, 2013), 98.

69. Caygill, *On Resistance*, 126.

6. UNLEASHED: SCHMITT AND THE *KATECHON*

The epigraph to this chapter is taken from W. B. Yeats, "The Second Coming," in *Selected Poems*, ed. Timothy Webb (London: Penguin, 1991), 124.

1. It has, of course, been the subject of significant readings by such diverse thinkers as Alain Badiou, Giorgio Agamben, Paolo Virno, Roberto Esposito, and Massimo Cacciari in the last years alone. See Alain Badiou, *Saint Paul: The Foundation of Universalism*, trans. Ray Brassier (Stanford, CA: Stanford University Press, 2003); Giorgio Agamben, *The Time That Remains: A Commentary on the Letter to the Romans*, trans. Patricia Dailey (Stanford, CA: Stanford University Press, 2005); Paolo Virno, *Multitude: Between Innovation and Negation* (New York: Semiotext(e), 2008); Roberto Esposito, "The Katechon," in *Immunitas: The Protection and Negation of Life*, trans. Zakiya Hanafi (London: Polity, 2011), 52–79; and Massimo Cacciari, *The Withholding Power: An Essay on Political Theology*, trans. Edi Pucci (London: Bloomsbury, 2017).

2. Carl Schmitt, *Glossarium: Aufzeichnungen aus den Jahren 1947–51*, ed. Eberhard Freiherr von Medem (Berlin: Duncker & Humblot, 1991), 63. See Marc de Wilde, "Politics Between Times: Theologico-Political

Interpretations of the Restraining Force (*Katechon*) in Paul's Second Letter to the Thessalonians," in *Paul and the Philosophers*, ed. Ward Blanton and Hent de Vries (New York: Fordham University Press, 2013), 105–26, 123.

3. Jacob Taubes, *The Political Theology of Paul*, trans. Dana Hollander (Stanford, CA: Stanford University Press, 2004), 103.

4. See Ward Blanton and Hent de Vries, eds., *Paul and the Philosophers* (New York: Fordham University Press, 2013); Theodore Jennings Jr., *Outlaw Justice: The Messianic Politics and Paul* (Stanford, CA: Stanford University Press, 2013); and Ward Blanton, *A Materialism for the Masses: Saint Paul and the Philosophy of Undying Life* (New York: Columbia University Press, 2014), for recent cutting-edge readings of Paul that have influenced my own.

5. See Heinrich Meier, *Die Lehre Carl Schmitts* (Stuttgart: J. B. Metzler, 1994); Günter Meuter, *Der Katechon: Zu Carl Schmitts fundamentalist-ischer Kritik der Zeit* (Berlin: Duncker & Humblot, 1994); Felix Gross-heutschi, *Carl Schmitt und die Lehre vom Katechon* (Berlin: Duncker & Humblot, 1996); and Ruth Groh, *Arbeit an der Heillosigkeit der Welt: Zur politisch-theologischen Mythologie und Anthropologie Carl Schmitts* (Frankfurt: Suhrkamp Verlag, 1998), for important assessments of Schmitt's account of the *katechon*.

6. Tertullian, *Apology*, trans. Terrot R. Glover (Cambridge, MA: Harvard University Press, 1977), 154–55.

7. Augustine of Hippo, *City of God*, trans. Henry Bettenson (Harmondsworth: Penguin, 1972), 20, 19, 933.

8. Taubes, *Political Theology of Paul*, 103.

9. Esposito, *Immunitas*, 63.

10. Carl Schmitt, *The* Nomos *of the Earth in the International Law of the Jus Publicum Europaeum*, trans. G. L. Ulmen (New York: Telos, 2003), 60.

11. Taubes, *Political Theology of Paul*, 103.

12. To be sure, we cannot do any justice here to the complexities of the Schmitt-Taubes debate. In lieu of a more detailed examination, let me simply say here that Taubes's own rejection of Schmittean political theology should not be interpreted as a rejection of the possibility of a political theology per se à la Eric Petersen: I prefer to follow Marin Terpstra and Theo de Wit's description of Taubes's philosophy as a

"negative political theology," where political power is theologically
delegitimized, in contrast to Schmitt's "positive political theology,"
which seeks theological sanction for politics. See Marin Terpstra and
Theo de Wit, "'No Spiritual Investment in the World as It Is': On the
Negative Political Theology of Taubes," in *Flight of the Gods: Philosophical Perspective on Negative Theology*, ed. I. N. Bulhof and L. ten Kate
(New York: Fordham University Press, 2000), 320–53.

13. See Julia Hell, "*Katechon*: Carl Schmitt's Imperial Theology and the
Ruins of the Future," *Germanic Review* 84, no. 4 (2009): 283–326;
Michael Hoelzl, "Before the Anti-Christ Is Revealed: On the Kate-
chontic Structure of Messianic Time," in *The Politics to Come: Power,
Modernity and the Messianic*, ed. Arthur Bradley and Paul Fletcher
(London: Continuum, 2010), 98–110; Michael Dillon, "Spectres of Bio-
politics: Eschatology, *Katechon* and Resistance," *South Atlantic Quar-
terly* 110, no. 3 (Summer 2011): 780–92; de Wilde, "Politics Between
Times"; and Peter Szendy, "Katechon." *Political Concepts: A Critical
Lexicon*, https://www.politicalconcepts.org/katechon-peter-szendy
/#fn5 (accessed October 16, 2018), for excellent recent discussions of
Schmitt and the *katechon* that have influenced my own.

14. Carl Schmitt, "Beschleuniger wider Willen, oder: Problematik der
westlichen Hemisphare," in *Staat, Grossraum, Nomos: Arbeiten aus den
Jahren 1916–1969*, ed. Gunter Maschke (Berlin: Duncker and Humblot, 1995), 431–36, 436. In calling this essay "Accelerator Despite Itself,"
I am following Julia Hell's elegant translation, but the title has been
equally translated as "Accelerator Against Its Will" or "Involuntary
Accelerator."

15. See William Hooker, *Carl Schmitt's International Thought: Order and
Orientation* (Cambridge: Cambridge University Press, 2009), 118–22,
for one of the only Anglophone discussions of Schmitt's essay. In the
following commentary, I am indebted to Hooker's excellent account.

16. Schmitt, "Beschleuniger wider Willen," 436.

17. Schmitt, "Beschleuniger wider Willen," 436.

18. See, for example, Carl Schmitt, "The Changing Structure of International Law," trans. Antonio Cerella and Andrea Salvatore, *Journal
for Cultural Research* 20, no. 3, special issue on Carl Schmitt, Political
Theology and Modernity, ed. Antonio Cerella and Arthur Bradley

(2016): 310–28. In this 1942 lecture, which was delivered in Madrid, Schmitt again documents what he sees as the United States' "oscillations between self-isolationist neutrality and pan-interventionism" (319).

19. Carl Schmitt, "The Age of Neutralizations and Depoliticizations," in *The Concept of the Political*, trans. George Schwab (Chicago: Chicago University Press, 2007), 80–96.

20. Schmitt, "Beschleuniger wider Willen," 436.

21. Schmitt, "Beschleuniger wider Willen," 436

22. Carl Schmitt, *Land and Sea*, trans. Simona Draghica (Washington, DC: Plutarch Press, 1997). In this 1942 text, Schmitt explicitly identifies the *katechon* with a number of historical figures and institutions. To begin with, the Eastern or Byzantine Roman Empire prevented the spread of Islam to Italy following the Arab conquest of Carthage in 698. If the Eastern Roman Empire had been absent, Schmitt argues, "Italy would have become part of the Muslim world, like North Africa, and all of the Ancient and Christian Civilization would have been destroyed" (8). Finally, Schmitt also argues that the German emperor Rudolf II (1552–1612) succeeded in keeping Europe's early modern religious wars outside of Germany's borders and held off the chaos of the Thirty Years' War.

23. Samuel Beckett, *Worstward Ho* (London: John Calder, 1999), 7.

24. See Marc de Wilde, "Politics Between Times," 117–19. In this paragraph, I am drawing on de Wilde's account of Schmitt and Hans Freyer.

25. Thalin Zarmanian, "Carl Schmitt and the Problem of Legal Order: From Domestic to International," *Leiden Journal of International Law* 19, no. 1 (2006): 41–67, 55.

26. Schmitt, *The* Nomos *of the Earth*, 59–60.

27. Hell, "*Katechon*," 292.

28. Agamben, *The Time That Remains*, 67. Emphasis in original.

29. Jean-François Lyotard, "Answer to the Question: What Is Postmodernism?," in *The Postmodern Explained to Children: Correspondence 1982–85* (London: Power Institute of Fine Arts, 1992), 11–15, 24.

30. Taubes, *Political Theology of Paul*, 70–76.

31. Walter Benjamin, "Theses on the Philosophy of History," in *Illuminations*, trans. H. Zohn (New York: Schocken, 1968), 253–64, 257.

32. Schmitt, *Political Theology*, 66.

33. See Michael Dillon, "Underwriting Security," in *Biopolitics of Security: A Political Analytic of Finitude* (London: Routledge, 2015), 99–122, for an indispensable discussion of the contemporary theory and praxis of security to which I owe this reference to Unisys Corporation.

34. Dillon, *Biopolitics of Security*, 104.

35. In recent Marxist and post-Marxist political discourse, the concept of "accelerationism" refers to the speeding up of technological processes to address the inherent or structural inequalities of the capitalist mode of production. See Robin Mackay and Armen Avanessian, *The Accelerationist Reader* (Berlin: Merve, 2014), for a range of responses to the accelerationist movement.

36. Dillon, *Biopolitics of Security*, 99.

37. Cacciari, *The Withholding Power*, 117.

38. Carl Schmitt, *Ex Captivitate Salus: Erfahrungen der Zeit, 1945–47* (Cologne: Greven, 1950), 12. In 1945, while interned in an American military prison, Schmitt described his fate thus: "It is the bad, unworthy and yet authentic case of a Christian Epimetheus."

39. Tony Blair, keynote speech to the Labour Party Conference, October 27, 2005, http://news.bbc.co.uk/1/hi/uk_politics/4287370.stm (accessed July 1, 2014).

7. UNDEAD: BENJAMIN AND THE PAST TO COME

The epigraph to this chapter is taken from Aristotle, *Nichomachean Ethics*, trans. and intr. Terence Irwin (Indianapolis, IN: Hackett, 1999), 1139b, 6–10, 87. In Aristotle's words: "We do not decide to do what is already past; no-one decides, for instance, to have sacked Troy. For neither do we deliberate about what is past, but only about what will be and admits of being or not being; and what is passed does not admit of not having happened. This is why Agathon is correct to say 'Of this alone even a God is deprived—to make what is all done to have never happened.'"

1. Walter Benjamin, *Selected Writings, Volume 2: 1927–1934*, ed. Michael W. Jennings, Howard Eiland, and Gary Smith, trans. Rodney Livingstone (Cambridge, MA: Belknap Press of Harvard University Press, 1999), 50.

2. Pietro Damiani [Peter Damian], Letter 119, "On Divine Omnipotence," in *Letters 91–120*, vol. 4 of *The Fathers of the Church*, trans. Owen J. Blum (Washington, DC: Catholic University of American Press, 1998), 344–86, 353.

3. Walter Benjamin, "Theses on the Philosophy of History," in *Illuminations*, trans. H. Zohn (New York: Schocken, 1968), 253–64, 254. Emphasis in the original.

4. Jacob Taubes, *The Political Theology of Paul*, trans. Dana Hollander (Stanford, CA: Stanford University Press, 2004), 103.

5. Jerome, *Epistle 22, Ad Eustochium*, in *Select Letters of Jerome*, ed. F. A. Wright (London: Heinemann, 1933), 62.

6. Damiani, "On Divine Omnipotence," 370.

7. Damiani, "On Divine Omnipotence," 383.

8. Damiani, "On Divine Omnipotence," 382.

9. Damiani, "On Divine Omnipotence," 353. See Irvin M. Resnick, *Divine Power and Possibility in St Peter Damian's "De Divina Omnipotentia"* (Leiden: Brill, 1992), for a detailed commentary on Damiani's letter. It is worth stressing that there is some critical disagreement about what exactly Damiani is arguing about divine omnipotence. According to the "weak" reading of his letter, Damiani never explicitly states that God *can* change the past, merely that it is not for human beings to presume any restriction whatsoever upon divine omnipotence. In the stronger reading, which I set out here, Damiani's defense of God's power to restore virginity to a woman who has lost it does indeed imply that God really can undo what has been done.

10. John D. Caputo, *The Weakness of God: A Theology of the Event* (Bloomington: Indiana University Press, 2006), 182–207, 183. In this excellent study, which offers the only other contemporary rehabilitation of Damiani I am aware of, Caputo reads the theologian as an important, if ambivalent, precursor for his deconstructive poetics of "the event" that anarchically exceeds all determinate ontology.

11. Quentin Meillassoux, *After Finitude: An Essay on the Necessity of Contingency*, trans. Ray Brassier (London: Continuum, 2008). In one respect, Damiani's divine anarchy is arguably even *more* contingent than Meillassoux's hyperchaos insofar as the former's God (unlike

Meillassoux's chaos) also possesses the power to break the principle of noncontradiction.

12. Damiani, "On Divine Omnipotence," 370–71.

13. See Francis Oakley, *Omnipotence, Covenant, and Order: An Excursion in the History of Ideas from Abelard to Leibniz* (Ithaca, NY: Cornell University Press, 1984); William J. Courtenay, *Capacity and Volition: A History of the Distinction of Absolute and Ordained Power* (Bergamo: Pierluigi Lubrina Editore, 1990); and Francis Oakley, *Natural Law, Laws of Nature, Natural Rights: Continuity and Discontinuity in the History of Ideas* (New York: Continuum, 2005), for classic discussions of the history of the theology of divine power.

14 Mika Ojakangas, "*Potentia absoluta* and *Potentia ordinate Dei*: On the Theological Origins of Carl Schmitt's Theory of Constitution," *Continental Philosophy Review* 45 (2012): 505–17, 510–11.

15. Giorgio Agamben, *The Kingdom and the Glory: For a Theological Genealogy of Economy and Government (Homo Sacer II, 2)*, trans. Lorenzo Chiesa (Stanford, CA: Stanford University Press, 2011).

16. Thomas Aquinas, *Summa Theologica*, 2nd rev. ed., trans. Fathers of the English Dominican Province (1920; New Advent: 2008), I.25.4, http://www.newadvent.org/summa/1025.htm (accessed March 29, 2019).

17. It is revealing that the nominalist challenge to Thomist Christian Aristotelianism is omitted from Agamben's theological genealogy of government in *The Kingdom and the Glory*—perhaps because it constitutes an exception (in every sense of the word) to Agamben's master narrative about the rise of economic theology as the paradigm for governmentality. In nominalism, of course, we find something much closer to Schmittean political theology than economic theology, because the immanent or domestic sphere has no autonomy, but always exists at the behest of a sovereign decision.

18. Michael Allen Gillespie, *Nihilism Before Nietzsche* (Chicago: University of Chicago Press, 1995), 1–32, 16.

19. Duns Scotus, *Contingency and Freedom: Lectura I 39*, trans. with intro. and commentary by A. Vos Jaczn, H. Veldhuis, A. H. Looman-Graaskamp, E. Dekker, and N. W. Den Bok (Dordrecht: Kluwer, 1994).

20. William of Ockham, *Predestination, God's Foreknowledge, and Future Contingents*, trans. Marilyn McCord Adams and Norman Kretzmann (Indianapolis, IN: Hackett, 1983).

21. See Nelson Pike, "Divine Omniscience and Voluntary Action," *Philosophical Review* 74 (January 1965): 27–46; "Of God and Freedom: A Rejoinder," *Philosophical Review* 75 (July 1966): 369–79; and "Divine Foreknowledge, Human Freedom and Possible Worlds," *Philosophical Review* 86 (April 1977): 209–16. In the fifty years since it was first proposed, Pike's distinction between "hard" and "soft" facts about the past in William of Ockham has been the subject of an extensive debate, which I cannot enter into here.

22. Courtenay, *Capacity and Volition*, 92.

23. To recall the famous poverty dispute between the Franciscan Order and Pope John XXII—the Franciscan argument was that Christ could embrace a life of poverty because he possessed the absolute power to contradict what God had originally ordained. In reply to Agamben's recent attempt to hold up a Franciscan form-of-life as a means of rendering sovereignty inoperative, then, we might argue that the highest poverty is made possible by a re-absolutizing of God's sovereignty: *ascesis* is merely a different kind of plenitude. See Giorgio Agamben, *The Highest Poverty: Monastic Rules and Form-of-Life*, trans. Adam Kotsko (Stanford, CA: Stanford University Press, 2013).

24. See Ojakangas, "*Potentia absoluta* and *Potentia ordinate Dei*," 505–17.

25. Banu Bargu, "Sovereignty as Erasure: Rethinking Enforced Disappearances," *Qui Parle: Critical Humanities and Social Sciences* 23, no. 1 (Fall/Winter 2014): 35–75.

26. Michel Foucault, *Discipline and Punish: The Birth of the Prison*, trans. Alan Sheridan (Harmondsworth: Penguin. 1977), 3–31.

27. International Convention for the Protection of All Persons from Enforced Disappearances, New York, December 20, 2006, Article 2, http://www.ohchr.org/EN/HRBodies/CED/Pages/Convention CED.aspx (accessed June 23, 2017).

28. For recent readings of Benjamin's philosophy of history, which have influenced my own, see Giorgio Agamben, "Benjamin and the Demonic: Happiness and Historical Redemption," in *Potentialities:*

Collected Essays in Philosophy, ed. and trans. Daniel Heller-Roazen (Stanford, CA: Stanford University Press, 1999), 138–59; Eric Jacobson, *Metaphysics of the Profane: The Political Theology of Walter Benjamin and Gershom Scholem* (New York: Columbia University Press, 2003); Werner Hamacher, "'Now': Walter Benjamin on Historical Time," in *Walter Benjamin and History*, ed. Andrew Benjamin, trans. N. Rosenthal (London: Continuum, 2005), 38–68; Peter Fenves, *The Messianic Reduction: Walter Benjamin and the Shape of Time* (Stanford, CA: Stanford University Press, 2010); Jelica Šumič, "Giorgio Agamben's Godless Saints: Saving What Was Not," *Angelaki* 16, no. 3 (2011): 137–47; Sami Khatib, "The Messianic Without Messianism: Walter Benjamin's Materialist Theology," *Anthropology and Materialism* 1 (2013), https://journals.openedition.org/am/159 (accessed April 10, 2019); and Miguel Vatter, *The Republic of the Living: Biopolitics and the Critique of Civil Society* (New York: Fordham University Press, 2014).

29. See Vatter, *The Republic of the Living*, 290–325, for an exception to this rule.

30. Walter Benjamin, "Theologico-Political Fragment," in *Reflections: Essays, Aphorisms, Autobiographical Writings*, ed. Peter Demetz, trans. Edmund Jephcott (New York, Schocken, 1978), 312–13.

31. Benjamin, "Theologico-Political Fragment," 312.

32. Benjamin, "Theologico-Political Fragment," 312.

33. Benjamin, "Theologico-Political Fragment," 313.

34. Vatter, *The Republic of the Living*, 318.

35. Benjamin, "Theses on the Philosophy of History," 261.

36. Benjamin, "Theses on the Philosophy of History," 255.

37. Benjamin, "Theses on the Philosophy of History," 253–54.

38. Walter Benjamin, *The Arcades Project*, trans. Howard Eiland and Kevin McLaughlin (Cambridge, MA: Belknap Press of Harvard University Press, 1999), N8, 1, 471.

39. Terry Eagleton, "Waking the Dead," *New Statesman*, November 12, 2009, https://www.newstatesman.com/ideas/2009/11/past-benjamin-future-obama (accessed March 29, 2019).

40. Slavoj Žižek, *The Parallax View* (Cambridge, MA: MIT Press, 2006), 78.

41. Giorgio Agamben, *The Time That Remains: A Commentary on the Letter to the Romans*, trans. Patricia Dailey (Stanford, CA: Stanford University Press, 2005), 41.

42. Benjamin, "Theses on the Philosophy of History," 255.

43. Benjamin, "Theses on the Philosophy of History," 255. Emphasis in original.

44. Karl Marx, "Theses on Feuerbach," in Karl Marx and Friedrich Engels, *Collected Works: Volume 5: 1845–47* (New York: International Publishers, 1976), 3–10, 8.

45. Benjamin, *The Arcades Project*, N8, 1, 471.

46. See Giorgio Agamben, "Bartleby, or On Contingency," in *Potentialities: Collected Essays in Philosophy*, ed. and trans. Daniel Heller-Roazen (Stanford, CA: Stanford University Press, 1999), 243–74, 254. In this essay, Agamben briefly alludes to a school of medieval theology "by which God can do anything (according to some, even evil, even acting such that the world never existed, or restoring a girl's lost virginity)."

47. Agamben, *The Time That Remains*, 39.

48. Šumič, "Giorgio Agamben's Godless Saints," 140.

49. See David King, *The Commissar Vanishes: The Falsification of Photographs and Art in Stalin's Russia* (London: Metropolitan, 1997), for a study of what Leon Trotsky (who knew whereof he spoke) famously called the "Stalin School of Falsification." For Stalin's state bureaucracy, I suspect the closest equivalent to Damiani's fallen woman was Nikolai Yezhov, the disgraced People's Commissariat for Internal Affairs chief who was quietly airbrushed out of a group photo with Comrade Stalin after his arrest and execution in 1939. In the unfortunate Yezhov's case, though, "virginity" took the form of a (presumably ideologically more sound) stretch of the Moscow-Volga canal, which occupied the place where he had once stood.

50. Bargu, "Sovereignty as Erasure," 43.

51. Damiani, "On Divine Omnipotence," 370–71.

52. Philip Roth, *The Plot Against America* (London: Jonathan Cape, 2004), 305.

53. Benjamin, "Theses on the Philosophy of History," 257.

54. Roth, *The Plot Against America*, 364–91.

55. Roth, *The Plot Against America*, 113–14.

56. Judith Thurman, "Philip Roth E-mails on Trump," *New Yorker*, January 30, 2017, http://www.newyorker.com/magazine/2017/01/30/philip-roth-e-mails-on-trump (accessed April 22, 2017). Emphasis mine.

57. Benjamin, "Theses on the Philosophy of History," 257–58.

CONCLUSION

1. Jane Mayer, "The Black Sites: A Rare Look Inside the C.I.A.'s Secret Interrogation Program," *New Yorker*, August 13, 2007, http://www .newyorker.com/magazine/2007/08/13/the-black-sites (accessed April 5, 2016).

2. Banu Bargu, "Sovereignty as Erasure: Rethinking Enforced Disappearances," *Qui Parle: Critical Humanities and Social Sciences* 23, no. 1 (Fall/Winter 2014): 35–75, 39. In her essay, Bargu also cites Patricio Galella and Carlos Espósito, "Extraordinary Renditions in the Fight Against Terrorism: Forced Disappearances?," *Sur: International Journal on Human Rights* 9, no. 16 (2012): 7–31.

3. United Nations Human Rights Council, "Report of the Working Group on Enforced or Involuntary Disappearances," A/HRC/30/38, http://www.ohchr.org/EN/Issues/Disappearances/Pages/Annual .aspx (accessed April 5, 2016).

4. To be sure, scholarly literature on enforced disappearance is now a very large field. In researching this conclusion, I have found the following particularly helpful: Jenny Edkins, *Missing: Persons and Politics* (Ithaca, NY: Cornell University Press, 2011); Gabriel Gatti, *Surviving Forced Disappearance in Argentina and Uruguay* (New York: Palgrave Macmillan, 2014); and Estela Schindel and Pamela Colombo, eds., *Space and the Memories of Violence: Landscapes of Erasure, Disappearance, and Exception* (New York: Palgrave Macmillan, 2014).

5. Bargu, "Sovereignty as Erasure," 43.

6. Michel Foucault, *"Society Must Be Defended": Lectures at the Collège de France, 1975–76*, trans. David Macey (New York: Picador, 2003), 240.

7. Ron Suskind, "Faith, Certainty and the Presidency of George W. Bush," *New York Times*, October 17, 2004, http://www.nytimes.com /2004/10/17/magazine/faith-certainty-and-the-presidency-of-george -w-bush.html?_r=0 (accessed April 4, 2016).

8. Judith Butler, *Precarious Life: The Powers of Mourning and Violence* (London: Verso, 2004), 33–34.

9. In its charter, the International Coalition Against Enforced Disappearances describes itself as "a global network of organizations of families of disappeared and NGOs working in a non-violent manner against the practice of enforced disappearances at the local, national

and international level." See the ICAED website at http://www.icaed
.org/home (accessed April 25, 2016).

10. The Invisible Committee, *The Coming Insurrection* (Los Angeles:
Semiotext(e), 2009).

11. See the Anonymous YouTube channel for more information on the
group and their activities: https://www.youtube.com/user/Anonymous
Worldvoce (accessed April 25, 2016).

BIBLIOGRAPHY

Adams, John, et al. *Adams Family Correspondence.* Vol. 2. Edited by L. H. Butterfield. Cambridge, MA: Belknap Press of Harvard University Press, 1963.

Agamben, Giorgio. "Bartleby, or On Contingency." In *Potentialities: Collected Essays in Philosophy*, edited and translated by Daniel Heller-Roazen, 243–74. Stanford, CA: Stanford University Press, 1999.

——. "Benjamin and the Demonic: Happiness and Historical Redemption." In *Potentialities: Collected Essays in Philosophy*, edited and translated by Daniel Heller-Roazen, 138–59. Stanford, CA: Stanford University Press, 1999.

——. *The Highest Poverty: Monastic Rules and Form-of-Life.* Translated by Adam Kotsko. Stanford, CA: Stanford University Press, 2013.

——. *Homo Sacer: Sovereign Power and Bare Life.* Translated by Daniel Heller-Roazen. Stanford, CA: Stanford University Press, 1998.

——. *The Kingdom and the Glory: For a Theological Genealogy of Economy and Government (Homo Sacer II, 2).* Translated by Lorenzo Chiesa. Stanford, CA: Stanford University Press, 2011.

——. *The Time That Remains: A Commentary on the Letter to the Romans.* Translated by Patricia Dailey. Stanford, CA: Stanford University Press, 2005.

Alker, Sharon, and Holly Faith Nelson. "*Macbeth*, the Jacobean Scot and the Politics of the Union." *Studies in English Literature, 1500–1900* 47, no. 2 (2007): 379–401.

Anidjar, Gil. *Blood: A Critique of Christianity*. New York: Columbia University Press, 2014.

Anonymous. https://www.youtube.com/user/AnonymousWorldvoce.

Appelbaum, Robert. "Shakespeare and Terrorism." *Criticism* 57, no. 1 (2015): 23–45.

——. *Terrorism Before the Letter: Mythography and Political Violence in England, Scotland, and France 1559–1642*. Oxford: Oxford University Press, 2015.

Aquinas, Thomas. *Summa Theologica*. 2nd rev. ed. Translated by Fathers of the English Dominican Province. 1920; New Advent: 2008. http://www .newadvent.org/summa/index.htm.

Arasse, Daniel. *La Guillotine et l'Imaginaire de la terreur*. Paris: Flammarion, 1987.

Arendt, Hannah. *The Human Condition*. Chicago: University of Chicago Press, 1958.

——. *The Origins of Totalitarianism*. 3rd. ed. New York: Harcourt, Brace, and World, 1973.

Aristotle. *Nichomachean Ethics*. Translated by Terence Irwin. Indianapolis, IN: Hackett, 1999.

Augustine of Hippo. *City of God*. Translated by Henry Bettenson. Harmondsworth: Penguin, 2003.

Badiou, Alain. "Meditation 32: Rousseau." In *Being and Event*, translated by Oliver Feltham, 345–54. London: Continuum, 2006.

——. *Saint Paul: The Foundation of Universalism*. Translated by Ray Brassier. Stanford, CA: Stanford University Press, 2003.

——. "What Is a Thermidorean?" In *Metapolitics*, translated by Jason Barker, 124–40. London: Verso, 2005.

Baecque, Antoine de. "Le tableau d'un cadavre. Les Récits de l'agonie de Robespierre: Du cadaver hideux au dernier héros." In *Robespierre: Figure-réputation (Yearbook of European Studies)*, edited by Annie Jourdan, 169–203. Amsterdam: Rodopi, 1996.

Bargu, Banu. "Sovereignty as Erasure: Rethinking Enforced Disappearances." *Qui Parle: Critical Humanities and Social Sciences* 23, no. 1 (Fall/Winter 2014): 35–75.

Barion, Hans. Review of *Saggi storici intorno al Papato dei Professori della Facoltà di Storia Ecclesiastica*. *Zeitschrift der Savigny- Stiftung für Rechtsgeschichte: Kanonistische Abteilung* 46 (1960): 481–501.

Becker, Jo, and Scott Shane. "Secret 'Kill List' Proves a Test of Obama's Principles and Will." *New York Times*, May 29, 2012. http://www.nytimes .com/2012/05/29/world/obamas-leadership-in-war-on-al-qaeda.html ?pagewanted=all&_r=0.

Beckett, Samuel. *Worstward Ho*. London: John Calder, 1999.

Benjamin, Walter. *The Arcades Project*. Translated by Howard Eiland and Kevin McLaughlin. Cambridge, MA: Belknap Press of Harvard University Press, 1999.

——. *Selected Writings, Volume 2: 1927–1934*. Edited by Michael W. Jennings, Howard Eiland, and Gary Smith. Translated by Rodney Livingstone. Cambridge, MA: Belknap Press of Harvard University Press, 1999.

——. *Selected Writings, Volume 4: 1938–40*. Translated by Edmund Jephcott. Edited by Howard Eiland and Michael W. Jennings. Cambridge, MA: Belknap Press of Harvard University Press, 2003.

——. "Theologico-Political Fragment." In *Reflections: Essays, Aphorisms, Autobiographical Writings*. Edited by Peter Demetz. Translated by Edmund Jephcott, 312–13. New York: Schocken, 1978.

——. "Theses on the Philosophy of History." In *Illuminations*, translated by H. Zohn, 253–64. New York: Schocken, 1968.

Bickerman, Elias. "Die römische Kaiserapotheose." *Archiv für Religionwissenschaft* 27 (1929): 1–34.

Bielik-Robson, Agata. *Jewish Cryptotheologies of Late Modernity: Philosophical Marranos*. London: Routledge, 2014.

Blair, Tony. Keynote speech to the Labour Party Conference, October 27, 2005. http://news.bbc.co.uk/1/hi/uk_politics/4287370.stm.

Blanchot, Maurice. "The Instant of my Death." In Maurice Blanchot and Jacques Derrida, *The Instant of My Death/Demeure: Fiction and Testimony*, translated by Elizabeth Rottenberg, 1–12. Stanford, CA: Stanford University Press, 2000.

——. "Literature and the Right to Death." In *The Work of Fire*, translated by Charlotte Mandell, 300–344. Stanford, CA: Stanford University Press, 1995.

Blanqui, Louis-Auguste. *Eternity by the Stars: An Astrological Hypothesis*. Translated by Frank Chouraqui. New York: Contra Mundum, 2013.

Blanton, Ward. *A Materialism for the Masses: Saint Paul and the Philosophy of Undying Life*. New York: Columbia University Press, 2014.

Blanton, Ward, and Hent de Vries, eds. *Paul and the Philosophers*. New York: Fordham University Press, 2013.

Blumenberg, Hans, and Carl Schmitt. *Briefwechsel 1971–1978 und weitere Materialien*. Edited by Alexander Schmitz. Frankfurt: Suhrkamp, 2007.

Bradley, Arthur. *Negative Theology and Modern French Philosophy*. London: Routledge, 2004.

——. *Originary Technicity: The Theory of Technology from Marx to Derrida*. London: Palgrave, 2011.

Bradley, Arthur, and Paul Fletcher. *The Messianic Now: Religion, Philosophy, Culture*. London: Routledge, 2011.

——. *The Politics to Come: Power, Modernity and the Messianic*. London: Continuum, 2010.

Brandon, Eric. *The Coherence of Hobbes' 'Leviathan': Civil and Religious Authority Combined*. London: Continuum, 2007.

Bredekamp, Horst. "Thomas Hobbes's Visual Strategies," in *The Cambridge Companion to Hobbes's "Leviathan,"* ed. Patricia Springborg, 29–60. Cambridge: Cambridge University Press, 2007.

Breyfogle, Todd. "Punishment." In *Augustine Through the Ages*, edited by Allan D. Fitzgerald, 688–90. Grand Rapids, MI: Eerdmans, 1999.

Brooks, Cleanth. "The Naked Babe and the Cloak of Manliness." In *The Well-Wrought Urn*, 21–46. London: Dennis Dobson, 1949.

Brown, H. F., ed. *Calendar of State Papers, Venice*. London Public Record Office. Vol. 10 (1900).

Brown, Wendy. *Politics Out of History*. Princeton, NJ: Princeton University Press, 2001.

Butler, Judith. *Frames of War: When Is Life Grievable?* London: Verso, 2009.

——. *Precarious Life: The Power of Mourning and Violence*. London: Verso, 2004.

Cacciari, Massimo. *The Withholding Power: An Essay on Political Theology*. Translated by Edi Pucci. London: Bloomsbury, 2018.

Cadava, Eduardo, Peter Connor, and Jean-Luc Nancy. *Who Comes After the Subject?* London: Routledge, 1991.

Campana, Joseph. "The Child's Two Bodies: Shakespeare, Sovereignty, and the End of Succession." *ELH* 81 (2014): 811–39.

Caputo, John D. *The Weakness of God: A Theology of the Event*. Bloomington: Indiana University Press, 2006.

Cavarero, Adriana. *Horrorism: Naming Contemporary Violence.* Translated by William McCuaig. New York: Columbia University Press, 2011.

Caygill, Howard. *On Resistance: A Philosophy of Defiance.* London: Bloomsbury, 2013.

Cazdyn, Eric. *The Already Dead: The New Time of Politics, Culture and Illness.* Durham, NC: Duke University Press, 2012.

Cerella, Antonio. *Genealogies of Political Modernity.* London: Bloomsbury, 2019.

Chateaubriand, François-René de. *Mémoires d'outre-tombe.* Paris: Flammarion, 1949.

Chiesa, Lorenzo. "The Bio-Theo-Politics of Birth." *Angelaki: Journal of the Theoretical Humanities* 16, no. 11 (2011): 101–15.

Clark, Sandra, and Pamela Mason. "Introduction" to *Macbeth*, The Arden Shakespeare, 116–21. London: Bloomsbury, 2015.

Coke, Edward. *A True and Perfect Relation of the Proceedings at the Severall Arraignments of the Late Most Barbarous Traitors.* London, 1606.

Coleman, Janet. *A History of Political Thought: From the Middle Ages to the Renaissance.* Oxford: Blackwell, 2000.

Comay, Rebecca. "Dead Right: Hegel and the Terror." *South Atlantic Quarterly* 103, nos. 2/3 (2004): 375–95.

Cooper, Melinda. *Life as Surplus: Biotechnology and Capitalism in the Neoliberal Era.* Seattle: University of Washington Press, 2008.

Courtenay, William J. *Capacity and Volition: A History of the Distinction of Absolute and Ordained Power.* Bergamo: Pierluigi Lubrina Editore, 1990.

Cowans, Jon. *To Speak for the People: Public Opinion and the Problem of Legitimacy in the French Revolution.* New York: Routledge, 2001.

Critchley, Simon. *Faith of the Faithless: Experiments in Political Theology.* London: Verso, 2012.

Damian, Peter. *Letters 91–120.* Vol. 4 of *The Fathers of the Church.* Translated by Owen J. Blum. Washington, DC: Catholic University of American Press, 1998.

Daston, Lorraine J., and Katherine Park. *Wonders and the Order of Nature.* Cambridge, MA: MIT Press, 2001.

Davis, Kathleen. *Periodization and Sovereignty: How Ideas of Feudalism and Secularization Govern the Politics of Time.* Philadelphia: University of Pennsylvania Press, 2008.

Deleuze, Gilles. *Negotiations, 1972–1990*. Translated by Martin Joughin. New York: Columbia University Press, 1990.

——. *Pure Immanence: Essays on a Life*. Translated by Anne Boyman. New York, Zone, 2001.

Derrida, Jacques. *The Beast and the Sovereign*. Vol. 1. Translated by Geoffrey Bennington. Chicago: University of Chicago Press, 2009.

——. *The Death Penalty*. Vol. 1. Translated by Peggy Kamuf. Chicago: University of Chicago Press, 2014.

——. "Declarations." In *Negotiations: Interventions and Interviews 1971–2001*, edited by Elizabeth Rottenberg, 46–54. Stanford, CA: Stanford University Press, 2002.

——. *Rogues: Two Essays on Reason*. Translated by Pascale-Anne Brault and Michael Naas. Stanford, CA: Stanford University Press, 2005.

Desmoulins, Camille. *Le Vieux Cordelier*. Edited by Henri Calvet. Paris: Armand Colin, 1936.

Dews, Peter. "The Return of the Subject in the Late Foucault." *Radical Philosophy* 51 (1989): 37–41.

Dickens, Charles. *Our Mutual Friend*. Ware: Wordsworth Classics, 1997.

Dillon, Michael. "Afterlife: Living Death to Political Spirituality." *Millennium: Journal of International Studies* 14, no. 1 (2013): 114–34.

——. *Biopolitics of Security: A Political Analytic of Finitude*. London: Routledge, 2015.

——. "Lethal Freedom: Divine Violence and the Machiavellian Moment." *Theory and Event* 11, no. 2 (2008).

——. "Spectres of Biopolitics: Eschatology, *Katechon* and Resistance." *South Atlantic Quarterly* 110, no. 3 (Summer 2011): 780–92.

Dillon, Michael, and Julian Reid. *The Liberal Way of War: Killing to Make Life Live*. London: Routledge, 2009.

Drakakis, John. "*Macbeth* and Sovereign Process." In *Macbeth: A Critical Reader*, edited by John Drakakis and Dale Townsend, 123–53. London: Bloomsbury, 2013.

Duns Scotus. *Contingency and Freedom: Lectura I 39*. Translated and with introduction and commentary by A. Vos Jaczn, H. Veldhuis, A. H. Looman-Graaskamp, E. Dekker, and N. W. Den Bok. Dordrecht: Kluwer, 1994.

Eagleton, Terry. "Waking the Dead," *New Statesman*, November 12, 2009. https://www.newstatesman.com/ideas/2009/11/past-benjamin-future-obama.

Edkins, Jenny. *Missing: Persons and Politics*. Ithaca, NY: Cornell University Press, 2011.

Elshtain, Jean Bethke. "Augustine." In *The Blackwell Companion to Political Theology*, edited by Peter Scott and William T. Cavanaugh, 35–47. Oxford: Blackwell, 2007.

Esposito, Roberto. *Bios: Biopolitics and Philosophy*. Translated by Timothy Campbell. Minneapolis: University of Minnesota Press, 2008.

——. *Communitas: The Origin and Destiny of Community*. Translated by Timothy Campbell. Stanford, CA: Stanford University Press, 2010.

——. "The Katechon." In *Immunitas: The Protection and Negation of Life*. Translated by Zakiya Hanafi, 52–79. London: Polity, 2011.

——. *Two: The Machine of Political Theology and the Place of Thought*. Translated by Zakiya Hanafi. New York: Fordham University Press, 2015.

Evans, Gillian R. *Augustine on Evil*. Cambridge: Cambridge University Press, 1990.

Fenves, Peter. *The Messianic Reduction: Walter Benjamin and the Shape of Time*. Stanford, CA: Stanford University Press, 2010.

Flower, Harriet I. *The Art of Forgetting: Disgrace and Oblivion in Roman Political Culture*. Chapel Hill, NC: University of North Carolina Press, 2006.

Foucault, Michel. *Discipline and Punish: The Birth of the Prison*. Translated by Alan Sheridan (Harmondsworth: Penguin, 1991.

——. "Is It Useless to Revolt?" Translated by Karen de Bruin and Kevin B. Anderson. In *Foucault and the Iranian Revolution: Gender and the Seductions of Islamism*, edited by Janet Afary and Kevin B. Anderson, 263–67. Chicago: University of Chicago Press, 2005.

——. "Omnes et Singulatim: Towards a Critique of Political Reason." In *Power: Essential Works of Michel Foucault*, edited by James D. Faubion and translated by Robert Hurley and others, 298–325. New York: New Press, 2000.

——. *Power/Knowledge: Selected Interviews and Other Writings, 1972–77*. Edited by Colin Gordon. New York: Pantheon, 1980.

——. *"Society Must Be Defended": Lectures at the Collège de France 1975–76*. Translated by David Macey. New York: Picador, 2003.

——. *The Will to Knowledge*. Vol. 1 of *The History of Sexuality*. Translated by Robert Hurley. London: Penguin, 1978.

Freud, Sigmund. *The Interpretation of Dreams, Part 1*. Vol. 4 of *Standard Edition of the Complete Psychological Works of Sigmund Freud*. Translated by A. A. Brill. London: Vintage, 2001.

Galella, Patricio, and Carlos Esposito. "Extraordinary Renditions in the Fight Against Terrorism– Forced Disappearances?" *Sur: International Journal on Human Rights* 9, no. 16 (2012): 7–31.

Gatti, Gabriel. *Surviving Forced Disappearance in Argentina and Uruguay.* New York: Palgrave Macmillan, 2014.

Gillespie, Michael Allen. *Nihilism Before Nietzsche.* Chicago: University of Chicago Press, 1995.

Girard, René. *Violence and the Sacred.* Translated by Patrick Gregory. Baltimore, MD: Johns Hopkins University Press, 1977.

Gransden, K. W. *Virgil: "Aeneid" Book VIII.* Cambridge: Cambridge University Press, 1976.

Gratton, Peter. *The State of Sovereignty: Lessons from the Political Fictions of Modernity*, 161–200. Albany: State University of New York Press, 2012.

Groh, Ruth. *Arbeit an der Heillosigkeit der Welt: Zur politisch-theologischen Mythologie und Anthropologie Carl Schmitts.* Frankfurt: Suhrkamp Verlag, 1998.

Grossheutschi, Felix. *Carl Schmitt und die Lehre vom Katechon.* Berlin: Duncker & Humblot, 1996.

Hallward, Peter. "The Will of the People: Notes Towards a Dialectical Voluntarism." *Radical Philosophy* 155 (May/June 2009): 17–30.

Hamacher, Werner. "'Now': Walter Benjamin on Historical Time." In *Walter Benjamin and History*, edited by Andrew Benjamin, translated by N. Rosenthal, 38–68. London: Continuum, 2005.

Hampton, Jean. *Hobbes and the Social Contract Tradition.* Cambridge: Cambridge University Press, 1986.

Han, Béatrice. *Foucault's Critical Project: Between the Transcendental and the Historical.* Stanford, CA: Stanford University Press, 2002.

Hegel, G. W. F. *Phenomenology of Spirit.* Translated by A. V. Miller. Oxford: Oxford University Press, 1977.

Hell, Julia. "*Katechon*: Carl Schmitt's Imperial Theology and the Ruins of the Future." *Germanic Review* 84, no. 4 (2009): 283–326.

Herman, Peter C. "'A Deed Without a Name': *Macbeth*, The Gunpowder Plot, and Terrorism." *Journal for Cultural Research* 18, no. 2 (2014): 114–31.

Heyking, John von. *Augustine and Politics as Longing in the World.* Columbia: University of Missouri Press, 2001.

———. "Augustine on Punishment and the Mystery of Human Freedom." In *The Philosophy of Punishment and the History of Political Thought*, edited by Peter Karl Koritansky, 54–73. Columbia: University of Missouri Press, 2011.

Hobbes, Thomas. *De Cive*. In *Man and Citizen: "De Homine" and "De Cive."* Edited by Bernard Gert. Indianapolis, IN: Hackett, 1991.

———. *The Elements of Law Natural and Politic*. Edited by Ferdinand Tönnies. 2nd ed. London: Cass, 1969.

———. *Leviathan or The Matter, Forme and Power of a Common Wealth Ecclesiasticall and Civil*. Edited by Richard Tuck. Cambridge: Cambridge University Press, 1991.

Hoelzl, Michael. "Before the Anti-Christ Is Revealed: On the Katechontic Structure of Messianic Time." In *The Politics to Come: Power, Modernity and the Messianic*, edited by Arthur Bradley and Paul Fletcher, 98–110. London: Continuum, 2010.

Holderness, Graham, and Bryan Loughrey. "Shakespeare and Terror." In *Shakespeare After 9/11: How a Social Trauma Reshapes Interpretation*, *Shakespeare Yearbook* 20, 23–56.

Honig, Bonnie. *Emergency Politics: Paradox, Law, Democracy*. Princeton, NJ: Princeton University Press, 2009.

Hooker, William. *Carl Schmitt's International Thought: Order and Orientation*. Cambridge: Cambridge University Press, 2009.

Hüning, Dieter. "Hobbes on the Right to Punish." In *The Cambridge Companion to Hobbes' "Leviathan,"* edited by Patricia Springborg, 217–40. Cambridge: Cambridge University Press, 2007.

Hunt, Lynn. *Politics and Class in the French Revolution*. Berkeley: University of California Press, 1984.

Hunter, Ian. *Rival Enlightenments: Civil and Metaphysical Philosophy in Early Modern Germany*. Cambridge: Cambridge University Press, 2001.

Hyppolite, Jean. *Genesis and Structure of Hegel's "Phenomenology of Spirit."* Translated by S. Cherniak and J. Heckman. Evanston, IL: Northwestern University Press, 1974.

International Convention for the Protection of All Persons from Enforced Disappearances. New York, December 20, 2006. Article 2. http://www.ohchr.org/EN/HRBodies/CED/Pages/ConventionCED.aspx.

The Invisible Committee. *The Coming Insurrection*. Los Angeles: Semiotext(e), 2009.

Israel, Jonathan. *Revolutionary Ideas: An Intellectual History of the French Revolution from the Rights of Man to Robespierre*. Princeton, NJ: Princeton University Press, 2014.

Jacobson, Eric. *Metaphysics of the Profane: The Political Theology of Walter Benjamin and Gershom Scholem*. New York: Columbia University Press, 2003.

Jennings, Theodore. *Outlaw Justice: The Messianic Politics and Paul*. Stanford, CA: Stanford University Press, 2013.

Jerome. *Epistle 22, Ad Eustochium*. In *Select Letters of Jerome*, edited by F. A. Wright. London: Heinemann, 1933.

Jordan, David P. *The Revolutionary Career of Maximilien Robespierre*. New York: Macmillan, 1985.

Jourdain, Annie. "Robespierre and Revolutionary Heroism." In *Robespierre*, edited by Colin Haydon and William Doyle, 54–74. Cambridge: Cambridge University Press, 1999.

Jung, Marc-René. *Hercule dans la littérature française du XVIe siècle: De l'Hercule courtois à l'Hercule baroque*. Geneva: Droz, 1966.

Kantorowicz, Ernst. *The King's Two Bodies: A Study in Medieval Political Theology*. Princeton, NJ: Princeton University Press, 1957.

Kastan, David. *Shakespeare After Theory*. New York: Routledge, 1999.

Kaufman, Peter Iver. "Augustine's Punishments." *Harvard Theological Review* 109, no. 4 (2016): 550–66.

Kermode, Frank. *Shakespeare's Language*. New York: Farrar, Straus & Giroux, 2000.

Khatib, Sami. "The Messianic Without Messianism: Walter Benjamin's Materialist Theology." *Anthropology and Materialism* 1 (2013).

King, David. *The Commissar Vanishes: The Falsification of Photographs and Art in Stalin's Russia*. London: Metropolitan, 1997.

Knights, L. C. "How Many Children Had Lady Macbeth? An Essay in the Theory and Practice of Shakespeare Criticism." In *Explorations*, 1–39. London: Chatto & Windus, 1946.

Kojève, Alexandre. *Introduction to the Reading of Hegel: Lectures on the "Phenomenology of Spirit" Assembled by Raymond Queneau*. Edited by A. Bloom. Translated by J. H. Nichols Jr. New York: Basic Books, 1969.

Kraynak, Robert. *History and Modernity in the Thought of Thomas Hobbes*. Ithaca, NY: Cornell University Press, 1990.

Laoutaris, Chris. *Shakespearean Maternities: Crises of Conception in Early Modern England*. Edinburgh: Edinburgh University Press, 2008.

Lefort, Claude. "The Permanence of the Theologico-Political?" In *Democracy and Political Theory*, translated by David Macey, 213–55. Minneapolis: University of Minnesota Press, 1988.

Levi, Primo. *Survival in Auschwitz: The Nazi Assault on Humanity*. New York: Simon and Schuster, 1996.

Lévinas, Emmanuel. *Existence and Existents*. Translated by Alphonso Lingis. Pittsburgh, PA: Duquesne University Press, 2001.

——. *Otherwise than Being*. Translated by Alphonso Lingis. Pittsburgh, PA: Duquesne University Press, 2001.

——. *Totality and Infinity: An Essay on Exteriority*. Translated by Alphonso Lingis. Pittsburgh, PA: Duquesne University Press, 1969.

Lilla, Mark. *The Still-Born God: Religion, Politics and the Modern West*. London: Vintage, 2007.

Livy, *The Early History of Rome, Books I–V*. Translated by Aubrey de Selincourt. London: Penguin, 2002.

Loriaux, Michael. "The Realists and Saint Augustine: Skepticism, Psychology, and Moral Action in International Relations Thought." *International Studies Quarterly* 36 (1992): 401–20.

Lyne, R. O. A. M. *Further Voices in Virgil's "Aeneid."* Oxford: Oxford University Press, 1987.

Lyotard, Jean-François. "Answer to the Question: What Is Postmodernism?" In *The Postmodern Explained to Children: Correspondence 1982–85*, 11–25. London: Power Institute of Fine Arts, 1992.

Mackay, Robin, and Armen Avanessian. *The Accelerationist Reader*. Berlin: Merve, 2014.

Markus, R. A. *Saeculum: History and Society in the Theology of Augustine*. Cambridge: Cambridge University Press, 1970.

Martinich, A. P. *The Two Gods of Leviathan: Thomas Hobbes on Religion and Politics*. Cambridge: Cambridge University Press, 1992.

Marx, Karl. "Theses on Feuerbach." In Karl Marx and Friedrich Engels, *Collected Works: Volume 5: 1845–47*, 3–10. New York: International Publishers, 1976.

Mautouchet, Paul. *Le Gouvernement révolutionnaire (10 août 1792–4 Brumaire an IV)*, 196–202. Paris: E. Cornely, 1912.

Mayer, Jane. "The Black Sites: A Rare Look Inside the C.I.A.'s Secret Interrogation Program." *New Yorker*, August 13, 2007. http://www.newyorker.com/magazine/2007/08/13/the-black-sites.

Mbembe, Achille. "Necropolitics." *Public Culture* 15, no. 1 (2003): 11–40.

McConnell, Terrance C. "Augustine on Torturing and Punishing an Innocent Person." *Southern Journal of Philosophy* 17 (1979): 481–92.

McQuillan, Martin. "Extra Time and the Death Penalties: On a Newly Arisen Violent Tone in Philosophy." *Derrida Today* 2, no. 2 (2009): 133–50.

Meier, Heinrich. *Die Lehre Carl Schmitts.* Stuttgart: J. B. Metzler, 1994.

Meillassoux, Quentin. *After Finitude: An Essay on the Necessity of Contingency.* Translated by Ray Brassier. London: Continuum, 2008.

Meuter, Günter. *Der Katechon: Carl Schmitts fundamentalistischer Kritik der Zeit.* Berlin: Duncker & Humblot, 1994.

Morgan, Llewelyn. "Assimilation and Civil War: Hercules and Cacus." In *Vergil's "Aeneid": Augustan Epic and Political Context*, edited by Hans-Peter Stahl, 175–98. London: Duckworth in association with the Classical Press of Wales, 1998.

Nancy, Jean-Luc. *The Truth of Democracy.* Translated by Michael Naas and Pascale-Anne Brault. New York: Fordham University Press, 2010.

Niebuhr, Reinhold. "Augustine's Political Realism." In *The Essential Reinhold Niebuhr—Selected Essays and Addresses*, edited by Robert McAfee Brown, 123–41. New Haven, CT: Yale University Press, 1953.

Nietzsche, Friedrich. *The Gay Science.* Translated by Walter Kaufman. New York: Vintage, 1974.

——. *Thus Spoke Zarathustra.* Translated by R. J. Hollingdale. New York: Penguin, 1973.

Norbrook, David. "Macbeth and the Politics of Historiography." In *The Politics of Discourse: The Literature and History of Seventeenth Century England*, edited by K. Sharpe and S. N. Zwicker, 78–116. Berkeley: University of California Press, 1987.

Norrie, Alan. "Hobbes and the Philosophy of Punishment." *Law and Philosophy* 3, no. 2 (1984): 299–320.

Oakley, Francis. *Natural Law, Laws of Nature, Natural Rights: Continuity and Discontinuity in the History of Ideas.* New York: Continuum, 2005.

——. *Omnipotence, Covenant, and Order: An Excursion in the History of Ideas from Abelard to Leibniz.* Ithaca, NY: Cornell University Press, 1984.

O'Donovan, Oliver, and Joan Lockwood O'Donovan. *Bonds of Imperfection: Christian Politics, Past and Present.* Grand Rapids, MI; Cambridge: Eerdmans, 2004.

Ojakangas, Mika. "Carl Schmitt and the Sacred Origins of Law." *Telos* 147 (Summer 2009): 34–54.

———. "Impossible Dialogue on Biopower: Agamben and Foucault." *Foucault Studies* (2005): 5–28.

———. "*Potentia absoluta* and *Potentia ordinate Dei*: On the Theological Origins of Carl Schmitt's Theory of Constitution." *Continental Philosophy Review* 45 (2012): 505–17.

Orwell, George. *Nineteen Eighty-Four*. In *The Penguin Complete Novels of George Orwell*. Harmondsworth: Penguin, 1983.

Palmer, R. R. *Twelve Who Ruled: The Year of the Terror in the French Revolution*. New York: Atheneum, 1969.

Pantucci, Raffaello. *We Love Death as You Love Life: Britain's Suburban Mujahedeen*. New York: Columbia University Press, 2013.

Patton, Paul. "Foucault and Agamben on Biopower and Biopolitics." In *Giorgio Agamben: Sovereignty and Life*, edited by Matthew Calarco and Steven DeCaroli, 203–18. Stanford, CA: Stanford University Press, 2007.

Pike, Nelson. "Divine Foreknowledge, Human Freedom and Possible Worlds." *Philosophical Review* 86 (April 1977): 209–16.

———. "Divine Omniscience and Voluntary Action." *Philosophical Review* 74 (January 1965): 27–46.

———. "Of God and Freedom: A Rejoinder." *Philosophical Review* 75 (July 1966): 369–79.

Pindar. "The *Nomos-Basileus* Fragment (169)." In *Early Greek Thought from Homer to the Sophists*, edited by Michael Gagarin and Paul Woodruff, 40. Cambridge: Cambridge University Press, 1995.

Pocock, J. G. A. *The Machiavellian Moment: Florentine Political Thought and the Atlantic Republican Tradition*. Princeton, NJ: Princeton University Press, 1975.

———. "Time, History and Eschatology in the Thought of Thomas Hobbes." In *Politics, Language and Time: Essays on Political Thought and History*, 148–201. New York: Atheneum, 1971.

Poole, Kristen. "Physics Divined: The Science of Calvin, Hooker and *Macbeth*." *South Central Review* 26, nos. 1–2 (2009): 127–52.

Pufendorf, Samuel von. *De jure naturae et gentium*. Edited by Frank Böhling. Vol. 4 of *Gesammelte Werke*, edited by Wilhelm Schmidt-Biggemann. Berlin: Akademie-Verlag, 1998.

Rancière, Jacques. *Disagreement: On Politics and Aesthetics*. Translated by Julie Rose. Minneapolis: University of Minnesota Press, 1999.

Remer, Gary. *Humanism and the Rhetoric of Toleration*. Philadelphia: Pennsylvania State University Press, 1996.

Resnick, Irvin M. *Divine Power and Possibility in St Peter Damian's "De Divina Omnipotentia."* Leiden: Brill, 1992.

Riley, Patrick. *The General Will Before Rousseau: The Transformation of the Divine into the Civic*. Princeton, NJ: Princeton University Press, 1986.

Robespierre, Maximilien. *Œuvres de Maximilien Robespierre*. 11 vols. Paris: Société des études Robespierristes, 1912–2007.

Rossi, Andrea. *The Labour of Subjectivity: Foucault on Biopolitics, Economy, Critique*. London: Rowman and Littlefield, 2015.

Roth, Philip. *The Plot Against America*. London: Jonathan Cape, 2004.

Rousseau, Jean-Jacques. "Discourse on the Origins and the Foundations of Inequality Amongst Men." In *The Discourses and Other Early Political Writings*, edited by Victor Gourevitch. Cambridge: Cambridge University Press, 1997.

——. *The Social Contract and Other Later Political Writings*. Edited by Victor Gourevitch. Cambridge: Cambridge University Press, 1997.

Rutter, Carol Chillington. "Remind Me: How Many Children Had Lady Macbeth?" In *Shakespeare Survey 57: Macbeth and Its Afterlives*, edited by Peter Holland, 38–53. Cambridge: Cambridge University Press, 2004.

——. *Shakespeare and Child's Play: Performing Lost Boys on Stage and Screen*. London: Routledge, 2007.

Santner, Eric L. *On Creaturely Life: Rilke/Benjamin/Sebald*. Chicago: University of Chicago Press, 2006.

——. *On the Pyschotheology of Everyday Life: Reflections on Freud and Rosenzweig*. Chicago: University of Chicago Press, 2001.

Schama, Simon. *Citizens: A Chronicle of the French Revolution*. New York: Knopf, 1989.

Schindel, Estela, and Pamela Colombo, eds. *Space and the Memories of Violence: Landscapes of Erasure, Disappearance and Exception*. New York: Palgrave Macmillan, 2014.

Schmitt, Carl. "The Age of Neutralizations and Depoliticizations." In *The Concept of the Political*, translated by George Schwab, 80–96. Chicago: Chicago University Press, 2007.

——. "Beschleuniger wider Willen, oder: Problematik der westlichen Hemisphare." In *Staat, Grossraum, Nomos: Arbeiten aus den Jahren 1916– 1969*, edited by Gunter Maschke, 431–36. Berlin: Duncker & Humblot, 1995.

——. "The Changing Structure of International Law." Translated by Antonio Cerella and Andrea Salvatore. *Journal for Cultural Research* 20, no. 3, special issue on Carl Schmitt, Political Theology and Modernity, edited by Antonio Cerella and Arthur Bradley (2016): 310–28.

——. *Ex Captivitate Salus: Erfahrungen der Zeit, 1945–47*. Cologne: Greven, 1950.

——. *Glossarium: Aufzeichnungen aus den Jahre 1947–51*. Edited by Eberhard Freiherr von Medem. Berlin: Duncker & Humblot, 1991.

——. *Land and Sea*. Translated by Simona Draghica. Washington, DC: Plutarch Press, 1997.

——. *The Leviathan in the State Theory of Thomas Hobbes: Meaning and Failure of a Political Symbol*. Translated by George Schwab and Erna Hilfstein. Chicago: University of Chicago Press, 2008.

——. *The* Nomos *of the Earth in the International Law of the Jus Publicum Europaeum*. Translated by G. L. Ulmen. New York: Telos, 2003.

——. *Political Theology: Four Chapters on the Concept of Sovereignty*. Translated by George Schwab. Chicago: University of Chicago Press, 2006.

Schrock, Thomas S. "The Rights to Punish and Resist Punishment in Hobbes's *Leviathan*." *Western Political Quarterly* 44, no. 4 (December 1991): 853–90.

Serres, Michel. *The Parasite*. Translated by Lawrence R. Schehr. Baltimore, MD: Johns Hopkins University Press, 1982.

——. *Rome: The Book of Foundations*. Translated by Felicia McCarren. Stanford, CA: Stanford University Press, 1991.

Seward, William H., Jr. *A Rhetoric of Bourgeois Revolution: The Abbé Sieyès and "What Is the Third Estate?"* Durham, NC: Duke University Press, 1994.

Shakespeare, William. *Macbeth*. Edited by Sandra Clark and Pamela Mason. London: Bloomsbury, 2015.

Sheehan, Jonathan. "Assenting to the Law: Sacrifice and Punishment at the Dawn of Secularism." In *After Secular Law*, edited by Winnifred Fallers Sullivan, Robert A. Yelle, and Matteo Taussig-Rubbo, 62–79. Stanford, CA: Stanford University Press, 2011.

Sieyès, Emmanuel-Joseph. *Qu'est-ce que le Tiers Etat?* Critical edition by Roberto Zapperi. Geneva: Librairie Droz, 1970.

Simondon, Gilbert. *L'individuation psychique et collective.* Paris: Aubier, 1989.

Sommerville, Johann P., ed. *King James VI and I: Political Writings.* Cambridge: Cambridge University Press, 1994.

Stiegler, Bernard. *Philosopher par accident: Entretiens avec Elie During.* Paris: Galilée, 2004.

Strauss, Leo. *Natural Right and History.* Chicago: University of Chicago Press, 1953.

Subcomandante Marcos. *Our Word Is Our Weapon: Selected Writings.* Edited by J. Ponce de León. Toronto: Seven Stories, 2001.

Šumič, Jelica. "Giorgio Agamben's Godless Saints: Saving What Was Not." *Angelaki* 16, no. 3 (2011): 137–47.

Suskind, Ron. "Faith, Certainty and the Presidency of George W. Bush." *New York Times*, October 17, 2004. http://www.nytimes.com/2004/10/17 /magazine/faith-certainty-and-the-presidency-of-george-w-bush.html ?_r=0.

Szendy, Peter. "Katechon." *Political Concepts: A Critical Lexicon.* https://www .politicalconcepts.org/katechon-peter-szendy/#fn5.

Tambling, Jeremy. "Lévinas and *Macbeth*'s 'Strange Images of Death.'" *Essays in Criticism* 54, no. 4 (2004): 351–72.

Taubes, Jacob. "Leviathan als sterblicher Gott: Zur Aktualität von Thomas Hobbes." *Evangelische Kommentare* 13 (1980): 571–74.

——. *The Political Theology of Paul.* Translated by Dana Hollander. Stanford, CA: Stanford University Press, 2004.

Terpstra, Marin, and Theo de Wit. "'No Spiritual Investment in the World as It Is': On the Negative Political Theology of Taubes." In *Flight of the Gods: Philosophical Perspective on Negative Theology*, edited by I. N. Bulhof and L. ten Kate, 320–53. New York: Fordham University Press, 2000.

Tertullian. *Apology.* Translated by Terrot R. Glover. Cambridge, MA: Harvard University Press, 1977.

Thompson, John L. *Writing the Wrongs: Women of the Old Testament among Biblical Commentators from Philo Through the Reformation.* New York: Oxford University Press, 2001.

Thurman, Judith. "Philip Roth E-mails on Trump." *New Yorker*, January 30, 2017. http://www.newyorker.com/magazine/2017/01/30/philip-roth-e -mails-on-trump.

Tierney, Brian. *The Idea of Natural Rights: Studies on Natural Rights, Natural Law, and Church Law, 1150–1625*. Cambridge: Eerdmans, 1997.

Trotsky, Leon. *The Stalin School of Falsification*. New York: Beekman, 2001.

——. *Trotsky's Diary in Exile: 1935*. Translated by Elena Zarudnaya. Cambridge, MA: Harvard University Press, 1958.

United Nations Human Rights Council. "Report of the Working Group on Enforced or Involuntary Disappearances A/HRC/30/38." http://www.ohchr.org/EN/Issues/Disappearances/Pages/Annual.aspx.

Vatter, Miguel. *The Republic of the Living: Biopolitics and the Critique of Civil Society*. New York: Fordham University Press, 2014.

Virgil. *Aeneid*. Translated by David West. Rev. ed. Harmondsworth: Penguin Classics, 2003.

Virno, Paolo. *Multitude: Between Innovation and Negation*. New York: Semiotext(e), 2008.

Waldron, Jeremy. "Hobbes on Public Worship." In *Nomos XLVIII: Toleration and Its Limits*, edited by Melissa S. Williams and Jeremy Waldron, 31–53. New York: New York University Press, 2008.

Walzer, Michael, ed. *Regicide and Revolution: Speeches at the Trial of Louis XVI*. New York: Columbia University Press, 1992.

Wilde, Marc de. "Politics Between Times: Theologico-Political Interpretations of the Restraining Force (*Katechon*) in Paul's Second Letter to the Thessalonians." In *Paul and the Philosophers*, ed. Ward Blanton and Hent de Vries, 105–26. New York: Fordham University Press, 2013.

William of Ockham. *Predestination, God's Foreknowledge, and Future Contingents*. Translated by Marilyn McCord Adams and Norman Kretzmann. Indianapolis, IN: Hackett, 1983.

Wills, Gary. *Witches and Jesuits: Shakespeare's* Macbeth. New York: Oxford University Press, 1995.

Wilson, Richard. "'Blood Will Have Blood': Regime Change in *Macbeth*." *Shakespeare Jahrbuch* 143: 11–35.

——. *Secret Shakespeare: Studies in Theatre, Religion and Resistance*. Manchester: Manchester University Press, 2004.

Yeats, W. B. "The Second Coming." In *Selected Poems*, edited by Timothy Webb. London: Penguin, 1991.

Zarmanian, Thalin. "Carl Schmitt and the Problem of Legal Order: From Domestic to International." *Leiden Journal of International Law* 19, no. 1 (2006): 41–67.

Žižek, Slavoj. *For They Know Not What They Do: Enjoyment as a Political Factor.* London: Verso, 1991.

——. *In Defense of Lost Causes.* London: Verso, 2008.

——. "Introduction: Robespierre, or the 'Divine Violence' of Terror." In Maximilien Robespierre, *Virtue and Terror*, vii–xxxix. London: Verso, 2007.

——. *The Parallax View.* Cambridge, MA: MIT Press, 2006.

INDEX

ACAED. *See* International Coalition Against Enforced Disappearances

accelerationism, in Marxist/post-Marxist political discourse, 228n35

Adams, John, 66

Adorno, Theodor, 173

Aeneid (Virgil). *See* Cacus-Hercules story, in *Aeneid*

Agamben, Giorgio: on abject body of *homo sacer*, 18; and bare life, 5, 35–36; on Benjamin, 158; on Dickens's *Our Mutual Friend*, 42; extension of Foucault's biopolitics theory, 35–36; on genealogy of government, 230n17; on Hercules-Cacus story, 205n16; on potentiality, 19; on redemption of history, 179, 181–82, 233n46; on Roman apotheosis, 1, 197n1; on sovereign power, 7–8, 108–9; on time, 157

American Revolution, Derrida on, 121

Amnesty International, 189–90

"Die andere Hegel-Linie" (Schmitt), 148, 154–55

Anonymous, 195, 196

apotheosis of emperors, 1–2, 197n1

Appelbaum, Robert, 88

Aquinas, Thomas, 168

Arcades Project, The (Benjamin), 178, 180–81

Arendt, Hannah: on natality, 19; on Nazi thanatopolitics, 5–6, 37–38, 93

Aristotle, 24

Augustine of Hippo: on *katechon*, 144, 146; and modern security dilemma, 66; on peace, universal human/animal desire for, 48–49; as philosophical architect of modern state, 65–66; on torture by political authorities, as imperfect but necessary tool, 60–62. *See also* Cacus-Hercules story, in Augustine

Augustine of Hippo, on political rule: and middle ground

Robespierre, Maximilien: and
biopolitics of retroactivity in
French Revolution, 129; and
Cacus-Hercules story, 67–69;
critics of politics of, 137–38; on
death as only proof of
revolutionary commitment,
134–35; execution of, 120; final
address to National
Convention, 135–36;
"Incorruptible" as nom de
guerre of, 119; lack of private
life, 218n3; and the "people," as
vanguard of the virtuous, 130;
reputation as either proto-
totalitarian fanatic or faithful
subject to truth, 120; as
something more or less than
human, 120–21; Thermidorean
accounts of, 218n4; as
unbearable life, 15; and
unbearable life as new
revolutionary subject to be
mobilized, 120
Robespierre, and execution of
Louis XVI: denial of need for
trial, 221n30; denial of popular
sovereignty in, 129–30; as enemy
of state, 223n61
Robespierre as already dead but
living martyr, 15, 119–20,
132–34; as basis for his
parrhesia, 133; as model
revolutionary subject, 133–34,
136–37, 139; multiple
deployments of, 133–34; and
perpetration of Reign of Terror
from subject position of

"death" itself, 132–33; and
retroactive self-annihilation of
final speech, 135–36
Romanov family, Red Army
execution of, as war on
children to control future,
91–92
Rome, ancient: apotheosis of
emperors, 1; *damnatio memoriae*
in, 2–3, 5, 19–20
Rome: The Book of Foundations
(Serres). *See* Cacus-Hercules
story, in Serres
Roth, Philip, 183–86
Rousseau, Jean-Jacques: and *beau
savage* as pre-human, 32; and
biopolitics of retroactivity, 122,
129; in Foucault's history of
birth of biopolitics, 31–34; on
general will, 122, 219nn12–13; on
king as foreigner among
citizens, 126; on sovereign and
general will, 18; on sovereign
power to declare unbearable
life, 33–34; on sovereign's right
of life and death, 33–34; and
theory of biopower, 26; on
violators of social contract as
enemies, 220n26. See also
Social Contract, The (Rousseau)
ruin-gazing, and *katechon*, 156–57
Rutter, Carol Chillington, 71, 78

Saeculum (Markus), 58–59
Saint-Just, Louis-Antoine, 126–28,
130–31, 136, 220n26
Santner, Eric, and creaturely life, 5
Schama, Simon, 120, 129

nihilopolitics, 35; on sovereignty
as power to kill, 7, 11, 24–25; on
sovereignty as power to make
live and let die, 6, 192–93;
theoretical unbearable life
posited in, 11, 18, 21–23
sovereign, life of: as unbearable
life, 9–10, 18–19; unliving
remainder within, 18
sovereign as Cacus: in *Aeneid*,
53–54; Augustine on, 46, 57–58,
64; Schmitt on, 51–52
sovereign power to declare life
unbearable, 4–5, 41, 192–93;
annihilation of resistance as
goal of, 9; annihilatory
violence as characteristic of,
193–94; and creation of
ontology, 193; genealogy of,
questions raised by, 4. *See also*
unbearable life
sovereignty: classical definition of,
4; Esposito on, 7; origin in right
of the father, 22; as power to
declare life unbearable, 4–5; as
void excepted from life/death
nexus, 19
sovereignty, Foucault on: as
power to kill, 7, 11, 24–25, 36; as
power to make die and let live,
6, 23, 192–93; as right of seizure,
23
sovereignty as erasure: and political
"disappearances," 171, 182–83,
233n49; and power to undo
past, 171
sovereignty as power to kill: as
common thread in biopolitical

thought, 7–8; Foucault on, 7, 11,
24–25, 36
Soviet Union, and political
"disappearances," 233n49
Spinoza, Baruch, 113
state of exception, permanent
extension of: Benjamin on, 158;
as type of *katechon*, 158–59,
161–62
Stiegler, Bernard, 32
Strauss, Leo, 32
subject, state of existence prior to
subject formation, 17–19
Šumič, Jelica, 181–82

Taubes, Jacob: on Bloch, 157; on
Hobbes, 112, 213–14n13; on
katechon, 148–49; on Schmitt,
142, 148–49, 225–26n12; on state
as *katechon*, 146
Tertullian, 145
thanatopolitics, *vs.* nihilopolitics, 8
"Theological-Political Fragment"
(Benjamin), 172, 173–74, 176
"Theses on the Philosophy of
History" (Benjamin), 129, 158,
164, 172, 175–76, 178–79, 180,
186–87
Thessalonians, First and
Second Letter of, on *katechon*,
143–44
Time That Remains, The
(Agamben), 179
Tiqqun, 195
Totality and Infinity (Lévinas), 5,
81–83
Trotsky, Leon, 91
Trump, Donald, 186

INSURRECTIONS: CRITICAL STUDIES IN RELIGION,
POLITICS, AND CULTURE

SLAVOJ ŽIŽEK, CLAYTON CROCKETT, CRESTON DAVIS,
JEFFREY W. ROBBINS, EDITORS